D0969126

Caribbean Contours

JOHNS HOPKINS STUDIES
IN ATLANTIC HISTORY AND CULTURE

RICHARD PRICE, GENERAL EDITOR

Caribbean Contours

EDITED BY

SIDNEY W. MINTZ AND
SALLY PRICE

The Johns Hopkins University Press
Baltimore and London

F
2169
.C365
1985

© 1985 The Johns Hopkins University Press
All rights reserved
Printed in the United States of America

The Johns Hopkins University Press, 701 West 40th Street, Baltimore, Maryland
21211
The Johns Hopkins Press Ltd, London

The paper in this book is acid-free and meets the guidelines for
permanence and durability of the Committee on Production Guidelines
for Book Longevity of the Council on Library Resources.

Library of Congress Cataloging in Publication Data
Main entry under title:

Caribbean contours.

(Johns Hopkins studies in Atlantic history and culture)
Bibliography: p.
1. Caribbean Area—Civilization—Addresses, essays, lectures.   I. Mintz,
Sidney Wilfred, 1922–   . II. Price, Sally.   III. Series.
F2169.C365   1985   972.9   84-43079
ISBN 0-8018-3271-3 (alk. paper)
ISBN 0-8018-3272-1 (pbk. : alk. paper)

Title page illustration:
Pre-Columbian bone spatula carved by Taino Indians.
Collection of
Fundación García Arévalo, Santo Domingo.

Augustana College Library
Rock Island, Illinois 61201

$\mathscr{C}ontents$

21406

Caribbean Contours

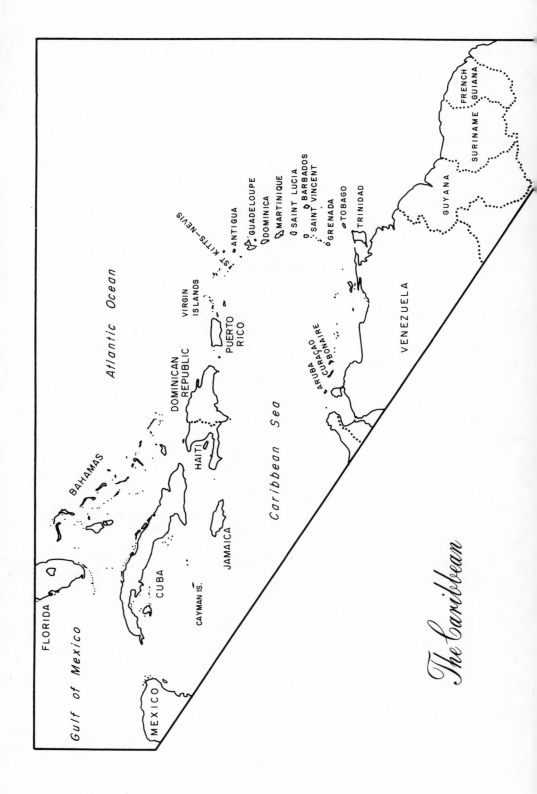

The Caribbean

Introduction

SIDNEY W. MINTZ AND
SALLY PRICE

Though the Caribbean region is commonly described as including both the several score islands that lie within the sea of the same name and the mainland to its west that stretches from Mexico to Panama, there exist other, more useful ways to define the Caribbean as a unified region. From the 1500s onward, the post-Conquest development of the mainland on the one hand, and of the islands on the other, proceeded quite differently, with but few exceptions, and left behind two rather distinct economic and social ensembles.

The Caribbean islands were the first colonial acquisition of the Europeans (in this case the Spaniards) in the New World. For about a century Spanish hegemony in the Antilles was unbroken. But Spanish conquests had been so swift and so successful, on the mainland as well as in the islands, that both governing institutions and military might were soon spread only thinly across a vast New World empire. By the first years of the seventeenth century, Spain had to pull back in some areas, and her control of the Antillean region grew slacker. Beginning around 1600, Great Britain and France, as well as the Netherlands, began to penetrate Spain's island world with more success. They concentrated first on the smaller, still unoccupied islands of the eastern Caribbean, such as Barbados, St. Lucia, St. Kitts, and Martinique. But soon after, more ambitious conquests in the Greater Antilles occurred. "After 1625," Newton noted, "swarms of English and French colonists poured like flies upon the rotting carcase of Spain's empire in the Caribbean, and within ten years the West Indian scene was changed forever" (1933:149). In 1655, Jamaica was wrested from Spain as part of Cromwell's Western Design; then, in 1697, Spain reluctantly ceded to France the western third of Hispaniola (St. Domingue, later called Haiti). By that time, Danish colonies were firmly established in addition to those of the Dutch, the English, and the French. Thus, in the course of much less than a century, but following more than one hundred years of Hispanic colonial monopoly, the dismemberment of the Spanish island world was realized.

We wish to thank Dr. Richard Morse, Secretary of the Latin American Program at the Woodrow Wilson Center, for useful critical comments.

Under Spain, the colonial presence in the islands had been at once tragic and transient. The utter destruction of the aboriginal peoples of the Greater Antilles, the exhaustion of the limited precious metal resources, and the establishment of feeble, largely self-sustaining and impoverished semipastoral forms of economic exploitation were nearly all Spain had to show for her efforts in the Greater Antilles when her domain there was challenged. In the Lesser Antilles (stretching from Trinidad northward to the islands off Puerto Rico's eastern tip), she had done no more than raid for Indians to enslave. But the North Europeans were motivated by radically different colonial conceptions.

Many writers have reflected on the differences between Spain and her enemies in these regards. Spain's laggard support for agricultural growth in the Caribbean has often been explained in terms of authoritarian government, a resistance to any autonomous economic development within her colonies, and a dominant interest in metallic extraction. But whatever the reasons, the Spanish colonies there were only poorly settled and developed in the mid-seventeenth century, even when compared to Spain's mainland settlements in Middle America and the Andes. In contrast, once the British, the Dutch, and the French had established themselves on the islands, they soon created thriving and lucrative plantation systems, based on forced labor. Within decades of the British occupation of Barbados, for instance, that colony had become a scene of intense activity where thousands of enslaved Africans were producing sugar for the exploding consumer markets of Western Europe. The same transformation was soon repeated in nearly every part of the region where the British, the Dutch, the Danes, and the French could seize islands. For centuries thereafter—in some places to this day—sugar was king.

Developments in some mainland areas were similar, and sugar plantations manned by slaves were also established there—for instance, in the coastal Guianas, between Brazil and what was to become Venezuela. Yet there were persisting differences that influenced the distinctive character of the mainland and insular Caribbean. Some of these differences are embodied in the contrast West and Augelli (1966:11–16) have drawn between Mainland and Rimland. In terms of topography, rainfall, soil, terrain, and the nature of post-Conquest occupation, only a thin coastal strip of the mainland—which West and Augelli aptly label the "rim"—belongs with the islands. But beyond this important geographic and economic distinction, there are the long-term consequences of Europe's invasion of the mainland and the islands, and the different topographic and demographic character of each locale.

The near-total destruction of the insular aboriginal population stands in clear contrast to the character of settlement in the mainland, where substantial indigenous populations, though reduced almost to extinction, were ultimately able to withstand the European apocalypse of war, enslavement, disease, and cultural destruction. In this regard, we need only compare Guatemala, for example, with its immense Indian population, to any Caribbean island. To be sure, Guatemala is an extreme case, but there are analogous differences in Mexico, Nicaragua, Panama, and elsewhere. Only a few bits of the mainland—in particular, Belize in Central America and the three Guianas on the South American coast—fell to Spain's enemies after 1625 and were subjected to the particular forms of forced development that had typified nearly all of the insular Caribbean.

While the metropolitan tradition has tied each Caribbean polity to one or another European power, such that the region is culturally and ethnically perhaps the most heterogeneous for its size in the whole world, the bulk of the mainland region can be described in some measure as a cultural counterposition of the Hispanic colonial tradition and the variant syntheses of aboriginal forms that set off one mainland society from another. The two regions, then, stand in a certain opposition, in spite of those broad underlying similarities that are shared by virtually every poor, agrarian, so-called Third World country. On the mainland, European enterprise in the form of haciendas and plantations employing mostly aboriginal labor was erected upon the ruins of the pre-Conquest indigenous economies. In contrast, on the islands, mostly black peasantries eventually achieved a fragile freedom from what had once been flourishing, slave-based European plantations. It is in light of this contrast that the Caribbean takes on some of its distinctive and particular character. A careful consideration of the differences helps to make clear why undertakings such as the Caribbean Basin Initiative (CBI) rest on such ethnocentric (and, ultimately, opportunistic) misunderstanding of the special nature of Caribbean life.

This volume is concerned primarily with the insular Caribbean, plus those mainland territories (Belize and the Guianas) whose colonial histories most resemble them. It deals broadly with a number of aspects of Caribbean life, some seemingly remote from the political, strategic, policy-oriented considerations that are the backbone of so many recent Caribbean studies. We must confess to both confusion and fatigue in the face of a seemingly endless succession of works purporting to "explain" the Caribbean, with analyses focusing on the play of military and political forces affecting the region, almost always from the perspective of U.S. interests. Important as these considerations are for any realistic grasp of the fate and future of the Caribbean, they cannot possibly explain all of it. In our view, such approaches cannot even satisfy their own goals, divorced as they usually are from a more broadly defined cultural context. These works generally tell us surprisingly little about the nearly twenty million who compose the populations of the Caribbean, about the histories and cultures of the dozens of societies that constitute it, or about the daily lives, languages, music, folklore, or beliefs (including, it needs stressing, the political beliefs) of its peoples.

A reading of a half-dozen such works might easily lead one to conclude that

Caribbean folk apparently have little to say for themselves. As pawns in a game (we are told by implication) far more important than their own lives and fates, their voices remain muffled—largely unheard and, again by implication, probably not much worth listening to. Of course, such views are never explicitly stated. Yet it is because of the implicit assumptions leading to such inferences, one suspects, that discussions about the destiny of countries such as Haiti, Cuba, Grenada, or Puerto Rico never seem to focus successfully upon what might otherwise seem an absolutely fundamental question: what do the international dialogues have to do with the daily experiences, the perceptions and aspirations, of the ordinary folk in the countries being described and manipulated?

While the essays in this book are intentionally wide-ranging in their subjects (treating matters that vary from the chemistry of sugar production to the ideological background of reggae music), many of the issues they discuss are recurring ones. Picking up on these common threads, we discern certain aspects of the development of Caribbean societies that justify discussion of the region as a unit in spite of the tremendous diversity of experiences represented by its various political, social, and cultural entities.

The concept of "creolization" may be a particularly apt illustration. The term "creole" (which probably came from the Portuguese *crioulo*) refers, on a general level, to something that comes from the Old World but is raised in the New (Friederici 1960:219; Arrom 1951; Cassidy and Le Page 1980:130; DeCamp 1971:15–16). In the languages of Caribbean people, variants of the term often imply this transplanted quality, but in numerous different ways. Haitians, for example, use the word "*Créole*" to refer to their national language, which was developed by people from the Old World (both Africa and Europe) interacting in the New. For people in the Hispanophone islands, a *pollo criollo* (creole chicken) is a fowl raised from old local stock, in contrast to one that has been recently imported or purchased in a modern supermarket; *ron criollo* (creole rum) identifies illegal, bootleg rum and carries a connotation of authenticity and local pride. Among the Maroons of the Suriname interior, *kióo* (creole) has always described the modern, somewhat rakish lifestyle expected of young men, as opposed to the more tradition-oriented involvements of their elders. In still other contexts, "creole" (and its variant forms) may refer to aspects of culture, from crops and cuisine to music and art, that arose from the complex encounters of people from four continents— encounters that shaped every island and mainland territory in the region. The term has also served in diverse ways as an ethnic label. In historical writing, "creole" has been used to distinguish slaves born in the Americas from their African-born contemporaries. In modern settings, it refers in some areas (e.g., coastal Suriname) to Afro-Americans and in others (e.g., Trinidad) to persons of European ancestry.

Even within a single domain, the word "creole" escapes simple definitions. As a linguistic term, it encompasses a range of mutually-unintelligible languages whose shared past consists of the fact that each one developed in response to a situation in which people speaking numerous different African, European, and other languages needed to communicate with one another. In Haiti and French *départements* such as Martinique and Guadeloupe, and even in some formerly French but subsequently British territories such as St. Lucia, variations of a creole language whose vocabulary comes mostly from French are spoken. Elsewhere, one finds several distinct creole languages spoken within a single territory. In Suriname, for instance, which was first settled by the British and then held by the Dutch until it achieved independence in 1975, one creole language (Sranan) is spoken in coastal areas and two others (Ndjuka and Saramaccan) in the interior. All three exhibit influences from West and Central African languages, from English, and from Dutch, and one has drawn on Portuguese as well, but the particular ways in which each of these languages has combined its linguistic heritages is unique, and the three are mutually unintelligible. Relationships among creole languages in other areas of the Caribbean are equally complex. Alleyne's essay in this volume introduces the reader to the shared properties of these languages, as well as to some of the ways in which people draw upon them—within the whole range of language possibilities that characterize most Caribbean speech communities— not only to communicate what they are saying, but also to reflect the social situations in which they are operating.

The notion of "creole" aspects of Caribbean culture comes up elsewhere in this volume as well. Hoetink's essay on the conceptualization of "race" and color directs attention to the ways in which the range of physical appearances in the Caribbean is conceptualized differently, depending on the historical settings in which they developed. Lewis's and Stone's essays remind us, by setting Caribbean political consciousness within the framework of ideas about "race," ethnic identity, and the tensions that hold contingents of Caribbean populations in balance, that the integration of European and African heritages has more than academic import. And Bilby's overview of musical life in the region underscores the ongoing complexities that characterize cultural traditions in which people living in the Western hemisphere draw on ancestral heritages from throughout the Old World.

The ways in which Caribbean peoples think about gender—that is, the particular distinctions they choose to draw between the places of men and of women in personal, social, and cultural terms—also reflect the region's complexity. Conceptions of the relative business acumen of women and men, for example, differ dramatically between Jamaica and Haiti on the one hand and Puerto Rico and the Dominican Republic on the other. Ideas about purity, virtue, and sexuality are equally varied, not only by class and locality, but also to some extent according to the colonial histories of nations and regions.

Further diversity is introduced into such distinctions by the passage of time, for "traditional" notions about men and women, like other cultural concepts, are not invulnerable to outside influences or to changing social and economic realities.

In terms of a now-popular perspective that ranges the status of women on a continuum from subservient to independent, it would not be possible to accord Caribbean women a particular position without an oversimplification of their lives and aspirations. While in many parts of the Caribbean women defer to their spouses in one or another arena of daily life, they also enjoy striking personal autonomy in others. Thus, Haitian market women, for instance, operate quite independently in terms of their freedom of movement and use of their own capital, yet accept their husbands' dominance in such matters as sexual freedom or certain kinds of economic decisions. Maroon women in Suriname are dependent on men for most of their material needs and conform to restrictive (and, from a Western perspective, oppressive) rules designed to protect men's ritual powers from the contamination associated with women's bodies, but they also conduct themselves with notable freedom in terms of personal mobility and are assured a prominence in the community through their special position in the strongly matrilineal kinship system that structures almost every aspect of life.

To date, literary works by Caribbean authors seem to have captured the special nature of women's experiences in the region more successfully than have academic analyses, and this is not altogether surprising. For gender seems to be an aspect of life where it is particularly difficult for observers to shed their own perspectives (whether sexist, feminist, or somewhere in between) in order to explore with an open mind the complex ensembles of goals and expectations concerning men and women that have developed over time in particular cultural settings.

The perception of "racial" categories is another issue that recurs repeatedly in these essays—not because it was pursued as such, but because it inescapably affects almost every aspect of Caribbean life. Hoetink's essay lays the groundwork here, exploring subtle differences in the classificatory frameworks used in various societies of the Caribbean, drawing broader contrasts between areas with Hispanic and non-Hispanic colonial pasts, and, finally, confronting the basic dissimilarities between understandings of "race" in Caribbean societies and in the United States. As we follow these variations on a theme and, in other essays, observe their influence on the political, linguistic, social, and cultural life of the region, we may find ourselves learning not only about the peoples of the Caribbean but also about ourselves. For in this comparative setting, we begin to see how much the deep division between "white" and "black" that holds sway in our own society is a cultural construct, one particular way of conceptualizing human diversity, rather than an objective or "scientific" classification. We also begin to empathize in a new way with the personal experiences of so many Caribbean individuals who venture outside of their home territories and find their own ethnic designations (always defined with subtlety and precision, and constituting an essential part of personal identity) replaced by a crude lumping together of persons not perceived as pure "white" under the single label of "black."

Venturing into "foreign" social systems is, however, a well-established pattern in Caribbean life, and the millions of Caribbean migrants now living in the United States have come from societies where frequent migration, even for lengthy periods, is a long-standing regional tradition. In Suriname, Maroon men from the villages of the interior spend months, years, and sometimes decades in coastal towns and in alien settings from Brazil and Venezuela to Martinique and Barbados. Haitian market women travel constantly between rural communities and the capital in their own country. They and their brothers seek employment not only in the United States, but throughout the Caribbean; the canefields and marketplaces of Guadeloupe, for example, are full of Haitian men and women. Martiniquan fishermen exploit the off-shore riches of St. Lucia, often establishing personal ties in coastal areas, and sometimes bringing back wives—whose subsequent adjustment in Martinique also rests on the matter-of-fact acceptance of geographical mobility and social adaptability as central features of life.

This pervasive and unceasing movement across geographical, social, and linguistic boundaries contributes further to the complexity of a region the demographic beginnings of which, after 1492, depended upon massive migrations, both forced and voluntary, from countless societies around the world. The resulting cosmopolitanism of Caribbean people gives the lie to the assumption that affluence brings sophistication, while poverty spells provincialism. Unlike most citizens of the United States, Caribbean people commonly grow up with a firm expectation that they will one day experience foreign cultures, learn to get along in other people's languages, and participate in work and leisure in unfamiliar social settings.

The personal experiences of early migrants to the Caribbean—enslavement, forced transportation, language learning, changes in diet, residence among strangers, adjustment to the plantation regimen, and acceptance of the outsider as ruler and master—represented a kind of forced-draft Westernization. And this is yet another way in which the region's unique historical origins have contributed to its special character in the twentieth century. Long before the common features of the industrial West (imported foods, time-conscious work regimes, factory production, impersonal work relations, etc.) had spread through much of Europe, they were commonplace aspects of life for Caribbean slaves. Today, and even in the most exotic corners of the Caribbean, from the riverain villages of the Guianese rain forest to the rural hamlets of the mountainous Haitian interior, European and North American interests contribute steadily and massively to the shaping of everyday life.

Two essays in this volume incidentally counterpose different aspects of the Caribbean history of Westernization. Hagelberg's detailed exploration of the place of sugar in the economies of the Caribbean demonstrates how the region remains linked to the world outside, continuing an agro-industrial tradition now almost five centuries old. Mintz's essay on the Caribbean peasantries shows how these rural adaptations have both stood against the West and, at the same time, integrated its demands within their design of local life—escaping the plantation regimen, yet seeking the various benefits of modernity for themselves and their children.

To characterize Caribbean peoples as sharing some kind of special personality or philosophy would be to vulgarize the complexity of their pasts and the much differentiated societies in which they live today. But it does seem significant that this region was involved so early in the development of a world system of production and trade, sponsored by the emergent nations of Western Europe, and expedited by the use of vast amounts of unpaid—that is, enslaved—and culturally heterogeneous, non-European labor. Accustomed to ethnic and cultural differences, to the movement of peoples into (and out of) their midsts, to migration itself as a way of life, to industrial tempos imposed on agricultural economies, and to the common contrasts between the lives of the privileged and the lives of the poor, Caribbean folk often seem more prepared for the modern world than other so-called Third World peoples.

Within the context of the Western world, the influence of Caribbean political thinkers and leaders, beginning with José Martí and Toussaint l'Ouverture and ending with Frantz Fanon, Fidel Castro, Luis Muñoz Marín, and Eric Williams, has been impressive. Caribbean societies have contributed disproportionately to political dialogue in the United States through people such as Marcus Garvey, Stokely Carmichael, and Shirley Chisholm. In literature, the names of Edward Kamau Brathwaite, Alejo Carpentier, Aimé Césaire, George Lamming, V. S. Naipaul, Derek Walcott, and many others are internationally known. The aesthetic and political products of the Caribbean, however, are perhaps particularly noteworthy because, while they have roots in the European cultural and linguistic traditions that permeate the privileged sectors of Caribbean life, they also show an originality and vitality all their own. One could argue that the ability of Caribbean peoples to react creatively to the cultural traditions around them is the quality that most sets them apart from other, older, and more intact, cultures.

The idea of assembling a series of essays by distinguished students of the Caribbean to introduce the region to nonspecialists was first suggested to us by Abraham F. Lowenthal and Louis W. Goodman, who sponsored the series through the Latin American Program of the Woodrow Wilson International Center for Scholars. We are grateful to both of them for the moral, intellectual, and financial support that they provided the project, from its original conception through to its final production. The essays that resulted were originally published as a series of pamphlets entitled *Focus: Caribbean,* which are available from the Wilson Center. In addition to those in the present volume, four other essays that deal with particular Caribbean nations (Cuba, Haiti, and Jamaica) and with migration from the Caribbean to the United States are available. Wayne S. Smith analyzed Cuba's responses to Soviet and U.S. policies toward the Caribbean in an essay entitled "Castro's Cuba: Soviet Partner or Nonaligned?" Michel-Rolph Trouillot explored the historical background of contemporary Haitian problems in "Nation, State, and Society in Haiti, 1804–1984." Evelyne Huber Stephens and John D. Stephens outlined the nature of recent political movements in Jamaica in "Jamaica's Democratic Socialist Experience." And Roy Simón Bryce-Laporte examined migration patterns to the United States in "Caribbean Immigrations and Their Implications for the United States." We encourage readers of the present volume to consult these four essays for authoritative introductions to subjects that are of central importance for an understanding of the place of the Caribbean in the contemporary world.

REFERENCES

ARROM, J.
1951   "Criollo: definición y matices de un concepto." *Hispania* 34(2):172–76.
CASSIDY, F. G., AND R. B. LE PAGE
1980   *Dictionary of Jamaican English.* Cambridge: Cambridge University Press.
DECAMP, DAVID
1971   "Introduction." *In* Dell Hymes (ed.), *Pidginization and Creolization of Languages,* pp. 13–39. Cambridge: Cambridge University Press.
FRIEDERICI, GEORG
1960   *Amerikanistisches Wörterbuch und Hilfswörterbuch für den Amerikansten.* 2. Auflage. Hamburg: Cram, De Gruyter & Co.
NEWTON, ARTHUR P.
1933   *The European Nations in the West Indies, 1493–1688.* London: A. & C. Black.
WEST, ROBERT C., AND JOHN P. AUGELLI
1966   *Middle America: Its Lands and Peoples.* Englewood Cliffs, N.J.: Prentice Hall.

· 1 ·

A Political Profile of the Caribbean

CARL STONE

INTRODUCTION

Most developing countries that achieved independence in the period following World War II inherited constitutions of the Western European type, with provision for elected government, parliamentary representation, competitive political parties, and liberal-democratic political and juridical traditions. That inherited legacy grew from the association with Western European colonizers. But the overwhelming majority of these states have since abandoned such a political inheritance in favor of military regimes, one-party rule, and wide-ranging forms of authoritarian rule.

The Caribbean remains the only area in the Third World where politics based on free elections, multiple parties, and liberal-democratic freedoms are still predominant. What makes the region so interesting politically is that there exists as well a wide variety of other political forms that provide sharp contrasts to the predominant pattern. The basis of this diversity is to be found in divergent historical experiences and political evolutions in the region. Much of the historical influence that separates the experiences and character of government and politics of the individual Caribbean states is due to the impact of divergent British, French, Spanish, Dutch, and U.S. colonization in the Caribbean and the residual legacy of their rule. In addition, some major differences in the nature of politics in these states arises from the character of the dominant political movements, their respective leadership, and their ties with major world powers in the post–World War II period.

The Caribbean represents a zone of intense political rivalry between Western capitalist and Eastern communist influences in their efforts to establish client states and international allies or to weaken the network of international support for the rival power bloc. The emergence of Cuba in the 1960s as a communist and radical Third World counterpoise to persisting dominant North American and Western European influences has been a major factor here. Also important is the growing connection between Caribbean political leaders and the Nonaligned movement in the Third World. The ideal of Third World neutrality competes with traditional Caribbean pro-Western stances and the newer leaning toward the Eastern bloc via the Cuban connection. Understanding Caribbean politics, therefore, depends very much on having a grasp of these regional ideological currents and their contemporary impact.

The Caribbean region consists mainly of ministates with small populations. The nature of their politics, therefore, reflects many of the features, problems, possibilities, and potentials of exercising authority and managing power within political communities that are even smaller than most cities and towns in industrial societies.

Caribbean societies have a long history of close contact with the North American mainland. The United States represents the most important source of imports for the region as a whole and the largest export destination. It has also been the major metropolitan center facilitating the economic linkages that result from the region's dependence on economic aid, foreign investment, and migration. The role played by U.S. interests in the region and the perspective these interests bring to bear on Caribbean political issues are, therefore, an important feature of the Caribbean political environment.

In the context of developing areas, the Caribbean has the largest concentration of territories that have voluntarily retained a colonial status, enjoying the benefits of colonial paternalism while postponing the burdens and responsibilities of independence. This compromise between the impulse for sovereignty and a pragmatic sense of economic realism represents an interesting aspect of the complex patterns of ambivalence that underlie the colonial connections in the Caribbean.

The states of the Caribbean are, of course, more than separate sovereign political entities. Political and ideological ties between them and between the more active political groupings in the region provide an important commentary on the alliances that shape Caribbean reality and the competition for power by opposing and adversary interests. These regional political alliances mirror the influence of both ideology and geography as well as the impact of language and culture on contemporary political groupings.

The fortunes of Caribbean economies, which are closely tied in to the world market, have fluctuated with the long- and short-term cyclical trends in the world economy. The decades between the early 1950s and the late 1960s were a period of growth, diversification, and expansion in trade, production, and real income for most territories in the region. The world price inflation of the 1970s and the world recession of the early 1980s have left a trail of declining incomes, reduced living standards, debt, and balance of payments problems, as well as debilitated public sectors with substantially reduced capacities to finance public expenditure. This pattern of economic crisis has tested the capability of these states to govern and sustain political stability under the stress of economic hardships, increasing social problems (crime, unemployment, social alienation, drugs, violence, etc.), and severely limited resources for public management.

A POLITICAL PROFILE OF THE CARIBBEAN

The 1970s were a period in which important changes in the character of political regimes occurred throughout the region, as governing coalitions and political leaders experienced increased difficulty in sustaining adequate levels of political support. The overall directions of these political changes express the dominant political and ideological impulses and trends that compete for ascendancy in the Caribbean. In some cases, competitive party systems that had been dominated for years by a single party witnessed electoral victories by opposition parties (St. Lucia, Antigua, and Dominica). In others, liberal-democratic rule collapsed and gave way to the installation of military rule and one-party states (Guyana, Suriname, and Grenada). In still others, stable political consensus broke down under the pressure of ideological polarization marked by increased levels of political violence (Jamaica and St. Lucia). An analysis of the political changes in the more important of these cases will provide a basis for assessing the strengths and weaknesses of the various types of political systems in the Caribbean.

As a region where liberal-democratic traditions are well established in political life, the Caribbean provides an arena in which to assess how the institutional legacy of parliamentary government, free elections, and multiple parties actually works in the context of Third World economic and social conditions. To be sure, these institutions have been adapted and modified by the social and cultural milieus of Caribbean societies and the contingent stresses and pressures of societies with limited social opportunities and surplus demand for jobs, social services, educational opportunities, and the creature comforts of modernity. The end result of this process of institutional adaptation has been the creation of political traditions that bear some similarities with parliamentary government in Europe and North America but also have distinctive, uniquely Caribbean features.

Caribbean society itself has been undergoing some fundamental patterns of change. The traditional plantation society, with its rigid social hierarchy dominated by a small handful of white landowners who presided over power structures with marked social inequalities and entrenched privilege has been modified over the present century. It has given birth to more open societies with upward social mobility, significant middle-class groupings, and a lower concentration of power in the hands of elites. Most importantly, in many societies in the region, the wealthy have had to begin sharing power with the emergent middle-class professional groups and to accept policy direction, control, and leadership from middle-class political leaders representing broadly based working-class and peasant interests. All of this has been facilitated by increasing urbanization, literacy levels, internal and external migration, mass media exposure, and shifts in the concentration of power from plantations to urban-based service and manufacturing activity. All of these social trends have served to sharpen political awareness and increase pressures for political expression and organization, especially among the lower socioeconomic groupings. Out of this have come vibrant expressions of party politics and highly politicized trade union movements. The long-term impact has been an enlargement of the role of the state in economic and social management and a shift in power from property owners to the political direc-torate, and to technocrats, who control the rapidly expanding domain of public power administered by state institutions.

The states in the Caribbean region may be divided into three major group-ings:

1. liberal-democratic states with competitive parties, high levels of civil and political rights, and a strong emphasis on social and economic reforms;
2. conservative nondemocratic or authoritarian regimes with low levels of political and civil rights; and
3. leftist regimes with highly organized mass supports, a ten-dency to advance social rights at the cost of civil and political rights, and a monopoly of power by the existing dominant leadership, invariably backed by a militarized and centrally controlled apparatus of power.

The overall trend in political change in the region between the early decades of the twentieth century and the contemporary period has been a transition from conservative-authoritarian regimes under European colonization to lib-eral-democratic states with either internal self-government or full indepen-dence. A second, less dominant pattern of change has been toward the emergence of leftist regimes transformed from either weak liberal-democratic states or conservative authoritarian political systems.

In spite of these regime changes over time and the accelerated shifts occur-ring in the 1970s, the overall pattern of politics in the region has been one of political stability, in contrast to nearby Central America. Clearly, there has been no overspill of Central American instability to the Caribbean, although some of the ideological issues that underpin that mainland agenda of conflicts are also to be found in political and ideological debates in the Caribbean.

A PROFILE OF REGIMES

Table 1 sets out a broad classification of Caribbean states into three main categories of political systems (liberal-democratic, leftist, and conservative-authoritarian). States are classified both for the beginning of the 1970s and for the early 1980s. The cross-tabulation permits an assessment of the nature of the changes that occurred over the decade as well as an appraisal of the current pattern of political regimes. Haiti is the only case of a conservative-authoritar-ian regime. Cuba, Guyana, and Suriname all fall into the category of leftist

TABLE 1.
Profile of Political Regime Types for Most of the 1970s and 1980–83[a]

Most of the 1970s	Conservative-Authoritarian	Leftist-Socialist	Liberal-Democratic (Independent)	Liberal-Democratic (Colonial)
Conservative-Authoritarian	**Haiti (1804)**		Dominican Republic (1844)	
Leftist-Socialist		**Cuba (1902)**		
Liberal-Democratic (Independent)		Guyana (1966) Grenada (1974)[b] Suriname (1975)	**Barbados (1966)** **Jamaica (1962)** **Bahamas (1973)** **Trinidad & Tobago (1962)**	
Liberal-Democratic (Colonial)			**St. Lucia (1979)** **Dominica (1978)** **St. Vincent (1979)** **Antigua (1982)** **Belize (1981)** **St. Kitts–Nevis (1983)**	**Puerto Rico** **Bermuda** **Martinique** **Guadeloupe** **Netherlands Antilles** **U.S. Virgin Islands** **Cayman Islands** **British Virgin Islands** **Montserrat** **Turks & Caicos Islands** **French Guiana** **Anguilla**

Source: Compiled by the author.

[a] Dates of independence are given in parentheses. Bold type indicates stable regimes.
[b] Occupied by the United States in October 1983.

regimes with militarized concentrations of power organized to express the hegemony (or monopoly control) by the dominant leftist intellectual leadership that claims sole right and authority to interpret the true interests of the majority classes (workers, peasants, etc.). The remaining political systems have preserved liberal democracy with varying levels of success.

It is of interest that thirteen of the twenty-eight territories in Table 1 remain under colonial rule. The French territories are administered as *départements* of the metropolitan government while the British and U.S. territories enjoy a high measure of internal self-government. Massive injections of economic aid that in several cases exceeds the income of the poorer territories in the region (in per capita terms) have made these territories reluctant to sever their colonial ties and the paternalistic links that go with them. The British territories receive the most modest inflows of economic aid through these colonial links, while the French, U.S. and Dutch territories have been most generously provided with economic assistance. As a result, it is the British territories that have been generating most of the drift toward independence. Here, the major constraining factor has been economic viability and the capacity to finance public expenditure in territories that had become accustomed to British budgetary support. Curiously, the largest single grouping of territories are the colonial liberal-democratic states where North American and European political influences remain very strong. (They represent, however, a minority of the Caribbean population.)

The major changes in the 1970s included the transition from colonial to independent liberal-democratic states (Belize, Antigua, St. Vincent, Dominica, and St. Lucia); shifts from liberal-democratic systems to leftist-socialist one-party states (Guyana, Grenada, and Suriname); and a change from authoritarian-conservative politics to liberal democracy in the Dominican Republic.

The breakdown of liberal democracy in Guyana and Grenada provides some interesting commentary on the conditions under which this type of political system is unlikely to survive. The case of Suriname also presents an important perspective on the issue of democratic collapse in the Caribbean.

Regime Changes (Grenada, Guyana, Suriname, the Dominican Republic)

In Grenada, although the government continued to exercise power under parliamentary constitutional authority in the 1970s, Prime Minister Eric Gairy turned that regime in the direction of authoritarianism between 1974 and 1979. Elections were rigged. Power was abused without any constraining countervailing forces being set in motion, and the entire bureaucracy and security forces were corrupted in order to support these changes. Opposition groups were subjected to violence and harassment. The scale of repression increased in the period leading up to 1979. As in countries such as Cuba and

Nicaragua before political revolution erupted, the major force destroying the established regime was the corruption and abuse of power by a dictatorial leader whose paranoia about real or imagined opposition forces led to a random escalation of repression directed at all classes and even at individuals within the governing coalition. The resulting rupture of the governing coalition and the considerable loss of legitimacy allowed a small group of determined opposition forces to seize power by force in March 1979. The seizure of power produced little bloodshed, for the security forces had not been sufficiently organized or armed to protect by armed might what had become a corrupt and inefficient regime.

In October 1983, however, a power struggle between Marxist deputy leader Bernard Coard and the more moderate party leader, Maurice Bishop, led to a military takeover of Grenada and the assassination of Prime Minister Bishop and three cabinet colleagues. Bishop was inclined to seek a negotiation of his country's differences with the United States and to lean more toward Western European support within the Socialist International than toward the Eastern European bloc. Faced with the slowdown of the economy due to declining foreign exchange earnings from tourism and nutmeg exports, Bishop was insistent on preserving a mixed economy in which the state sector coexisted with a strong private sector.

Although Bishop had much popular support from the citizens of Grenada and was the main link between the population and the governing New Jewel movement, he was relatively isolated by the dominant hard-line Marxist tendencies (influenced by strong Cuban connections) within the movement. Unfortunately, the movement had directed its organizational expansion more toward creating a popular militia (some 4,000 strong) than toward broadening the base of its party membership (approximately 400). The imbalance of military over political organizational strength led the military to assume control when faced with a deep internal division in the movement. After being placed under house arrest, Bishop refused to yield to the military takeover. The result was that his popular support rallied to his defense and released him. But the militia mounted a massive attack on Bishop and his followers that left close to 200 persons dead when armored cars and heavy weapons were opened up on a large crowd of some 5,000 loyal pro-Bishop Grenadians.

Bishop surrendered, but he and three cabinet colleagues were led away and shot. The assassination of Bishop sent shock waves of anger, protest, and concern throughout the Caribbean. The small Caribbean states in the Windward and Leeward island groups were fearful of the arms build-up taking place in Grenada under Cuban and USSR sponsorship. Bishop was seen as a force for restraint and moderation. His death and its circumstances triggered a panic reaction that resulted in the small states around Grenada inviting Barbados, Jamaica, and the United States to join them in invading Grenada in order to liberate the people from oppressive military rule. A Caribbean force of 300 provided a cover of legitimacy for what was in reality a U.S. invasion designed explicitly to eliminate the island's potential to mature into "another Cuba" in the region.

The invasion served to divide the Caribbean into a majority of hard-line anti-Marxist states aligning with the United States in seeking to eliminate the threat of Marxist subversion in the region and a smaller group that refused to support the effort for a variety of different reasons. Trinidad and Tobago, Belize, the Bahamas, and Guyana opposed the invasion. The other English-speaking Caribbean countries strongly supported the move.

Public opinion polls have confirmed that the people of the English-speaking Caribbean strongly supported the invasion. In Jamaica a national poll revealed 58 percent in favor and 34 percent against, while in Trinidad and in Grenada itself the support levels for the invasion were 61 percent and 90 percent respectively. The invasion initiative was promoted initially by Barbados, Dominica, Jamaica, and the United States. The prime ministers of Jamaica and of Dominica (as head of the Organisation of Eastern Caribbean States) played key roles in convincing the members of the OECS (St. Vincent, St. Lucia, Montserrat, Antigua, and St. Kitts-Nevis) to join and support the U.S.-led invasion. The severity of the fighting and the discovery of large stocks of arms of Cuban and Soviet origin has been used to confirm the fears of these small states that regional subversion was being planned in Grenada. As a result, military and political links between these English-speaking Caribbean states and the United States will increase significantly in the 1980s.

As a result of the invasion and the removal of the military junta after ten days of fierce battle between U.S. marines (5,000 strong) and local militia (4,000 in number) supported by some 600 Cubans, an interim regime has been set up with a view to engineering Grenada's transition back to liberal-democratic rule and free elections.

Cuban and Soviet arms supplies and military training had turned Grenada into a garrison state with military capability to defeat all of the English-speaking Caribbean states combined. This drastic alteration of the balance of military capability in the region combined with the perceived Marxist threat (to weak ministates without effective armies or other security forces) left the door open for U.S. leadership to assume the role of protector of small and weak democratic states against international Marxist insurgency and military threats.

The brutal nature of the political murders in Grenada has already had the effect of discrediting Marxism/Leninism throughout the region. Cuban implication in the removal of Bishop has increased fears about Cuban political interference in other territories. Even leftist Suriname broke diplomatic relations with Cuba over developments in Grenada.

Grenada has provided the United States with an opportunity to assert its political and military strength in the Caribbean and to cement ties of loyalty and support from English-speaking countries that live in fear of communist subversion. Division over the invasion, however, has had the effect of shattering what little regional political unity existed among the English-speaking countries.

In the case of Guyana, a liberal-democratic state was gradually converted into a militarized leftist-socialist regime by the governing party, rather than through the seizure of power by opposition groups, as in Grenada. Here, the liberal-democratic system was corrupted to sustain one-party rule. But whereas in Grenada the main opposition (the New Jewel movement, led by Maurice Bishop) refused to be relegated to the status of a permanent and powerless opposition, the opposition parties in Guyana have not resisted their fate as symbolic decorations of a competitive party façade designed to disguise the reality of one-party rule. The racial balance in Guyana permitted this manipulation of power by a party identified with the black population—the People's National Congress party (PNC) led by President-for-life Forbes Burnham. The Guyanese political community is sharply divided along racial lines, with the East Indians supporting the opposition People's Progressive party (PPP), led by the avowed communist Cheddi Jagan, and the blacks supporting Burnham's PNC party. The Indians are strong in commerce, agriculture, and the professions, but the blacks control the bureaucracy, the security forces, and the administrative machinery of the state. Fear of Indian control of state power provides a secure base of black support for Burnham's PNC. A minority Marxist party (the Working People's alliance), led by university intellectuals, has so far not been able to challenge Burnham's one-party regime and the Marxist-led PPP has been both docile and compliant. In contrast to Grenada, where the main parties competing for power were ideologically divided, the major political parties in Guyana are controlled by the middle-class leftist intelligentsia and are prosocialist. In both cases liberal democracy broke down because political leaders were unwilling to share power or to abide by the rules of the game of liberal-democratic politics, which limit power.

The experience of Suriname adds a somewhat different dimension to this story of democratic collapse in the Caribbean. Here as in Guyana, sharp polarization of the society along racial lines had debilitated an already weak and fractured party system and had reduced consensus within the elite to a rather low level. Mutual distrust between the racial blocs (black and East Indian) has facilitated the abandonment of competitive politics and the consolidation of a leftist and military regime that has yet to build a strong base of popular support. What began between the black-dominated governing coalition and the armed forces as a pay dispute suddenly escalated into a military takeover in 1980. The new regime led by leftist army officers and intellectuals had established strong ties of support with both Cuba and Grenada. In Suriname, there was convincing evidence of Cuban leftist support in the periods both before and after the political revolution. This external support had led to anti-U.S. regional alliances and had intensified Cuban political and military influences in these territories. The alliance aroused the hostility of the United States which mounted a strong diplomatic and political offensive against both Suriname and Grenada, eventuating in the military occupation of Grenada. U.S. economic aid was first cut off and both states were attacked by aggressive U.S. rhetoric on the subject of their links with Cuba and their ostensible role as platforms for communist military attacks on the U.S. mainland. Developments in Grenada have eliminated the problem by removing the Marxist-Cuban influence there and causing the rupture of Cuba-Suriname ties.

The Dominican Republic represents a fascinating case of a shift from an authoritarian political regime to liberal democracy. Substantial traces of authoritarianism remain intact, but the liberal-democratic tendencies have been quietly taking root in the 1970s. As in Grenada and Suriname, the attempt to achieve regime change was influenced by external factors, but here the major input came from the United States. The human rights foreign policy of President Carter, which sought to promote liberal democracy in some countries, was activated decisively in the 1970s by the threat of a withdrawal of aid to the Dominican Republic when the military seemed poised to prevent the reformist Democratic Revolutionary party (PRD) from taking power after the 1978 election.

The collapse of the dictatorship after Trujillo's assassination in 1961 presented an opportunity for the Dominican Republic to move toward liberal democracy. The active opposition forces that sought power under the banner of the PRD were led by a section of the leftist intelligentsia that was socialist in ideological outlook yet liberal-democratic and anticommunist in its political views. These democratic socialists were opposed to communism but embraced strong nationalist and anti-U.S. sentiments. If the United States had sanctioned their election victory in 1962 and defended the integrity of the liberal-democratic system, political change would have taken shape much earlier. Instead, the Johnson administration backed a military coup, which removed the chances of either a stable liberal-democratic system or rule by a reformist center-left party. The army was on the verge of preserving power in the hands of the remnants of the Trujillo dynasty when President Carter intervened and permitted the PRD to take power in 1978.

Democracy in Ministates

Among the regimes where liberal democracy was stabilized, the pattern of politics in the 1970s suggests that there are weaknesses in the functioning of this European political model in these small Caribbean states. What precisely are these weaknesses and how can we account for them?

Political loyalties in these ministates are highly personalized. Individuals and groups are often intimidated from adopting positions they believe in on political issues out of a reluctance to seem unsupportive of the dominant political leaders and personalities to whom they owe allegiance. These loyalty ties are usually part of patron-client networks and heavy dependency between private interests and the state in economies with government spending ranging between 35 percent and 50 percent of the gross national product and the state being the major source of employment.

The problem is compounded by small size. Close face-to-face relationships and friendship networks often inhibit individual political freedom. The ability of the politician to use these networks to restrain and control the political behavior of individuals is quite significant. Small size and the consequent personalization of any political act increase the visibility of all political actors and the ability of the authorities to undertake surveillance of political activity. Political loyalties are often extensions of deeply felt racial, community, or family loyalties, and these primordial attachments often discourage coalition formation, flexible issue positions, and willingness either to negotiate issues or to see them as negotiable.

While these factors inhibit the role of public opinion in politics, the effects are not fundamental where there exist organizations, associations, and institutions that cannot be muzzled and controlled by governing elites. These include the church, trade unions, the mass media, commodity organizations representing farmer interests, interest groups, and professional associations. Such institutions and groups have played a significant role in the consolidation of liberal democracy in the Caribbean.

In my view, there are three main dangers to the survival of liberal democracy in the region. The first consists of a cultural residue or survival from the value system of the early plantation society with its emphasis on paternalism, authoritarianism, and elitism. The authoritarianism inherent in the culture, social ideology, and social relations of the traditional plantation society have in some subtle (as well as overt) ways carried over into the contemporary value system. There is a strong tendency to elevate and defer to political leaders as if they were transcendental authority figures standing at some great distance above the political system. These leaders are (in their moments of high popularity) invested with extraordinary qualities of wisdom and pampered with emotional displays of ritual subservience by party followers. Party leaders are put on a pedestal by cabinet members, parliamentarians, party activists, and other members of the party elite. The effect is a tendency for the party leader to assume a sense of personal authority and power that is inconsistent with leadership accountability and a strong democratic system. Those personalities who have an extraordinary need for either power or the ego gratification that comes from acting out this role have both the means and the temptation to try to corrupt the liberal-democratic system into something that can guarantee their commanding role. That was precisely what happened in

Grenada under Gairy and in Guyana under Burnham. Such a tradition of leadership is especially strong in Jamaica and has been held in check there only by the evenly balanced two-party system. Beyond this, the tradition of transcendental leadership stifles internal party democracy.

A second area of weakness in the liberal-democratic systems of the Caribbean is the high-handed, nonbargaining, nonconsultative, and nonresponsive tradition of decision making and policy formulation inherited from the colonial civil service system. This tradition has yet to be eliminated from the inherited legacy of state institutions that have grafted a superstructure of Western European liberal political institutions onto a substructure of authoritarian colonial administration. The contradiction between the traditions of the state bureaucracy and those of liberal-democratic politics represents an area of severe tension and weakness in these democratic systems. The very character of these administrative and bureaucratic institutions makes it easy for leaders to subvert the liberal-democratic system. That more states have not drifted into either conservative-authoritarianism or leftist single-party states is due partly to the ideological attachment of the present generation of leaders to liberal democracy and to the strength of the network of independent organizations and institutions (trade unions, church, interest groups, etc.).

The third area of weakness, political violence by military and police or by organized paramilitary and terrorist groups, is still a potential threat to Caribbean democracy. This danger has emerged in Jamaica and to a lesser extent in Antigua, St. Lucia, and Dominica through the arming of political activists. But the danger has been great only in Jamaica, where the foreign connections of the two rival parties facilitated an extensive arming of political gunmen on a scale that threatened the capability of the army and the police to contain political killings and public disorder. In this liberal-democratic state both major political parties (the People's National party and the Jamaica Labour party) have the means to destabilize the political system through activists who have been heavily armed with high-powered submachine guns and sophisticated assault rifles. In both Grenada and Guyana, the corruption of the security forces was a major factor in the dismantling of the liberal-democratic system as the armed forces became the political tool of a repressive and paranoid chief executive.

COMPARING THE INDEPENDENT STATES

Social Modernization

In those states that have a long tradition of authoritarian rule, wage workers still represent less than half of the labor force; here, the working class assumes a minority status and small peasants and petty commodity producers are numerically predominant. This situation characterizes both Haiti and the Dominican Republic, societies in which the middle class and lower middle class (consisting of professionals, managers, and administrative and clerical workers) constitute a relatively small proportion of the labor force. Literacy levels in these countries are still quite low in spite of the considerable advances that have been made since 1950. There is, therefore, a considerable cultural gap and status distance between, on the one hand, the small elite and middle class and, on the other, the large grouping of illiterate or semiliterate low-income peasants and petty commodity producers. This social profile is typical of societies with a continuing predominance of paternalistic social tendencies. Also typical of such social systems is the predominantly rural-agrarian character of the labor force, a section of which tends to come into the social and political power domain of the big landowners. Although significant social changes (such as urban expansion and increased literacy) have occurred in these societies, their essential paternalistic features remain unchanged. Authoritarianism is, therefore, entrenched. While the institutional forms of liberal democracy can be developed (as they have been in the Dominican Republic), many of the features and important attributes of liberal democracy are not likely to develop in the short run. These include strong independent interest groups representing a wide array of interests, independent centers of public opinion, and high levels of political freedom or individual political rights. Belize, which also falls into this category but has maintained a long tradition of liberal democracy, is the exceptional case.

Those societies where paternalism has been eroded fall into two main groupings. The first consists of the most socially advanced countries of the region. These are very small open societies with socially egalitarian values, large middle-class and lower-middle-class groups, an overwhelming preponderance of wage labor in the labor force, and only a small proportion of that labor force either in agriculture or in the petty commodity sector. Within this group, Cuba is the only independent Hispanic society and the only country with a relatively large population. These societies can appropriately be classified as very modernized in their social structure. Income levels are high, and adult literacy has been widespread since as early as 1950. (Barbados is the exceptional case of high literacy and high working-class living standards.) Such a level of social modernization is incompatible with an authoritarian political regime. The breakdown of the authoritarian state system in Cuba and the growth of the first stable leftist-socialist model of political development in that country is perhaps quite understandable in light of its level of social development. The other modernized social systems in the Caribbean all have stable and highly developed liberal-democratic state systems.

The second grouping of societies where paternalism has been eroded include some that have features similar to the modern small open societies just described, combined with strong residues and traces of paternalist social values and social relations. These will be referred to here as dualistic societies. Liberal democracy tends to operate under great stress in these societies, as the authoritarian value system often runs counter to the values of liberalism. In particular, social violence, authoritarian styles of leadership, authoritarian institutions, nonbargaining attitudes to political conflict, and tendencies toward political religiosity and fanaticism introduce high levels of stress in the workings of the liberal-democratic model. On the other hand, there are strong social forces that seek to democratize political power in order to make it responsive to mass needs and interests and to enlist mass participation. These societies represent an intermediary level of social development in the region and include significant concentrations of isolated rural communities, illiterate adults, and petty commodity producers as well as agricultural workers. Table 2 groups Caribbean countries by level of social modernization and presents their political and social profiles.

Political Freedom

Annual surveys of political and civil rights for most states, conducted by Freedom House, an independent New York–based political institute, provide what are probably the best available rankings of civil liberties in different countries (Gastil 1982). The Freedom House civil liberties scale ranks countries, with the highest levels of civil liberties as level 1 and the lowest as level 7. The scale essentially measures individual citizens' freedom of expression, association, and movement, the degree to which these freedoms are protected by the administration of justice, and the extent to which violations of them occur through arbitrary sanctions, coercion, and harassment by the state. Most Western democratic-pluralist states are ranked at level 1. Communist states are mainly ranked between levels 4 and 6, while oppressive authoritarian dictatorships are usually ranked at level 7.

The Freedom House index of civil liberties is ideally designed to measure the degree to which liberal-democratic rights have developed in a state. The scale, therefore, permits us to compare the differences between the three main types of state systems in the achievement of individual civil liberties. Since the Carter administration, the emphasis on human rights and civil liberties has generated legislation in the United States requiring the executive to certify satisfactory levels of civil liberties as a condition for legislative support for foreign aid to individual countries.

Part of the rationale for this requirement was the recognition that pre-Carter, post–World War II U.S. policy in the region concentrated on the civil liberties violations of communist states and the threat that ideology posed to individual freedom while ignoring the violations of human rights that were pervasive in authoritarian states. The ascendancy of a liberal position on human rights during President Carter's administration brought sharply into

TABLE 2.

Profile of Independent Political Communities

Social Development	Per Capita Income ($U.S.) 1980	Political Regime[a] 1980	Percentage of White Collar Workers 1978	Percentage of Wage Laborers 1978	Percentage of Agricultural Workers 1978	Percentage of Literate Adults		Percentage of Population Isolated from Urban Centers 1980
						1980	1950	
Paternalistic								
Haiti	270	authorit.	10	20	70	23	10	80
Dominican Republic	1,140	lib.-dem.	15	44	57	67	60	55
Belize	950	lib.-dem.	17	67	40	75	n.a.	n.a.
Highly modernized								
Bahamas	3,300	lib.-dem.	48	96	6	98	73	25
Barbados	3,040	lib.-dem.	32	96	17	99	91	28
Trinidad & Tobago	4,370	lib.-dem.	42	86	12	95	74	20
Suriname	2,840	left.-soc.	33	75	18	80	73	22
Cuba	1,407	left.-soc.	31	98	30	96	78	24
Dualistic								
Jamaica	1,030	lib.-dem.	26	58	29	50	40	30
St. Lucia	850	lib.-dem.	23	75	40	88	n.a.	50
Dominica	620	lib.-dem.	20	70	50	n.a.	n.a.	60
Grenada[b]	690	left.-soc.	22	72	38	80	n.a.	45
Guyana	690	left.-soc.	19	79	22	86	74	30

Sources: Banks and Overstreet 1980, Central Intelligence Agency 1981, International Labour Office 1978–80, Kidron and Segal 1981, World Bank 1980.

[a] Political regimes: lib.-dem. = liberal-democratic, left.-soc. = leftist-socialist, authorit. = authoritarian.

[b] This table represents information gathered prior to the U.S. occupation in October 1983.

relief the issue of whether communist or authoritarian states posed greater threats to human rights and political freedoms.

Some critics of this liberal position have implied that authoritarian states have the potential to evolve toward liberal democracy but that communist states represent a "terminal case" of the degeneration of political freedom. The application of the civil liberties scale to the countries in the region thus provides some basis on which to assess the influence of type of political regime on the level of civil liberties. Among the liberal-democratic states the rankings will provide an indication of how far these political systems have moved toward achieving, in Third World conditions, levels of individual political freedom like those associated with Western industrial states.

Table 3 represents my own adaptation of the Freedom House civil liberties scale for 1980 for the various regime types in the Caribbean. It will be noted that only three of the eight liberal-democratic states listed are classified as having the highest level of individual civil liberties. These include the Bahamas and Barbados, both of which fall within the grouping of most highly modernized social systems. Other highly ranked states are Trinidad and Tobago and Dominica—also former British colonies. Among the liberal-democratic states are three that enjoy only medium levels of civil liberties. These are Jamaica, St. Lucia, and the Dominican Republic. The first two are dualistic social systems subject to internal stress and tensions, which are expressed through the mechanism of intense political party animosities, factionalism, and political violence. In Jamaica, not only is the degree of political stress somewhat higher but the incidence of violence against persons and property is considerably amplified because of extensive possession of guns by political activists.

The Dominican Republic reflects the impact of continuing paternalism and authoritarianism during the slow transition to liberal-democratic politics. Considerable power still rests with institutions and interests that are not fully supportive of these changes. To that extent, the change is still tenuous and could be reversed in the face of severe internal political crises. The development of individual civil liberties advances only as this slow process of political change moves forward.

Leftist-socialist regimes are characterized by the lowest level of civil liberties. Their average ranking for 1980 was level 5 compared to level 2 for the liberal-democratic and level 4 for the authoritarian regimes. Although only one communist state (Cuba) is included in the leftist-socialist grouping, the civil liberties ranking of these states is similar to that for the sole authoritarian regime (Haiti). In Guyana (and in Grenada before the occupation) systematic state control of the mass media served to limit the free flow of political information and ideas. Opposition political groups are also subjected to violence and harassment. Guyana, however, unlike Haiti, or Grenada before the occupation, tolerates a loyal opposition party, while circumscribing the politi-

TABLE 3.

Regime Type and Political Indicators

| | Civil Liberties 1980[a] | Trade Union Membership | | Political Role of Military 1982 | Military Spending as Percentage of Budget Expenditure 1980 | Armed Forces per 1,000 1980 | Military Spending over GNP 1980 |
		Percentage of Wage Laborers 1979	Status 1980				
Liberal-Democratic							
Belize	1	8	free	neutral	n.a.	n.a.	n.a.
Bahamas	1	26	free	neutral	0.3	n.a.	0.1
Barbados	1	33	free	neutral	0.6	4.0	0.2
Trinidad & Tobago	2	31	free	neutral	1.3	0.8	0.4
Jamaica	3	43	free	neutral	3.0	1.8	0.7
St. Lucia	3	27	free	neutral	0.1	n.a.	0.2
Dominican Republic	3	5	not free	politicized	10.0	3.8	2.0
Dominica	2	34	free	neutral	n.a.	n.a.	n.a.
Leftist-Socialist							
Cuba	6	n.a.	not free	politicized	18.0	23.0	5.0
Guyana	4	40	free	politicized	5.0	8.1	3.0
Grenda[b]	5	39	free	politicized	n.a.	n.a.	n.a.
Authoritarian							
Haiti	5	8	not free	politicized	5.0	1.2	1.0

Sources: Banks and Overstreet 1980, Central Intelligence Agency 1981, Sivard 1981.

[a] Civil liberties scale: 1 = most free, 7 = least free.
[b] This table represents information gathered prior to the U.S. occupation in October 1983.

cal effectiveness of its one-party system by press censorship, electoral manipulation, and widespread use of the army and police as instruments of
controlled harassment.

In the newly established leftist-socialist regimes, the rationale for restrictions on civil liberties is somewhat different from the justification used for
their permanent retardation as a necessary feature of the new regime. In the
early stages the state's position on civil liberties tends to be ambiguous and
ambivalent at best. Because many liberals support the new regimes in the
early stages, lip service is paid to civil liberties and individual political freedoms as legitimate political ends while the restrictions placed on them are
promoted as a temporary exigency demanded by the dangers of counterrevo-
lution. These restrictions acquire both urgency and legitimacy very quickly if
the state is able to point to threats from foreign enemies or alliances between
foreign enemies and supporters of the dismantled regime. This happened in
Grenada, where the United States was associated in a supportive way with the
political leadership of the discredited Gairy regime from which power was
seized in 1979. U.S. hostility to the new regime probably encouraged the drift
toward rigid restrictions on civil liberties: fears of possible U.S. intervention
created a climate of political paranoia and insecurity that discouraged the
relaxation of restrictions on civil liberties. The threat of the external enemy
and the potential link to internal sabotage are powerful political forces that
stand in the path of any progress toward higher levels of civil liberties. They
constitute a strong inducement toward the militarization of the political system and the development of repressive systems of internal security that will
destroy any potential for real and effective citizens' participation in the political process. If this trend continues, political mobilization (which is still
impressive in that country) will fail and eventually be limited to a small
minority of activist and militarized cadres supporting the regime while most
citizens will withdraw, out of fear of harassment by the state.

The long-term trend in such regimes is for initial restrictions on civil liberties to give way to a new pattern of freedom to participate within the rules, the
codes of conduct, and the organizations that support (and are controlled by)
the state, by its party and bureaucratic agencies, and by the vanguard leadership. A new system of political rights therefore emerges in the long run; this
has happened, for example, in Cuba. It has also happened in Guyana, but by
the route of bending and adapting forms of participation in the liberal-democratic model to make them compatible with a state system based on leftist-
socialist principles. The low ranking of these countries on the Freedom House
scale of civil liberties is therefore misleading because it fails to account for the
trade-off between new channels of controlled participation that are offered by
the state (within the mass party, community groups, mass organizations, and
production organizations) and the tight restrictions on civil liberties. Compared to the authoritarian state, the leftist-socialist regimes in the region are

very participatory. Moreover, in all of them workers have access to participation in the decisions made to implement state policies, and community groups have access to involvement in the process of implementing state policy at a level that has no parallel in the liberal-democratic states in the region. In liberal-democratic regimes, voting and party membership are the limits to which opportunities for participation are developed.

Systematic state control of social and economic relations, economic controls through planning, and state economic management are all inherent features of the leftist-socialist political regime, whether communist or noncommunist. The communist version abandons the market mechanism of allocating goods, services, and prices and substitutes centralized or decentralized procedures of state control. Its essence, therefore, is the command economy controlled by the state through planning machinery. The noncommunist version retains the market mechanism as the vehicle for price determination and for the distribution of goods and services but organizes the economy around a preponderance of public ownership, which requires a powerful political apparatus of public management and political controls to make it workable.

Political goals and objectives are often articulated in the language of Marxism or Marxism/Leninism, and this has given rise to a tendency to equate all leftist-socialist regimes with communism. The confusion is also partly due to the fact that the communist cases have led the way toward the development of the machinery of political controls, which means that the institutional forms of both versions are very similar on a superficial level. Further, the balance between domestic and international political alignments more often than not locates the leadership of the noncommunist regimes in strong anti-U.S. alliances, and this also encourages the confusion.

To the extent that the noncommunist version has a wide option to increase or decrease the size of the state sector or the private sector or to determine the relative sizes of these two areas of the economy's ownership, the noncommunist populist-statist regime will have a more varied power structure in which private ownership interests can be co-opted into the political elite or into the centers of decision making. One critical difference in the command political structure of the communist and noncommunist regimes is that in the long run the state bureaucrats tend to have more power than the party cadres in the noncommunist systems, while the party cadres will tend to have more power under communism. In noncommunist systems that lack competitive politics, party structures tend to weaken and degenerate over time. Weakness inherent in the Guyanese ruling PNC and the evident signs of weakening within the Grenadian People's Revolutionary government before the regime's collapse support this interpretation. In Grenada the new regime was installed by a movement that did not have a strong party structure. The Grenadian New Jewel movement was hardly more than a socialist electoral party before a military coup swept it into power without much preparation in the management of state power outside of the British parliamentary system. Hence it is not surprising that this state tried to accelerate its learning process by drawing on assistance from Cuba. The Grenadian People's Revolutionary movement was engaged in trying to consolidate its power base, and was therefore reluctant to permit open election and challenge by an opposition party. Failure to do so meant that many Caribbean states treated the regime as illegitimate.

The Cuban model developed along the lines of a noncommunist leftist-socialist model until increasing reliance on the Soviet Union and the insertion of strong Soviet influences between the middle 1960s and early 1970s converted it into a communist version. Subsequently, this Soviet influence developed and consolidated a strong Cuban party state that gradually replaced the power structure in which the state bureaucrats were dominant.

The leftist-socialist state involves a process of managing power in any political system in which power is both appropriated on behalf of the masses or majority classes and highly concentrated and unregulated by legal or constitutional means.

Table 3 also lists the level of union membership among wage laborers, in order to assess the effect of regime types on levels of labor organization. To the extent that labor develops strong channels of participation through trade union activity, the imbalance in the power of the capitalist and labor interests will tend to be reduced. That imbalance tends in the long run to favor capitalists where they control a large or dominant share of the economy. Part of the ideological case made for liberal democracy is that it permits and stimulates political organization by the poorer classes in ways that are blocked or retarded in authoritarian regimes. Under the noncommunist leftist-socialist regime, free labor organization is permitted, which is unlike the situation under communism. It is therefore of interest to examine whether these regimes retard or advance labor organization.

The data shown in Table 3 suggest that levels of union organization within the region are influenced by the political regimes. The consistent pattern is one of high levels of trade union membership among the more modernized societies and low levels among the societies with strong paternalistic value systems and a long history of recent authoritarian tendencies. Traditional Hispanic influences in the Caribbean discouraged a rapid development of working-class efforts and achievement in class representation through trade unionism. In the non-Hispanic Caribbean, where capitalist and Western liberal political influences were strong, independent and more advanced trade unionism was the norm. But a decade of competitive party politics has not significantly influenced levels of union membership in the Hispanic Dominican Republic. This low level of union membership in the Hispanic states is a very significant indicator of continuing paternalistic values among the working class, among whom large sections continue to rely on employer paternalism rather than collective bargaining power through unions to protect their interests.

Table 3 also classifies the relative freedom of trade union movements in these states. The historical differences between the English-speaking and Dutch-speaking states, on the one hand, and the Hispanic states on the other are as evident here as they were in levels of union membership. In the Hispanic states the labor movement was not only tightly controlled but in fact repressed by the state. In contrast, all of the English-speaking states, as well as the one Dutch-speaking state, have trade unions that enjoy a status of freedom not unlike that extended to labor in Western European and North Atlantic liberal-democratic states. Haiti and Cuba reveal the impact of political regime and historical influences in the common regimented state control of labor. As a peasant society, Haiti never developed a strong working class, and its authoritarian state was hostile to a free labor movement. In Cuba, the Hispanic tradition together with the centralizing tendency of communism brought labor under strict state regulation.

The Military

The nature of a state's political regime also affects the role of its military. The liberal democracies are the only states in the Caribbean in which the army is both politically neutral and under civilian control. This is a most important factor in enabling citizens to hold their government accountable to them, to hold it subject to their opinions, and to make it responsive to the threat of a withdrawal of legitimacy in the event that state power is abused. In both Dominica and St. Lucia during the 1970s, for example, unpopular governments were forced to resign by organized citizens' protests when those governments were perceived by vocal and active centers of public opinion as having lost legitimacy. In both cases, representatives of trade unions, the church, the civil service, the business community, and the working class, supported by school children, mounted nationwide protests and shutdowns. These actions were not the expression of sectional positions or points of view, but rather the articulation of the political will and consensus of the majority in small communities with extensive networks of face-to-face communication. The resignation of the government led in each case to the calling of new elections in which opposition parties and alternate personalities were voted into office. The withdrawal of legitimacy by public protest action had served to accelerate changes in political succession, which made for a stabilization of the political community. The articulation of such a consensual political will, which generates a virtual moral majority (in a literal sense), is possible only in small states of the size that exist in the Caribbean (50,000–250,000 citizens).

Where the state is militarized and the military overdeveloped, as is the case with both the authoritarian state and the leftist-socialist regimes, the expres-

CARL STONE

sion of this sort of spontaneous political will is not possible, even in very small societies such as those in the Caribbean. As is shown in Table 3, military expenditure and military personnel are high in leftist-socialist regimes and low in liberal-democratic regimes, where the tendency toward militarism is brought under civilian control.

Militarization is clearly minimized in the states that have developed liberal-democratic systems, while it is clearly most advanced in the state systems that are based on leftist-socialist principles. The consistency of the limited data on military spending and the number of military personnel confirm the evident difference in the political role of the military in these types of state systems. Where the military is brought under civilian control, as in liberal-democratic systems, it is unable to claim a large share of national resources, and this minimizes its capacity to operate as a means of intimidating citizens. The case of the Dominican Republic suggests that, where the military *is* able to do that, it is quite difficult to bring it under control. The high degree of militarization in states such as Guyana (where the government maintains itself partly through military support) and Cuba (where increasing militarization has redefined the whole character of the regime) raises serious questions about the claims by these regimes to be moving toward democratic goals. The fact that militarism was predominant in the leftist-socialist regimes (Suriname and, formerly, Grenada) confirms the contradictions between democratic goals and the garrison state character of these revolutionary governments. The Cuban case illustrates even further the high costs that are incurred when such states get involved in major international power struggles, for this requires them to arm extensively for self-defense and for the deployment of military resources regionally or globally. Under these conditions, extreme political vigilance, tightly organized secret police methods, systematic suppression of dissent, and the discouraging of the free flow of ideas become necessary to satisfy the external revolutionary political imperative. But the effect is to convert a state conceived in the lofty ideals of democracy into a military command structure in which democracy is sometimes forgotten and in which citizens often merely take orders. The close alliance between Cuba and both Suriname and Grenada before Grenada's occupation suggests that these trends were sustained by regional power struggles with the United States. Perhaps the very hostile posture of the United States government under President Reagan makes the prospects for increased militarism inevitable in these states.

Ideology

Ideological tendencies and inclinations have also been influenced by the balance of social forces that support and sustain the distinctly separate regime types in the Caribbean. Table 4 lists a variety of ideological and ideologically related attributes of the three types of political regime. A content analysis of

TABLE 4.
Regime Types and Political Attributes

	Pro-U.S. Votes on East-West Issues in UN 1975–78[a]	Dominant Ideological Tendency 1970s	Dominant Ideological Tendency 1982	Membership in Nonaligned Movement 1979	Main Opposition 1982	Index of Political Stability 1982	Policy Toward U.S. 1982
Liberal-Democratic							
Belize	n.a.	reformist	reformist	no	legitimate	1	pro-U.S.
Bahamas	5	reformist	reformist	no	legitimate	1	pro-U.S.
Barbados	4	reformist	reformist	no	legitimate	1	pro-U.S.
Trinidad & Tobago	2	reformist	reformist	no	legitimate	1	anti-U.S.
Jamaica	2	socialist	reformist	yes	legitimate	2	pro-U.S.
St. Lucia	n.a.	reformist	reformist	no	legitimate	2	pro-U.S.
Dominican Republic	5	conservative	reformist	no	legitimate	2	pro-U.S.
Dominica	n.a.	reformist	reformist	no	legitimate	2	pro-U.S.
Leftist-Socialist							
Cuba	1	Marxist	Marxist	yes	none	1	anti-U.S.
Guyana	1	socialist	socialist	yes	legitimate	3	neutral
Grenada[c]	n.a.	socialist	socialist	yes	none	2	anti-U.S.
Suriname	n.a.	reformist	socialist	yes	underground	3	anti-U.S.
Authoritarian							
Haiti	5	conservative	conservative	no	underground	2	pro-U.S.

Sources: Banks and Overstreet 1980, Central Intelligence Agency 1981, United Nations 1975–79.

[a] UN-votes scale of rankings: 5 = 60% or more voting with the U.S.
4 = 40%–59% voting with the U.S.
3 = less than 40% voting with both USSR and the U.S.
2 = 40%–59% voting with the USSR
1 = 60% or more voting with the USSR

[b] Index of political stability: 1 = stable
2 = low political stress
3 = high political stress
4 = factional violence & instability
5 = internal war & instability

[c] This table represents information gathered prior to the U.S. occupation in October 1983.

country reports from a variety of secondary sources was used to construct a scale of ideological tendencies for the various countries. Assessments are given for the dominant ideological tendencies both during the 1970s and in 1982 in order to give a sense of the stability of those trends over time.

Four main ideological trends were identified: conservative, reformist, socialist, and Marxist. The conservative tendency has concentrated on maximizing economic growth and studiously avoiding any policies aimed either at restructuring the society and its political institutions or at redistributing income or the ownership of assets on a large enough scale to influence the relative power of classes in the society. The reformist ideological orientation supports all of these priorities but tries to push for social changes that ease the burdens on the poor without attempting to change asset distribution, income distribution, or the distribution of power. Reformist regimes place primary emphasis on education, skill training, and upward social mobility, as well as improved social services generally. Their goal is to balance these social priorities with efforts to increase economic growth. Like the conservative orientation, then, the reformist point of view gives high priority to economic growth. The socialist position involves attempts to introduce policies that would redistribute wealth or assets or power in favor of the poorer classes. Some of its main policy instruments are large-scale cooperatives, land reform, worker ownership, limitations on private ownership, and extensive nationalization of assets held by foreign corporations or local capitalists. Also included are extensive subsidies for reducing the living expenses of the poor and pricing policies designed to redistribute income in favor of the poorer classes. The Marxist approach involves efforts at installing or consolidating a planned or command type economy that dismantles the market mechanism. Here, prices, wages, production targets, and the distribution of goods and services are determined by central planners rather than by supply and demand.

Throughout the 1970s the predominant tendency among liberal-democratic states was reformist. The two exceptions were Jamaica, where a foreign policy tie-up with Cuba accelerated a shift to the left in domestic policy goals, and the Dominican Republic, where the political system continued to be dominated by a coalition of interests that controlled state power in the earlier authoritarian Trujillo period. It is noteworthy that in both Jamaica and the Dominican Republic elections held toward the end of the decade (1978 and 1980 respectively) shifted these two states toward the mainstream tendency in the liberal-democratic grouping.

Liberal-democratic regimes in the Caribbean generally conform to the dominant ideological tendency of this regime type in Western capitalist states to move between center and center-left. The reformist posture represents a level of relative independence from powerful capitalist class interests. Majority class supports through party politics encourage and develop policy priorities that seek social reforms to benefit the masses. On the other hand, reformist

political leaderships are committed to the capitalist system of economic management, and therefore to according capitalists a significant voice in policy
making and defending their interests as long as these do not conflict with the
public welfare or the public interest. The liberal-democratic regimes in the
region all have political leaders and state bureaucrats who have developed an
agenda of policy priorities based on some notion of the public interest. Capitalists and other private interests usually have to make policy demands within
this framework. From time to time the interests of specific capitalist groups
are adversely affected, and to that extent the policy-making process develops
a moderate degree of autonomy from private interests. Table 4 shows that the
liberal-democratic states have the highest levels of political stability in the
region, are mainly pro–United States in their foreign policy, and tend not to be
members of the Third World's Nonaligned movement. With the exception of
Jamaica (under Manley) and the nationalist and anti-U.S. Trinidadian state,
they all voted heavily with the United States on East-West issues in the United
Nations in the second half of the 1970s. In these states political stability is
based partly on the fact that opposition groups are legitimate and function
within established political parties that have a stake in the political system and
are not averse to functioning as a loyal opposition. Liberal democracy provides, moreover, an outlet and safety valve for political alienation by giving
citizens political choices and alternatives when they grow disenchanted with a
governing coalition.

The experience of relative political calm in these states in the 1970s while
political instability was rampant in neighboring authoritarian Central American states points further to the important role of political institutions in stabilizing political life. This is a factor that is more often than not ignored entirely
in newspaper and media coverage of the region, which forecasts political
instability whenever economic trends deteriorate, unemployment levels seem
to be increasing, and economic growth and income trends look gloomy, as
they did for many countries in the 1970s and early 1980s. Even more absurd
are sensationalist attempts to raise alarms about potential communist
takeovers in the Caribbean as a consequence of economic declines. During the
latter half of the 1970s and early 1980s in St. Lucia, Jamaica, Barbados, and
Dominica, the most conservative among competing political parties and candidates won national elections against those with leftist-socialist ideological
tendencies. In Dominica, Antigua, and St. Vincent recently established leftist
parties (which had carried out extensive community and organizational work)
were badly defeated by the middle-of-the-road parties, in spite of the high and
increasing levels of unemployment and the severe economic recession that has
created enormous problems for these small states.

Leftist-socialist regimes in the region tend, on the contrary, to be supportive
of radical economic and social policies, to have membership in the Nonaligned movement, to vote against the United States in the United Nations on

East-West issues, and to be anti-U.S. in their foreign policy. They represent the regional opposition alliance to U.S. regional power and influence. As resentment against the United States builds up over north-south issues and Central America, the political leverage of these states in hemispheric politics may well increase. Except for Guyana and Suriname, where weak regimes rely heavily on coercion, these states, in contrast to the authoritarian state (Haiti), are very stable and have substantial mass support.

Clearly, the leftist-socialist regimes have the widest degrees of freedom to implement economic and social policy and enjoy the highest degree of independence from private property-owning interests. That fact alone makes such regimes inherently attractive to people who see the capitalist system and the landowning class as the main obstacles to policies that can benefit the majority interest. But it is possible that these political factors play no key role in influencing either the flow of benefits to the masses or success in economic management. The Guyanese economy is on the verge of bankruptcy, and living standards have fallen dramatically since the 1970s. The Cuban economy has stagnated since the mid-1970s and has been kept afloat by massive economic aid from the Soviet Union, although it has performed no worse than nonsocialist economies in the region. Leftist regimes clearly offer no easy path to improving the quality of life for the poor.

Underlying all of these issues is the controversial question of what role the state has played and continues to play in determining the balance of power between classes in the region and in retarding or advancing competing class interests. The colonial history of the beginnings of the state in all territories in the region and the preeminent interests of powerful planters, landowners, and foreign corporations throughout most of the history of all Caribbean states have left a legacy of biases that favor capitalism and the private sector in the functioning of the main state institutions and in their formulation of public policy. The exceptions are, of course, the leftist-socialist regimes.

However, in those states in which capitalist interests continue to be dominant, countervailing influences have limited private sector control of the political systems. Alliances between emergent middle-class political leadership and working-class and peasant support established the basis on which liberal democracy emerged as an alternative to authoritarian or colonial state systems where planter, landowner, or foreign interests exercised monopoly political power. In the contemporary liberal-democratic state system, capitalists and foreign interests continue to exercise considerable political influence subject to challenge by other competing interests such as labor and small farmers.

The three types of state systems reflect predictable differences in the size of the public sector and the level of public spending and taxation. Tax or state resource control levels are lowest in the conservative-authoritarian state of

Haiti. The liberal-democratic states have a significantly higher level of taxation of national wealth, while the leftist-socialist regimes have the highest level of taxing and resource mobilization because of the dominant state interventionist ideology. The data shown in Table 5 confirm these generalizations.

In the Bahamas, a preponderance of foreign hotel ownership in an economy based mainly on tourism produces the lowest level of taxation among the English-speaking states. In oil-rich Trinidad, the highly nationalistic government collects the highest level of revenue in the region. The Dominican Republic, whose powerful U.S. conglomerate, Gulf and Western, owns over 30 percent of its sugar and most of its tourist industry, shows a low level of taxation. Under the reinvigoration of planter export interests that occurred in the late nineteenth and early twentieth centuries, the entrenchment of that class has made liberal democracy quite ineffective in significantly increasing the taxing levels in the Hispanic states. This contrasts with the English-speaking states, where there has been a political ascendancy of middle-class technocrats and political leaders and promotion by the latter of a larger and more expanded state bureaucracy. Communist Cuba, of course, represents the highest level of political control by the technocracy and the most complete elimination of capitalist influences.

TABLE 5.
Regime Type and Central Government Revenue

	Total Government Revenue as Percentage of GDP (1980)[a]
Liberal-Democratic	
Bahamas	19
Barbados	32
Trinidad & Tobago	42
St. Lucia	29
Dominica	22
Dominican Republic	13
Belize	27
Leftist-Socialist	
Grenada[b]	39
Guyana	40
Cuba	75
Authoritarian	
Haiti	17

Source: Inter-American Development Bank 1981.

[a] Note that GDP (gross domestic product) is the total value of goods and services produced; unlike GNP (gross national product) it excludes income transfers.
[b] This table represents information gathered prior to the U.S. occupation in October 1983.

As the numerical majority among Caribbean territories (both independent and colonial), the states of the English-speaking Caribbean are at the center of the region's politics and political trends. It is therefore appropriate to focus on their main political and ideological tendencies in building an understanding of Caribbean politics.

For most of the postwar period in the Commonwealth Caribbean territories, sharp differences over political ideology did not emerge, and political parties, party leaders, and party activists gave minimal attention to the subject of political ideology. The decade of the 1970s has, however, witnessed a dramatic reversal of this pattern. Clearly defined divisions and conflicts over ideology have emerged between competing political parties in some territories, between factions of states in the region, and between groups with divergent approaches to national development strategies.

In the period between the 1940s and the 1960s the party movements in the English-speaking Caribbean were mainly preoccupied with decolonization, the development of political rights and freedoms within the framework of liberal-democratic political institutions, and the formation of competitive party systems to give political expression to the newly enfranchised electorates and majority classes of workers and peasants. In this period of liberal-democratic institution building, two dominant ideological tendencies emerged. A social democratic ideology was promoted mainly by the emergent British-educated, middle-class party leaders, who represented the intelligentsia among the new party leadership, while a working-class- and peasant-based populism was advocated by working-class and lower-middle-class leaders who emerged out of the trade union movement.

The social democratic movement drew its inspiration mainly from the ideas and political traditions of the British Labour party and the political course charted by other anticolonial party movements within the British Empire. Parties and party leaders of this persuasion identified with the socialist label. The commitment to socialism embraced support for policies promoting equality of social opportunity, an active role for the state in economic management, a more equal distribution of wealth, land reform, cooperative ownership, and specific social rights akin to those achieved by the European welfare state.

The competing ideology of worker- and peasant-based populism had less clearly defined political goals and tended to be anchored in policies supporting labor demands for better pay and working conditions, programs geared to improving the quality of life and social opportunities available to the majority classes of workers and peasants, and policies advocating state support for small farmers and small business. Whereas the social democrats attempted to formulate political positions within a structured framework of European social democratic ideas, the leadership of the trade union–based party, which was both less educated and less Europeanized, developed pragmatic policy concerns in response to social pressures from working-class and peasant constituents.

Typical of the social democratic tendency were the People's National party in Jamaica, the Democratic Labour party and Barbados Labour party in Barbados, the People's National movement (PNM) in Trinidad and Tobago, the People's Progressive party in Guyana, and the People's United party of Belize. In general, the social democratic parties led by the British-educated intelligentsia were dominant in the larger and more developed Caribbean territories. Examples of the more populist trade union– and peasant-based parties were the St. Kitts Labour party, the Antiguan Labour party, the St. Lucia United Workers party, the Grenada United Labour party, the Jamaica Labour party (JLP), and the Dominica Labour party. These populist union- and peasant-based political parties dominated party politics in the smaller and less developed Caribbean territories in the decades before the 1970s.

The two main types of party movements and ideological tendencies had a great deal in common. Both believed in the political ideas and principles identified with European liberalism, and they shared a nationalist concern as expressed in their support for political decolonization. Both tended to see the future of the Caribbean and their individual territories as tied into close collaborative relationships with Western capitalist interests, and both attached great importance to the political and economic ties with Britain as these were articulated through membership in the multiracial British Commonwealth and through colonial ties for territories that were not yet independent.

In essence, they represented dual types of centrist ideological tendencies that supported economic and social reform on behalf of the majority classes but rejected either right-wing conservatism or left-wing Marxism / Leninism. To be sure, some minority impulses of the far right and the far left did find political expression in the politics of the region before the 1970s. In Jamaica, weak Marxist impulses developed in the center-left People's National party in its early development between 1938 and 1952. In Guyana the racial split within the People's Progressive party resulted in a strong Marxist faction, which took over the East Indian segment of the party movement, and a social democratic faction, which continued to be dominant in the Afro-American segment. The original PPP, therefore, split into a Marxist-led, racially based PPP and an Afro-American–supported PNC, controlled mainly by a social democratic inclined leadership. In the countries with significant white populations (the Bahamas and Bermuda), the privileged and affluent white business elite formed parties whose ideologies were right of center. These tourist economies provided a basis for business-oriented political parties led by affluent members of the white business elite—the United Bahamian party and the United Bermuda party. Although these are not far-right parties, their distinctly probusiness and antilabor tendencies placed them somewhat right of center and at some ideological distance from the mainstream social democratic and populist union- and peasant-based center parties.

To some extent, the ideological spectrum of Caribbean party movements reflected dominant reformist center tendencies and weak conservative or leftist ideological tendencies, which are to be expected in the context of competitive electoral politics. In this respect the pattern is similar to the overall trends in Western, North Atlantic, parliamentary democracies, where center tendencies have been the dominant forces in the party arena.

For most of the period up to the 1970s, these ideological splits amounted to little more than divergent issue positions for electoral debates, as no really sharp or fundamental differences in public policies emerged between the dominant party movements in each territory. With the exception of Bermuda, where the right-of-center United Bermuda party held power in the decade leading into the 1970s, the governing parties in the Commonwealth Caribbean and their main opposition challengers shared a broad consensus about public policy, political values, and ideology. For most of the period between the end of World War II and the 1970s, ideological developments were mainly symbolic. Under the paternalist eye of the British Colonial Office, there was not much room for radical changes in public policy directions that could give expression to these ideological impulses, and in any event the main preoccupation was with political decolonization and institution building. The British managed to induce the party leaders of the region to accept a slow and gradual apprenticeship in self-government, and there was no desire to rock the boat with radical policy directions. The exception, of course, was Guyana, where the original social democratic PPP tried to chart some new directions and was removed from power through constitutional manipulations by the Colonial Office.

External Influences

Although decolonization was high on the agenda of concerns of the party leaders of the region, the nationalist sentiment that informed it was both ambivalent in content and moderate in intensity. No strong feelings of antagonism toward the British Empire or the British monarchy existed in the region during the postwar colonial period. Many looked to the British connection with pride and positively identified with British culture, values, and institutions. Some doubted the capacity of these small island territories either to run their affairs or to become economically viable. The sense of territorial nationalism was relatively weak, and there was little feeling of common interests with other Third World countries, except within small sections of the intelligentsia and minority social movements such as the African-Rastafarian politico-religious movement in Jamaica.

During the postwar period, the pattern of trade and economic ties shifted from a predominance of linkages with Great Britain to a predominance of economic ties with the United States and Canada through oil, bauxite, tourism, foreign investment, and imports, especially in the larger and more economically developed territories of Jamaica, Trinidad and Tobago, Guyana, and Barbados. This redirection of external economic ties took place in the context of a period of economic expansion and diversification in the region, as these territories benefited from the postwar upturn in economic activity in Western capitalist economies. These economic relationships were, therefore, viewed in very positive terms.

At the beginning of the 1960s, no English-speaking Caribbean territory had attained political independence. By the end of the 1970s, all Commonwealth Caribbean territories had either attained self-government or were in the advanced stages of some form of internal self-government and on the path toward independence. This assumption of greater local responsibility for public management and especially the charting of economic policies during the 1960s and 1970s provided more room for political ideology to become less purely symbolic and to exert a positive force in guiding public policy in some territories. This was especially true in territories in which disillusionment with the existing pattern of political economy (on both domestic and international dimensions)induced and provoked a search for alternate, noncapitalist development models and economic directions. Guyana, Jamaica, and later Grenada led the way in this direction.

Unlike the earlier postwar years, the 1970s were a period of economic contraction in the region as world inflation and escalating oil prices generated mounting indebtedness, massive balance of payments difficulties, slow growth, and increased unemployment. These years of economic crisis forced Caribbean states to reassess their economic ties with Western capitalist countries and to review their real and potential areas of common interest with other Third World countries, as more and more Third World states organized themselves into global and regional lobbies to bargain for a reform of the world economic system.

Greater contact and dialogue with Third World countries modified and weakened the legacy of British-influenced political ideas, values, and ideology throughout the region. The idea of one-party states, the seizure of political power by extraconstitutional means, an increased role for the state in economic management, serious questioning of the role of private interests and foreign capital in economic development, and concern about ties of economic dependency with rich North Atlantic countries were no longer dismissed as heresies by important segments of opinion in the region. As Third World states embraced noncapitalist ideas, experimented with political alternatives to liberal democracy and competitive party systems, and carved out a larger role for the state in economic management, the impact of these trends generated new ideological currents in the Commonwealth Caribbean. As linkages with Europe declined in importance and as ties with the United States and Canada yielded less than optimal results or expectations for economic advancement, a greater sense of being part of the Third World emerged.

To be sure, all these new political and ideological currents had to compete with the dominant ideas and ideological tendencies that were the legacy of a long association with Great Britain and strong socialization into the values, beliefs, norms, and frames of reference passed on to Caribbean leaders and political culture. These included British traditions of political liberalism and capitalist political economy, and the British-induced view of benevolent paternalism in the relationships between the Commonwealth Caribbean and Western capitalist interest. Within individual territories, therefore, and between territories in the region a sharp ideological split has emerged. It has divided traditional and established frames of reference of political and economic thought, on the one hand, and these new currents of thinking, on the other. This factor has formed the basis of some of the ideological divisions in the region that came to the forefront in the 1970s.

The currents of socialism that were inserted in the political culture of the Commonwealth Caribbean in the 1970s reached beyond social democracy to embrace elements of Marxism / Leninism, and socialist notions developed from the experience and thought of Third World countries and leaders. While these new socialist impulses represented minority tendencies, they nevertheless had great impact in countries such as Guyana, Grenada, and Jamaica and set in motion an intense regionwide ideological debate about political alternatives.

That debate has been informed both by the mounting ideological hemispheric confrontation between communist Cuba and the region's dominant capitalist power, the United States, and by the impact of the Cuban political influence. As the United States and Cuba have competed for allies in the Commonwealth Caribbean and as many have looked to the successes or failures of the Cuban political economy as an example of an alternative model of development, the ideological debates and conflicts between noncapitalist and antiimperialist ideological tendencies, on the one hand, and procapitalist and antisocialist tendencies, on the other, loomed large in the Commonwealth Caribbean in the 1970s. As new cadres of national leadership educated at the University of the West Indies have replaced the British-educated intelligentsia, influential centers of opinion in the region have become more receptive to new currents of thinking and new ideological frames of reference.

Paralleling these developments were the intense racial and ethnic divisions that were emerging between blacks and nonwhite immigrant groups in the United States. These conflicts served both to influence the frame of reference of U.S.-educated leaders in the Caribbean and to develop a wider sensitivity in the Caribbean to the racial problems of white North America. These perceptions and experiences sharpened the distrust of U.S. interests in the region—as has the build-up of public attacks on big corporations in the United States by journalists, academics, and leftist activists. The United States has come to be viewed by many (especially among the intelligentsia, the radical clergy, university students, trade union leaders, journalists, and the younger, university-trained middle class) as indistinguishable from greedy, profit maximizing, transnational corporations.

These views and perspectives tend not to be shared by the majority of the working class and the lower strata mass public, who continue to view the United States as a land of opportunity and abundance, and as a country where the dispossessed Commonwealth Caribbean working-class immigrant can achieve personal advancement in terms of employment, income, education, and living standards. More importantly, opinion polls conducted in the Caribbean among lower-class and working-class sections of the electorate (e.g., in Jamaica) showed that the United States was generally viewed as a friendly country whose potential for giving aid to Caribbean territories should be courted.

Economic Management

Ideology has had a major impact also on the profile of political economies in the region. Very low levels of state economic intervention were operative in Barbados, the Bahamas, Dominica, Bermuda, Antigua, St. Vincent, and St. Lucia, while high levels were found in Guyana and to a lesser extent in Jamaica under the People's National party (PNP) and Grenada under Bishop. The highest levels were found in countries where the political directorate was influenced by the new currents of Third World socialist thinking (Guyana and pre-occupation Grenada). Countries where the traditional social democratic tendencies have been dominant and those where populist worker- and peasant-based parties were in the ascendancy do not show any tendency toward high levels of state economic intervention. The two exceptions are, of course, Trinidad and St. Kitts, where there is a significantly high level of state ownership.

Although much of the U.S. foreign policy thrust toward the Caribbean is inspired by fears of communist expansionism in the region, the political party trends suggest that such fears are grossly exaggerated. With the exception of Grenada, where the pre-occupation government came to power by a "coup," and Guyana, where the government has remained in office through electoral fraud, the dominant ideological framework in the Commonwealth Caribbean states continues to be the center position shared by traditional social democratic parties and labor-based populist parties. In Guyana the ruling PNC has shifted from traditional social democracy to noncapitalist notions about development and an embrace of Marxist-tinged Third World socialism. Not surprisingly, therefore, the people of Guyana have broken from the open competitive party system of the inherited liberal-democratic model of parliamentary politics and have institutionalized a one-party dominant state system. Grenada followed the Guyanese example and attempted to establish the political infrastructure of a militarized one-party state with a strong mass base committed to socialist and noncapitalist development goals.

In Jamaica under the PNP, some elements of Marxist and noncapitalist thinking came to influence the regime in the 1970s, but these represented minority tendencies within the party's parliamentary leadership, and sharp internal party divisions over ideology limited the degree to which this ideological tendency could by translated into program and policy directions. Indeed, these influences appear to have been manifest more in the PNP's rhetoric than in its policies and programs in Jamaica in the 1970s.

In electoral contests in which these new currents of socialist impulses challenged the existing center parties in Antigua, Dominica, and St. Vincent, the new leftist parties failed to win a single parliamentary seat. In both Jamaica and Trinidad leftist parties lost elections in the early 1980s to political parties that were to their right on the ideological continuum, the PNP to the JLP in Jamaica and the United Labour Front (ULF) to the PNM in Trinidad. In the case of Trinidad, a newly emergent, right-of-center, business-oriented political party (the Organisation for National Reconstruction) failed to win a seat but won a larger proportion of the popular vote than the ULF with its heavy concentration of support in Indian areas. While new currents of leftist political ideology have abandoned their traditional disdain for competitive electoral politics and have openly challenged the traditional center parties for electoral supports (except for Jamaica, where those tendencies infiltrated a traditional social democratic party), no real gains were registered by leftist groups in the 1970s in terms of strong mass support.

The reversal from PNP socialism to JLP free enterprise ideology in Jamaica, after the massive sweep of the Jamaican electorate by the JLP in the elections of 30 October 1980, represented a major setback for the socialist thrust in the Caribbean, especially since the vote against the PNP was heavily influenced by explicit rejections of communist ties within the PNP and by feelings that socialism under the PNP had resulted in considerable mismanagement of public affairs.

The large-scale migration of disaffected citizens from Cuba to the United States also represented a setback to the promotion of socialism in the English-speaking Caribbean, bringing sharply into relief indications of problems with the quality of life under Cuban communism.

The growth of newer socialist trends resulted in a regional counteroffensive by anticommunist religious and secular groups, which attempted to identify these more radical socialist impulses as alien to the region and to its culture and institutional and social traditions. These reactions to modest socialist advances bolstered to some degree the ideological offensive mounted by the

United States against Cuba and radical socialist movements in the Caribbean more generally.

The U.S. offensive culminated in the Caribbean Basin Regional Aid Plan, which offers economic assistance while seeking to increase the political isolation of Cuba and its allies in the Caribbean. In this effort the U.S. administration under President Reagan has developed close links with the JLP government in Jamaica and has massively increased aid to that country as part of its design to use Jamaica as a spearhead in its anticommunist offensive. These pro-U.S. gains are, likely to be short-lived, however, since Jamaica is a two-party system in which each government has only a limited tenure, and the PNP will inevitably return to power.

Indeed, given the petty jealousies over aid allocations, the fear of U.S. domination in the region, and the modest increases in aid offered by the Reagan administration, Jamaica, Barbados, Dominica, and Antigua appear to be the only states that are lining up enthusiastically with the United States.

The overall ideological balance in the Caribbean still reflects a predominance of centrist ideological tendencies, but Third World and noncapitalist socialist impulses became dominant in two states that lacked free elections (Guyana and pre-occupation Grenada), while minority tendencies have emerged in several states in support of the new framework of socialist thinking. In the case of Jamaica, the leftist infiltration of and influence over a traditional social democratic party provided an important symbolic victory for the new wave of socialism in this, the largest Commonwealth Caribbean territory, during the Manley regime in the 1970s.

A most important ideological change was the increasing sense of Third World links and political affiliation as the paternalist ties to Great Britain withered in most territories. Related to these trends were political and economic initiatives toward establishing ties with communist Eastern European countries through trade, diplomatic ties, and even party-to-party ties of collaboration. These last political initiatives were strategically promoted by Cuba under Castro's skillful diplomacy, which offered a hand of friendship and modest economic assistance to governments advocating nonalignment and antiimperialism. Guyana, Jamaica, Grenada, and Trinidad became active members of the Nonaligned movement, and other independent states such as St. Lucia and Barbados acquired observer status.

The Non-English-speaking Group

Although liberal democracy is predominant in the English-speaking Caribbean, this is not the case with the non-English-speaking independent Caribbean states. Among these four states (Cuba, Haiti, the Dominican Republic, and Suriname), only the Dominican Republic has an executive that came to power by free and openly competitive elections. The other European colonizers in the Caribbean were less successful than the British in implanting firm and stable support for liberal democracy among the emergent Caribbean political elite.

The Hispanic territories inherited a tradition of military-dominated authoritarian politics from Spain, which itself has only recently moved toward adopting a Western type of liberal democracy. The process of social change in these societies has tended, nevertheless, to generate demands for democratic change and to undermine corrupt, personalized, and repressive military rule. These pressures come from labor leaders, students, unionized workers, the middle class, and the urban poor, all of whom seek greater channels of political expression than are available under military rule.

With the dismantling of an authoritarian military regime, political change can move toward either leftist socialism or liberal democracy. Societies with a strong authoritarian tradition such as the Hispanic countries in the Caribbean can adopt leftist socialism more easily than liberal democracy. They can easily achieve the transition toward one-party states with centralized and highly concentrated power structures and unified and militarized leadership hierarchies. The change toward liberal democracy, tolerance of opposition, free public opinion, the free flow of information and ideas, free elections, and politically neutral bureaucracies and security forces is much more traumatic and difficult.

For many countries, the nature of external support has been important in determining which path is taken out of the restrictive politics of military rule. In the case of Cuba, economic and political dependence on the Soviet Union accelerated the transition to leftist socialism by strengthening the leadership opposed to liberal democracy. That alliance was consolidated in the face of U.S. economic hostilities after the nationalization of U.S. corporate assets in Cuba.

In the Dominican Republic the U.S. influence has been decisive in supporting the leadership groups favoring liberal democracy and in weakening those favoring a return to militarism or revolutionary changes toward leftist socialism. There as in Cuba, a shift toward leftist socialism could have occurred only after a political revolution. But the balance of social forces in the Dominican Republic would not support any such development. On the contrary, a political accommodation has been arrived at between the powerful rightist interests and the political center to develop liberal-democratic political reforms without substantially weakening the economic and social power of the landowners, big corporations, and rich families. This political truce has set severe limits on how far liberal-democratic reforms can go in changing the distribution of power in the Dominican Republic. In other words, democracy has not displaced the traditional elite, and this has guaranteed cautious support for democracy within these powerful conservative interests. The impact of the political truce has been to isolate the left, which has become increasingly disenchanted with the conservative policy of the elected center governments. This minority leftist tendency is likely to become more militant and disenchanted in the future and will clearly be cultivated and encouraged by the region's leftist-socialist alliance (Cuba, Suriname, etc.).

With its cheap labor, close alliances with U.S. corporate and political interests, and abundant opportunities for lucrative investments, the Dominican Republic's economy is likely to expand, diversify, and industrialize during the 1980s. That probable economic trend will strengthen support for the liberal-democratic system. More than any other independent Caribbean state, the Dominican Republic is a country where private foreign capital feels welcome, secure, and unthreatened by socialist impulses to economic nationalism. Within the region, it is the country where the government-to-government ties with the United States are deepest and where the U.S. presence is most evident.

Haiti represents a typical Third World right-of-center dictatorship presiding over an impoverished and illiterate peasantry in which the middle-class political overlords rule with an iron fist, abuse power by extensive corrupt practices, and treat the state as if it were their private property. After the collapse of the plantation system in Haiti following the revolution in the nineteenth century, the country has had a series of military dictatorships with varying degrees of stability. The drift of the economy into subsistence agriculture and the consequent impoverishment of the people served to set the stage for political authoritarianism. State power is used neither to promote national development nor to foster economic progress, but to enrich the politically powerful. Haiti emerged in the twentieth century as a prototype of the weak, corrupt, authoritarian state.

Earlier periods of political instability left both Haiti and the Dominican Republic vulnerable to external political intervention. An expanding and aggressive United States seized the opportunity to occupy these territories with a view to stabilizing them by a combination of military presence, administrative and political controls, and the installation of new hand-picked political leaders. In contrast to the Dominican Republic, where the U.S. influence continued to be dominant after the occupation period, Haiti reasserted its nationalism and has considerably diminished the residue of U.S. influence. The main impact of the U.S. occupation was to consolidate the army's political control and to establish an ideological bond of conservatism between Washington and successive Haitian governments. However, Haiti's constant violation of political rights, its abuse and mismanagement of aid funds, and the large flows of illegal migrants seeking to enter the United States to escape from a backward and starvation-ridden peasant economy have been sources of stress and tension in that relationship.

As the first state in the region to develop a socialist revolution and the only Caribbean country that is a major active international force (both in its own right and as an ally of the Soviet Union), Cuba is the only non-English-speaking Caribbean country with extensive links and channels of influence among the majority English-speaking group of states. The Cuban Revolution has been a major factor legitimizing Marxist ideas and political thinking in the region. As that revolution has become consolidated and has succeeded in eliminating unemployment and the grosser forms of poverty so rampant in Latin America, it has aided the spread of Marxist groups throughout the Caribbean—minority political parties and trade unions, student groups, and social action groups within the radical clergy.

Of interest is the fact that the earlier but now severed Cuban-Grenadian-Surinamese alliance was the only close political bond among Caribbean countries that cut across the traditional language barriers. In order to grasp opportunities to expand that alliance, the Cubans cultivate and encourage fledgling leftist fringe groups in other territories in the hope that political instability or turmoil might set the stage for their emergence as power brokers or controllers of state power, as in Suriname and Grenada. Political stability is therefore seen as the enemy of leftist-Marxist expansionism and political instability its natural ally.

Colonial Status

As Table 6 makes clear, the level of civil liberties and political freedoms is relatively high among the nonindependent states, where liberal democracy remains the exclusive basis on which political authority has been established. The very long period of colonization and the consequent deepening of European and U.S. political influences should mean that these territories will remain on the liberal-democratic path after they have attained independence. Several of these states seem, however, to be choosing to remain colonies, although the impulse for sovereignty is being felt increasingly in Bermuda, the Netherlands Antilles, Puerto Rico, and elsewhere.

As the only Spanish-speaking territory in the region with a stable and well-developed liberal democracy, Puerto Rico is in a politically important position, but its potential to bridge the communication gap between the English-speaking and non-English-speaking territories in the Caribbean is as yet unfulfilled. Because Puerto Rico continues to operate in the shadow of the United States, it has been unable to exercise its full influence as a large middle-income territory with the most industrialized economy in the region, and a developed, large, and highly educated middle class. Until Puerto Rico becomes an independent state, it will not be able to assume the regional leadership role it could enjoy to counterbalance Cuban influences and to take some of the pressure off the United States in building and enlarging the alliance of pro-Western states in the Caribbean region.

Puerto Rico's political profile is similar to that of the typical Caribbean

TABLE 6.
Freedom House Measures of Political Freedoms among Nonindependent Caribbean Territories

		Civil Liberties Scale				
HIGH . . . . *LOW*						
1	2	3	4	5	6	7
Bermuda	French Guiana	St. Kitts–Nevis				
Puerto Rico	Guadeloupe	U.S. Virgin Islands				
	Martinique					
	Netherlands Antilles					
	Anguilla					
	British Virgin Islands					
	Montserrat					

Source: Gastil (1982:14).

English-speaking liberal democracy. Its main political parties and leaders are located at the ideological center rather than at the extreme left or right. It has strong and free trade unions, a free press, well-developed political and civil rights, and high levels of mass political participation.

Much of this is due to the close connection with the United States and the internalization by the Puerto Rican middle class of U.S. democratic political culture, values, and institutional forms. Underlying it, however, is a deep tension between excessive Americanization and the search for Puerto Rican nationalism. The latter is a growing force that will eventually demand expression through greater Puerto Rican political autonomy. What is likely to remain undisturbed is the deep attachment to liberal democracy and political freedoms.

CONCLUSION

The political profile of the Caribbean as a whole is one of stability. A dominant liberal-democratic tradition has combined with increasing political diversity and ideological rivalries between proleftist and antileftist groupings of states, both variously influenced by Havana, and Washington, the main contenders for regional political influence. This pattern is likely to continue in the future, provided political stability can be maintained and the economic viability of the region assured. Disruptions of these two interrelated factors could easily push the Caribbean toward more leftist and authoritarian regimes in the long run.

It seems likely that most political regimes in the Caribbean will be able to sustain political stability in the 1980s in spite of the increasing levels of economic hardship and consequent political stress. Unlike most Third World regions, the Caribbean has established strong political institutions that reflect both the depth of the Western European influences and the adaptability of these political institutions to Caribbean political culture.

A good index of the strength of these political systems can be gleaned from the levels of comparative voting between the Caribbean and other Third World states that had elections in the early 1980s; in this context, voter turnout is 35–100 percent higher in the Caribbean.

The Caribbean indeed represents an interesting political balance between Western European and Third World influences that is unique in the modern world. After the unfortunate events in Grenada, more militant efforts are going to be mounted regionwide to protect the European legacy of liberal democracy. This will aid the U.S. policy of trying to insulate the region from Cuban and communist penetration.

REFERENCES

BANKS, ARTHUR S., AND WILLIAM OVERSTREET
 1980 *Political Handbook of the World.* New York: McGraw Hill.

CENTRAL INTELLIGENCE AGENCY
 1981 *Handbook of Nations.* Detroit: Grand River Books.

GASTIL, RAYMOND (ED.)
 1982 *Freedom in the World: Political Rights and Civil Liberties.* Westport, Conn.: Greenwood Press.

INTER-AMERICAN DEVELOPMENT BANK
 1981 *Economic and Social Progress in Latin America (1980-81).* Washington, D.C.: IADB.

INTERNATIONAL LABOUR OFFICE
 1978–80 *International Labour Statistics.* Geneva.

INTERNATIONAL LABOUR ORGANISATION
 1980 *International Labour Statistics.* Geneva.

KIDRON, MICHAEL, AND RONALD SEGAL
1981   *The State of the World Atlas.* New York: Simon and Schuster.

SIVARD, RUTH LEGER
1981   *World Military and Social Expenditures.* Leesberg: World Priorities.

UNITED NATIONS
1975–79 *Annual Reports.* New York: United Nations.

WORLD BANK
1980   *World Bank Atlas.* Washington, D.C.: World Bank.

· 2 ·

"Race" and Color in the Caribbean

H. HOETINK

INTRODUCTION

In defining the Caribbean region, and considering how much of its population now resides in New York and Miami, should we begin at home? Or, looking back at the historical formation of Caribbean society, molded by plantations, black slave labor, and white planters, should we also include the Deep South? Or, finally, should we adopt a recently developed notion and speak of the Caribbean basin as including not only the islands between North and South America, but also Central America, with its entirely different economic history, ethnic composition, and cultural geography?

Some scholars justify this last possibility by noting that all the countries it includes share a large number of economic and political problems, and that Central America and the Caribbean archipelago are also similar in their remarkable internal variety (Pastor 1982:1039–40). But such arguments are perhaps too broad for our present purposes, since they could easily be extended to much of the so-called Third World at large. Clearly, the fact that both areas form part of the weak underbelly of the United States' political anatomy means that they pose a set of common problems to that country. But a political criterion of this sort can serve only limited purposes in a definition of the region and is not particularly helpful in coming to grips with the widely different social and cultural complexities it encompasses.

It may be best, then, in a brief essay dealing with the evolution of racial relations, to focus on the Caribbean archipelago as the historical and geographical core of Afro-America, and to undertake only occasional excursions to other parts of the hemisphere.

In trying to understand different patterns of race and ethnic relations in the contemporary Caribbean, we shall have to delve into its history, not with the intention of burying the reader under details, numbers, and dates, but in the hope of excavating whatever is necessary to fill the historical vacuum in which present-day structures and attitudes would otherwise be floating.

HISPANIC AND NON-HISPANIC REGIONS

For nearly two centuries after its European conquest, *all* of the Caribbean belonged to the Spanish Empire and was governed from Santo Domingo on the island of Hispaniola. The Caribbean Sea was considered to be a Spanish, "closed" sea. It was not until the seventeenth century that British, French, and Dutch intruders succeeded in seizing some of the small islands along the sea's eastern rim and off the coast of what is now Venezuela. Of the larger islands, only Jamaica was surrendered to the British during that period, while France claimed sovereignty over the western part of Hispaniola (Saint-Domingue) in 1697. Trinidad remained Spanish until the end of the eighteenth century.

All of the islands, then, have an archaeology with at least two common layers—one Amerindian and one Hispanic. Much of these historical legacies has been erased by time, but fragments still remain. The local names for flora, fauna, and topographical features in many islands, for example, contain words of both Amerindian and Spanish origin, even where Spanish rule was long ago supplanted by that of other colonial powers. It is remarkable that a weakening Spain, whose Caribbean possessions were constantly being threatened by the emerging new European colonial powers, succeeded in clinging to the better part of the larger islands for so long. Cuba and Puerto Rico remained Spanish until 1898, nearly a century longer than the Spanish colonies on the South American mainland, and the Dominican Republic declared its independence in the middle of the last century. In all three of these countries the Spanish presence had been prolonged and intense enough to leave a strong, durable imprint on their culture. One might argue somewhat disingenuously, then, that the Hispanic Caribbean of today, as the direct heir to the Spanish imperial venture, represents the "old" or "real" Caribbean, as it took shape under the tutelage of its first European conquerors. From this perspective, the rest of the area—which for the sake of convenience we shall call the non-Hispanic Caribbean—might be viewed as merely a deviation from the Spanish path, a creation of marauding buccaneers and upstart colonial powers, whose total population today is less than half that of Cuba, and barely equals the six million inhabiting the Dominican Republic. Although I am not endorsing such a view, it strikes me as being no more biased than the notion of many authors who flaunt the word "Caribbean" or "West Indies" in the titles of their books and articles without so much as mentioning the Hispanic parts of the region. Generally dealing with the British or Commonwealth Caribbean, they have taught the English-speaking public everywhere to associate the Caribbean primarily with its English-speaking areas. This bias is found among scholars as well, for many "Caribbeanists" suffer from a single-language focus and some are apt to make Caribbean-wide generalizations based on comparative research in, for example, Jamaica and St. Kitts, leaving the study of the Hispanic islands to another academic tribe, the Latin Americanists. These latter tend to view the Spanish-speaking Antilles as mere appendages to a vaster and ultimately more fascinating continent (except when a revolution such as that in Cuba inspires both the best and the worst of them). In more general terms it is fair to say that scholars both from the Caribbean and from abroad, with few exceptions, tend to suffer from a narrowness of focus, as the paucity of works on the region as a whole will attest. The insularism, so characteristic of the area, is thus reflected in much of the work written about it.

It is not only the language used that distinguishes the Hispanic Caribbean from the rest of the archipelago; there is also a difference in language diversity. Cubans, Dominicans, and Puerto Ricans all speak Spanish and understand each other, regional and class distinctions notwithstanding. In the territories colonized by Britain, France, and the Netherlands, such a linguistic unity is often lacking. The upper classes generally speak an approximation of the standard European language, while the lowest strata speak a creole language; between these two poles there exists what has been described as a linguistic continuum. In some Dutch islands and in Suriname (where the official language is Dutch), the vernacular is an English-based creole, and in some British Commonwealth islands it is a French-based creole. In Trinidad, Guyana, and Suriname, descendants of contract laborers from British India and (in Suriname) the Dutch East Indies speak their own languages, as do the maroons in Suriname and French Guiana and the small Indian tribes in Suriname, French Guiana, and Guyana. Only in the small islands of Curaçao, Aruba, and Bonaire, off the Venezuelan coast, has the local creole, Papiamentu, become accepted as the language of all social classes and of government. There Dutch, although still the official language, is quickly losing importance. Linguistically, then, the diversity in the non-Hispanic societies is in marked contrast with the homogeneity of the Hispanic Caribbean.

A similar difference may be observed in religion. In the Hispanic Caribbean, evangelical sects have made some inroads and Afro-American cults may flourish in some areas, yet the overall picture is one of a nationally unified religious culture. This is a Hispanic-American variant of Catholicism that entails not only religious beliefs, ideas, and rites, but also an important system of ritual kinship—a network of social ties among godparents and godchildren, which are created at birth, communion, and marriage, with well-defined rights and obligations for each participant. In the non-Hispanic Caribbean (except the French Antilles, which are predominantly Catholic), we tend to find a proliferation of Protestant churches and sects, the upper classes traditionally belonging to one of the more prestigious metropolitan churches, while the lower classes attend a variety of smaller, often less formal and more emotional ones. There are also instances where the traditional elites are Protestant but the mass of the population Catholic. In Haiti, Roman Catholicism and the syncretic *vodun* occupy similar social rankings. In the countries with Asian populations, such as Guyana, Suriname, and Trinidad, Islam and Hinduism enliven and complicate the picture even more.

There is, finally, a difference between the Hispanic and non-Hispanic Caribbean in terms of the rhythm of economic evolution. Ultimately, virtually all Caribbean societies have witnessed the introduction of modern, large-scale sugar plantations producing for the world market and dependent on black labor, but the paths followed by the two areas in this regard were different. It was not the fact that the modern sugar plantation was introduced relatively late in the Hispanic Caribbean that made the difference; other societies (Trinidad and the southern United States) were also latecomers. It was rather that the Hispanic Caribbean had *two* periods of booming plantation economy, with a lengthy dividing interregnum between.

The first period started immediately after the conquest and lasted about three-quarters of a century. Many slaves were imported then, and these, together with the remnants of the aboriginal population, had to work in the modern sugar mills of the day. In the long period of economic decay that followed, blacks, Amerindians, and whites were heir to abundant lands and, away from the cities, they were out of sight and control of metropolitan power. It was in this primitive, largely autarchic rural economy that there developed a type of peasantry that is known by such names as *guajiro, jíbaro, montero,* and *campesino.* Culturally, it was syncretic, adopting Amerindian and African-derived cultural objects and ideas, but it retained Spanish as its language and its own brand of Catholicism, centered on the worship of saints and on private altars, as its religion. Genetically, it was an interweaving of European, African, and Amerindian strands. These multiple influences were reflected in a local conceptualization in which physical traits ranged from "dark" to "light," different "types" of which could well manifest themselves within a single family. "Pure" types gave way to a racial continuum in which, however, the higher social prestige of "light" color did not disappear. When, at a much later time, the economy once again became centered on the sugar plantations and immigration of foreign (mostly black) labor was again stimulated, the basis for a national culture and for a particular, fluid type of socioracial structure was already set. Surface changes were inevitable under the impact of so many newcomers and new institutions, but the existence of a socioracial continuum was preserved.

In the non-Hispanic Caribbean, plantation economy knew no such interruption, and "racial" divisions there were generally more clear-cut, as we will see later in this essay. Small wonder, then, that comparison of the homogeneous "creole"[1] culture of the Hispanic Caribbean and the linguistic and religious diversity of the other islands, as well as discussions of the seemingly more flexible structuring of race relations in the Spanish-speaking area, have played a central role in studies of the region.

Were the differences attributable to economic and demographic elements, or were there perhaps significant variations in colonial policy, in metropolitan culture, or in the roles of Catholicism and Protestantism? Could the greater incidence of marriage (as opposed to sexual liaisons) between whites and "light coloreds"[2] in the Hispanic region have something to do with Spanish-Moorish relations far back in history, or to related considerations, such as norms of physical beauty, which were perhaps slightly different from those of the more endogamous Northwest Europeans? And, to mention a more policy-oriented question, and comparing the Caribbean as a whole with the United States, might not the scales of racial labeling that we find in the Caribbean today be disadvantageous to the blacks because leaving the line between *black* and *colored* ambiguous makes it more difficult for blacks to organize politically along color lines, as happens in the United States?[3] These and similar questions (discussed in Mintz 1974 and Hoetink 1973) may be pertinent not only in furthering our understanding of Caribbean phenomena but also in unraveling the much larger problem of why, among all the European colonizers, only the Iberians have become an integral and integrated presence in the societies that they have founded in the New World.

There is one island, the second largest of the archipelago, where a Hispanic and a non-Hispanic society live side by side. This is Hispaniola, the western third of which forms the Republic of Haiti, and the eastern two-thirds the Dominican Republic. Since these two societies may be said to present in extreme form two of the main Caribbean "models" of race relations, let us look at their formation and development in some detail.

The first century after the Spanish conquest witnessed great activity on the island; Hispaniola was the first Caribbean island to be colonized and it was from here that the expanding empire was governed. Here, the viceroy had his seat, the first hospital and university of the New World were established, the first treaties with the Amerindians were signed, and the first wars with them were fought. Economically, mining and the cultivation and processing of sugar cane (imported by the Spaniards) gave vigor to the island. This activity also gave rise to the importation of the first slaves, initially from Spain (where slavery still existed), and soon after from Africa. It is perhaps not surprising, then, that in addition to its other "firsts," Hispaniola also had (in 1522) the first black slave rebellion in the New World.

However, by the end of the sixteenth century, the island was no longer a vital center of Caribbean activity. Many colonists had left, some with their slaves, for the more promising, newly conquered mainland, leaving Hispaniola with a sparse population, a weak defense, and a tiny colonial bureaucracy that was dependent on *situados* (subsidies) handed down by the Spanish crown. Agriculture regressed to more primitive forms, and cattle, fruits, and vegetables kept the small population alive. There was neither the money nor the need to import large contingents of new slaves. Slavery did continue to exist de jure, but outside of the remaining sugar mills relations between each master and his few slaves tended to be of a personal, paternalistic nature. Slaves could buy their freedom and settle on the land, or even run away, without much chance of being pursued, let alone captured.

In the course of several generations, the descendants of Amerindians, black slaves, and Spanish settlers formed a relatively homogeneous rural population. This population was removed from the small colonial and ecclesiastical urban centers, whose inhabitants aspired to maintain and cultivate strict distinctions of rank and social status, the latter based largely on whether a person was Spanish or locally born (*peninsular* or *criollo*) and, for those born locally, on physical traits as well.

The main problem for this isolated population was a lack of commerce by which they could obtain those goods (iron implements, textiles, and weapons) they could not make themselves. The economic policy of the Spanish crown forbade trade with foreigners, but Spain itself was unable to provide such necessities with any regularity. Hence, as early as the late sixteenth century, on the north and west coasts of the island, far from the capital in the south, a busy contraband trade developed. French, British, and Dutch merchants filled the commercial vacuum, with the Dutch, moreover, propagating the faith of the Reformation by handing out large numbers of bibles. Rather than changing its economic policy in response to this problem, the Spanish crown adopted a scorched-earth strategy. In 1605–6 it ordered all cities on the northwestern coast burned and their inhabitants moved to the central part of the island. By giving up part of its colony in this way, Spain actually opened herself up to her enemies, who, operating from the nearby island of Tortuga, used it at first as a base for provisioning their buccaneering ships. After the western part of the island had become a French colony in 1697, with the name Saint-Domingue, it developed quickly into a sugar colony of great prosperity, based on the labor of tens of thousands of African slaves, severely regimented and exploited. The eastern (Spanish) part of Hispaniola served in the eighteenth century as a provider of cattle for the slave economy of Saint-Domingue. It also served as a haven for many fugitive slaves from the western part, who established maroon communities just across the border.

In Saint-Domingue, colonial society was characterized by a hierarchy of classes, the formation and boundaries of which were shaped by both economic and racial considerations; it was more complicated than the simple twofold division of black slaves and white slave owners that one might envisage. True, the overwhelming majority of the population was slave and black. But some blacks were set free, and a considerable group of coloreds (born of the sexual relations between masters and female slaves) received preferential treatment as slaves (working as house rather than field slaves) or had been manumitted as well. A portion of these "free coloreds" were allowed to acquire a European education and material prosperity and owned land and slaves themselves. The whites were divided also into several classes, ranging from small shopkeepers and artisans (*petits blancs*) to large plantation owners, colonial bureaucrats, and professionals. Not only did there exist the type of tension and friction that one might expect in any society based on enforced agricultural labor, repression, and cruel treatment of laborers, but there also developed fatal tensions between the prosperous and educated colored elite,

Colored elite vs.
Petits blancs

"RACE" AND COLOR IN THE CARIBBEAN

on the one hand, and the French whites, perhaps especially the *petits blancs,* on the other. In the latter half of the eighteenth century, the colored elite was increasingly discriminated against and subjected to humiliating legislation.

Thus, by the last quarter of that century, two entirely different models of economic development and of race relations had developed within a single island. In the Spanish colony of Santo Domingo, the economy at that time might be termed one of self-reliance. With the colonial power limiting access to the open international market, the economy was predominantly autarchic, even though some cattle trade with its western neighbor did exist. Without a plantation economy geared to export, and hence without a need for massive importation of slaves or their strict regimentation, with a rural population not pressured by scarcity of land, and with only a tiny urban section trying to preserve the nice distinctions of colonial officialdom and ecclesiastical rank, a particular socioracial structure developed (helped, in all probability, by cultural factors at which we hinted earlier). Whites (and especially those from the metropolis) were clearly favored socially over blacks, it is true, but the vast majority of the population had amalgamated sufficiently to leave no room for fixed color lines. Rather, a color continuum developed within which subtle differences in skin color, hair texture, and facial features were noted and essentially catalogued in an extensive vocabulary, with all its social implications, but without any group striving after (or succeeding in) the maintenance of strict endogamy, which might have created a clear separation from all others. If, in such a structure, there was any area of tension, it would have been one between the various shades of whites and lighter coloreds, on the one hand, and the darkest groups, on the other.

The French colony of Saint-Domingue at the same time was an export-oriented plantation economy with a large majority of black slaves, a tiny minority of whites of different class positions, and further minorities of free blacks and free coloreds. (Some of these last achieved considerable prosperity and a high level of education without, however, being accepted on a footing of social equality by the white community.) Saint-Domingue was characterized by potentially explosive lines of division, not only between the oppressed slaves and their masters, but also between whites and coloreds.

The two models briefly described here illustrate the main differences between the Hispanic and non-Hispanic Caribbean during the last quarter of the eighteenth century. If we could have traveled in the Caribbean at that time, we would have recognized the Santo Domingo model in Cuba, Puerto Rico, and Trinidad (then still Spanish), as well as parallels between Saint-Domingue and most of the islands that were now British, French, Dutch, or (as in the case of the U.S. Virgin Islands) Danish, and which had been lost by Spain in the previous century.

Before exploring more recent developments in the two societies of Hispaniola, I would like to make two more general remarks.

First, my description of the models in terms of their economic development and socioracial structure might be taken to imply a causal connection between the two, as if a pastoral or autarchic economy would always lead to a racial continuum of the Santo Domingo type, and a plantation economy producing for the world market to sharp divisions like those in Saint-Domingue. Yet we should note that a continuum like that in Santo Domingo also developed in northeast Brazil, where an export-oriented sugar economy had been established at an early date. Furthermore, some small islands in the archipelago, such as Curaçao, were characterized by a socioracial stratification like that in Saint-Domingue but proved to be unfit for export agriculture; their economy was based on commerce rather than crops, and slavery, though it existed, could not be considered a pillar of their economy. These cases may serve to remind us that, even though economic development seems to exert a strong influence on racial structures and relations, it is not the only shaping force.

Second, it is clear that there is a close correlation between the prevailing type of economy and the character of master-slave relations (as distinct from racial relations). A plantation economy, particularly one based on sugar, with its contracted periods of labor-intensive harvesting when hundreds of laborers have to live and work together, creates greater duress, deprivation, cruelty, and harshness than an economic system where the slaves are herdsmen of free-roaming cattle. However, there is no clear connection between the type of slavery (traditionally ranged on a continuum from "cruel" to "mild," though the latter of course fails to reflect slavery's inherent inhumanity) and the positions attained by *free* blacks or coloreds in the society where such slavery exists or has existed. Without going into a detailed argument here, we may observe that there are cases of societies with a history of extremely severe slave treatment, and yet with an early formation of a relatively prosperous and powerful class of coloreds. Conversely, there are instances of "mild" slavery with, simultaneously, strenuous efforts on the part of the white community to place firm limits on upward mobility by the (free) coloreds (Hoetink 1973:5–9).

To sum up: neither the connection between slavery and race relations nor the relation between economy and socioracial stratification is as clear or simple as has sometimes been suggested. What is much harder to contest, however, is the linkage between the prevailing type of economy and the general treatment of the slaves.

I deliberately interrupted our brief survey of the two colonies of Hispaniola at a point when the different paths they were to follow had become clearly established but before the French colony erupted in a revolution whose reverberations were to be felt for a long time both within and beyond the Caribbean. In the long revolutionary process that culminated in the proclamation of the independent Republic of Haiti in 1804, both the blacks (slave and free) and the coloreds (poor and elite) took an active part even though the precise nature of their alliances shifted repeatedly; the whites were killed or expelled.

Since then, the country (often called a black republic by those who think in terms of only two "racial" groupings) has witnessed the uneasy coexistence of a traditional elite of French cultural orientation and a poor, mostly rural population, the majority of whose ancestors were eighteenth-century African slaves and whose folk culture consequently contains many ingredients of African origin. At one time in its early days, the country was split into a black kingdom in the north, and a colored republic in the south.

Despite initial efforts to preserve the colonial plantation system, it gradually gave way to one in which small peasants worked on an increasingly eroded soil. But this did not change the castelike structure (Leyburn 1966) of privileged coloreds and poor blacks, nor the elite's preference for the culture (and even for the physical traits) of the colonial people they had driven out. Of course, the structure had its anomalies and did, over time, change; many leading army officers of the nineteenth century were black rather than colored, and at the end of that same century enlightened voices already could be heard clamoring for the equality of all races and pointing to the intrinsic beauty of the blacks. Furthermore, the coloreds and blacks never lived in isolated compartments; between them many-stranded relations (economic, political, sexual) existed. In the identity crisis caused by the United States' occupation of the country in 1915–34, a nationalist renaissance led some members of the elite to develop an ideological focus on their African roots long before Aimé Césaire and others from the French Antilles attracted international attention by urging a similar point of view. But it was only after World War II that this cultural program found its political counterpart and was supported by the growth of a black middle class. In this respect, the harsh regime of the rural doctor, François Duvalier, was of greater significance for the evolution of Haitian race relations than is commonly acknowledged. The once rigid, castelike structure slowly grew into a more complex stratification in which changing alliances between different sections of the former "castes" became possible without, however, the color factor losing its social significance in a country without native whites.

In the Haitian context, then, the terms *noir* and *mulâtre* do not refer to
ethnic type exclusively. They also carry social and political connotations.
Social, because while the illegitimate child of a Black working woman
and a White sailor on shore leave might be described as *mulâtre* in
appearance, he would certainly not be considered as belonging to the
mulâtre (i.e., upper) class. Conversely, a Black high government official
or successful businessman would make certain he was by marrying into a
mulâtre family. Political, because Haitian political factions have traditionally formed along class- and therefore color-lines. This is tacitly
understood rather than openly admitted, and the *mulâtre* group makes it a
point to include some ethnic Blacks in the government when it is in
power, while the *noir* group does the same for Mulattos when its turn
comes. (Hoffmann 1980:31)

Although larger in size, the eastern part of the island, Santo Domingo, remained weaker than Haiti, both in population and organization, for much of the nineteenth century; in 1822–44 it was occupied by Haiti, an annexation that is vividly and antagonistically depicted by most of the nation's traditional historiographers as well as by all who prefer to emphasize the country's Hispanic rather than its African heritage and its ethnic links with Europe rather than with Haiti.

In the last decades of the nineteenth century (when slavery had long since been abolished) the country's long economic interregnum ended with the establishment of modern sugar plantations, mostly on the southern plains. The immigration of thousands of foreign cane cutters from Haiti and from the Eastern Caribbean was encouraged, and many of these remained and were absorbed into the lower strata of society. The "modernization" of the country in this period, the growth of its cities, and the increased opportunities for commerce and the professions further led to the immigration of whites from the Caribbean, Europe, and the Near East.

Even though this influx of whites was far smaller, in numerical terms, than that of the cane cutters, it seems fair to say that, in the wake of the country's integration into the world sugar market, a certain "blackening" of the poorest strata went hand in hand with a "whitening" of the incipient national bourgeoisie. While this did not produce a rupture in the socioracial continuum, it did strain it, producing a greater sensitivity in the relations between its two extremes. This was, not surprisingly, especially true in the southern cane-growing region (Hoetink 1982:191); in the Central Cibao Valley, where tobacco, coffee, and cacao are produced, the traditional Santo Domingo model has not come under pressure from massive labor immigration.

This may change soon, however; in the last several years the number of Haitians residing in all parts of the country has greatly increased, and is not estimated at 200,000–400,000. Yearly, some 15,000 Haitian cane cutters are legally allowed to enter the country on a temporary basis, and many of them have remained there in the past. Uncounted others participate in what has been termed a "peaceful invasion." Since the end of the nineteenth century, power relations between the two countries have been reversed. Haiti, now the poorest country of the hemisphere, with a dramatic population pressure on its poor soil, sees its people seek work (miserably paid, to be sure, even by Dominican standards) in the same neighboring state that had been so easily invaded and dominated only a century and a half earlier.

In the 1920s and 1930s, a "peaceful invasion" similar to the one now under daily discussion in the Dominican press had also taken place; land had been occupied, cattle had been stolen, and the Haitian *gourde* had become the main currency in the western part of the Republic. The ensuing massacre of thousands of Haitians on Dominican soil in 1937 during the early years of the Trujillo regime, was only the most recent and most abhorrent in a series of tragic incidents in Dominican-Haitian relations that have been perpetrated by both sides over the last two centuries. In Dominican society, where the presence of dark-skinned bureaucrats and military officers next to light-colored peasants attests to the lack of a rigid hierarchy based on color, but where incidents of discrimination on the basis of physical appearance are common as well, it is hardly surprising that racial tensions tend to be projected upon the Haitians. Haitians are viewed by Dominicans not only as a blacker people (a stereotype that would be hard to refute) but also as culturally inferior.

It is perhaps interesting to note, in this context, that one of the most powerful Dominican politicians of today is not only unequivocally black but also believed to be of Haitian descent. While few Dominicans would deny his political sagacity and astuteness, many (including the leader himself) doubt whether it would be expedient to propose his presidential candidacy in the near future, precisely because of the potential political cost of his appearance and alleged descent to both him and his party. Recently, however, a letter to the editor of a leading newspaper advocated such a step.

> It would be progress if we could rid ourselves of our complex, knowing that we are negroes and mulattoes even though we have a light skin. If you do not believe so, look at your grandmother, grandfather, or uncle, your cousin, or in many cases your own brother. It would be progress if one day, not far away, the Dominican people would vote unhampered by complexes or by fear for the color of their own skin. . . . Progress would be the courage this people needs to vote for a pure specimen of its origin. . . . Progress it is to follow our Black Diamond. (*Listin Diario,* 6 June 1983)

The country has had a few dark-skinned presidents in the past, whose star had risen during civil war and political turmoil (situations that generally favor mobility), and perhaps the future will produce one by peaceful means. But the people's reluctance to acknowledge its partially African roots is great in a country that traditionally highlights its Hispanic heritage and its racial intermingling (which, as the above letter points out, makes itself visible within many families). It will be hard to overcome the prevalent idea that black "purity" (an untenable notion in itself, of course) points to the old Haitian adversaries rather than to part of the Dominican population. Yet there is some slight change, very slow to be sure. I cite just two (largely symbolic) examples. Recently, the two statues in front of one of Santo Domingo's larger museums (one depicting a Spaniard, the other an Amerindian) were joined by a third, representing a black. And the formerly exclusive Good Friday procession in the capital has undergone some changes as well. "A generation ago, the procession recruited its Roman guards from among the best students of the city's Catholic colleges, and those selected had to possess certain physical characteristics similar to those of the old Romans. . . . Nowadays . . . the selection of its members is less strict . . . and its ranks include young people of the most varied appearance" (Yaryura 1983:32).

THE HISPANIC CARIBBEAN

In Cuba, the Caribbean's most powerful and populous island, the modernization and rapid expansion of the sugar sector began in the second half of the eighteenth century, a hundred years before that of the Dominican Republic. Massive slave imports (partly illegal) continued well into the nineteenth century, drastically changing the racial composition of the population. Slavery was abolished only in the 1880s. Even before abolition, other sources of unfree labor were tapped: tens of thousands of Chinese contract laborers were recruited, and many Amerindians from Yucatán were forcibly transported to Cuba. After abolition, a still expanding sugar area—increasingly under United States ownership—encouraged further immigration of cane cutters from nearby islands where the plantation economy had declined. In the first decades of the present century, tens of thousands of British West Indians and Haitians arrived in Cuba.

Similar to the Cibao Valley in the Dominican Republic, parts of Cuba's Oriente region, dominated by smaller farms and by crops other than cane, preserved much of the racial structure of the preceding period; most of the new waves of migration were initially directed to the western half of the island, where the large sugar plantations predominated. Here, a tense relationship developed between the whites and light coloreds on the one hand and, on the other, the "dark coloreds" and the mass of black slaves and their descendants. (The line of division between whites and light coloreds continued to be blurred according to the Santo Domingo model, though it was complicated by the higher prestige alloted to the Spanish-born in the continuing colonial situation.) In this western part of Cuba, the intermediate range of coloreds ultimately constituted only a tiny proportion of the total population. This polarization, begun during slavery, continued after abolition and was aggravated by an occasional questioning of the "Cubanness" not only of the slaves and their descendants, but also (and more urgently) of the many black immigrants from elsewhere in the Caribbean. Perhaps the increasing U.S. presence, including its perspective on race relations, contributed to the polarization, although it might be argued that sheer weight of numbers, cultural diversity, and the unbalanced economic structure alone would be sufficient to account for it. Elsewhere in the Hispanic Caribbean, Havana and the Cuban sugar area had acquired a reputation for racism by the end of the nineteenth century. In 1912 some 3,000 Afro-Cubans, demanding more economic and political power and the right to organize a black political party, were ruthlessly killed by government troops. In the 1930s, no doubt influenced by the economic depression, legislation was adopted to "Cubanize" the (sugar) work force and to send the foreign laborers home. The pattern of increasingly harsh, partly public discrimination was overcome only by the Cuban Revolution, whose successful efforts at distributive justice (rather than at increased productivity) generally proved beneficial to the lower and darker-skinned strata of society, even though an early postrevolutionary effort to establish a black Communist party was quickly suppressed. Both Marxist and traditionally Hispanic convictions converged to deemphasize racial diversity and tensions, a phenomenon that was disappointing to some visiting U.S. black militants during the early years of the new regime. Part of the benefits for lower-class Cubans was the result of the exodus of middle-class professionals and bureaucrats, which, together with expanded education facilities, made for increased mobility among the revolution's first generation of adults. On the other hand, and without minimizing the positive effects of the revolution, it should be observed that blacks have not become conspicuous by their increased presence in the upper echelons of the Cuban government, no matter how much this government (in a remarkable parallel with Brazil) tries to stress the country's African roots in its dealing with countries in Africa and in the non-Hispanic Caribbean.

While Cuba represents a variation on the Santo Domingo model because of the dramatic increase in discriminatory practices resulting from a proportionately much larger immigration of black sugar workers (both slaves and "free" immigrants), Puerto Rico during the nineteenth century presents a variant in the other direction. By the time that modern sugar plantations started being established there in the early nineteenth century, the population density and the general poverty in the rural areas were such that the need for cane cutters could be filled largely by the island's own labor force. Together with the importation of new slaves, a system of antivagrancy regulations was introduced that obliged able-bodied men without proven regular jobs to enter the plantation work force. This *régimen de la libreta* ("workbook system," named after the books in which the laborer's work contracts were noted down) mobilized thousands of Puerto Rican *jíbaros* as de facto unfree laborers who had to work side by side with de jure slaves, creating an interracial work situation for the first time in the Caribbean since the middle of the seventeenth century, when white indentured laborers in the British and French islands had worked together with recently imported slaves.

In Puerto Rico, as in Cuba, the booming sugar economy made for harsh treatment of the slaves and enforced laborers, but in the years after abolition, the relatively small number of former slaves was absorbed fairly easily into the mass of the population, the large majority of which belonged to the intermediate sectors of the socioracial continuum that had been formed prior to the advent of sugar. While in Cuba, as Knight observes, the intermediate free colored population was "swamped by the immigrants" and "restricted to the towns and the eastern part of the island where work opportunities were more abundant," in Puerto Rico the predominance of a "large intermediate group of free colored persons" made social mobility possible "for most people who suffered from no practical inequalities and were not visually and culturally distinct from the elite" (Knight 1970:191). It should be kept in mind, however, that while such mobility was easy (as far as visual distinctions are concerned) for most people, it was not for all. Even if the sugar industry today is no longer the mainstay of Puerto Rican economic life, it is in the traditional sugar areas of the coastal plains, and increasingly in the poorer sections of the burgeoning cities as well, that parts of the lower strata give physical evidence of slavery's impact on the population. They do not escape from the prejudices that such a status seems to provoke everywhere.

While it makes sense, as we have argued, to stress the underlying unity of the Hispanic Caribbean, we should not lose sight of the very real differences in race relations among the three societies that make it up. They have in common the circumstance that a considerable part of their population developed socially and culturally prior to (and later, to some extent, apart from) the impact of the modern sugar plantation, with its ensuing new waves of black immigrants, slave or otherwise, that came to be the main work force of this agrarian sector. This impact was different in each of these societies. The socioracial continuum and the relatively homogeneous culture (especially in terms of language and religion) that had evolved since the early sixteenth century, came under pressure, different in intensity for each of them. In the case of the Dominican Republic, an unusually long presugar phase and the presence of a relatively open border with Haiti led to a continuous color scale on which the darker mixed strata appear to predominate; in Puerto Rico, the lighter-colored intermediate strata are more numerous; and in Cuba the extreme ends of the continuum appear to be more visible and more numerous now than the population in between. Yet in all three societies, the newcomers and their cultural baggage were largely absorbed into a common culture, and the effects of the traditional fluidity between the many contiguous color distinctions, though subject to very severe strains (especially in Cuba), seem at this point not to have disappeared entirely.

THE NON-HISPANIC CARIBBEAN

If it was not easy to encompass in a brief sketch the Hispanic Caribbean's unity and diversity in terms of race relations, a similar attempt with regard to the non-Hispanic part of the area will be even more difficult. The sheer number of its societies (many of them very small islands, and each with its own peculiarities in both historical development and the nature of contemporary life) defies any effort at a compact synthesis. To simplify our task somewhat, let us first set aside Trinidad, Suriname, and Guyana for later discussion. Even though the early history of these countries shows parallels with that of the other non-Hispanic societies, the arrival in the nineteenth century of massive groups of Asian contract laborers drastically changed their ethnic physiognomy.

The Lesser Antilles and Jamaica

To the remaining islands—most of the Lesser Antilles, and Jamaica—sugar came early. From the area around Recife, Brazil, where modern sugar agriculture and processing techniques had been introduced under Dutch auspices in the second quarter of the seventeenth century, the plantation system spread northward in that same century, first to Barbados, then to the other recently conquered British, French, Dutch, and Danish islands in the eastern rim, and to Jamaica. In the next century, as we have seen, it was to arrive also in Saint-Domingue. Earlier efforts at agriculture in some of the British and French islands, where crops such as tobacco and indigo were cultivated by unfree laborers from the metropolitan countries (indentured laborers, *engagés*), quickly gave way to the new and profitable crop. This led to an immediate and long-lasting importation of black slaves, who came to form the vast majority in virtually all of these societies.

A basic pattern evolved in which a tiny minority of whites (owners or overseers of plantations, some technical staff, colonial bureaucrats and clergy, large and small traders and their clerks, and some artisans) occupied the highest rungs of the social ladder (though they were internally divided into classes and factions according to wealth, education, and occupation). The mass of slaves and their descendants were at the other end of the scale, while a mixed, colored section, although often desperately poor, received preferential treatment from the dominant whites whenever there were intermediate jobs that no whites could or would take. In this way some coloreds succeeded in time in obtaining positions of a certain prestige and remuneration without, however, being accepted as social equals by the whites. The ultimate reflection of the durable social distance between these two groups is the continuing aspiration of the white group to preserve its racial endogamy.

> Of all instrumentalities that separate classes, the most deliberate and durable is endogamy. Nowhere in the Caribbean is miscegenation legally banned or publicly censured. None the less white Creole [i.e., native] intermarriage remains customary if not mandatory; whites who marry nonwhite West Indians are, in the main, expatriates unconstrained by Creole family ties.
>   In the French Antilles endogamy is vital to *béké* [native white] economic as well as social dominance and demands social exclusion against the risk of forbidden attachments. Male friendships across colour lines, however warm and enduring, never extend into family lives. (Lowenthal 1972:133)

This endogamy certainly does not mean that there were no sexual relationships between white men and black or colored women. Such relationships were common, sometimes even taking the form of durable unions, the children of which helped swell the ranks of the prosperous and "respectable" coloreds. But marriages of this type that recognized the children as legitimate heirs have always been exceedingly rare.

In the context of intergroup relations, then, the position of the intermediate group of coloreds is a peculiar one.

> As he sat down, an elderly coloured man said, just to open the conversation, "A lot of these black fellers in Tobago are damn intelligent, you know."
> We were in the West Indies. Black had a precise meaning; I was among people who had a nice eye for shades of black. And the elderly coloured man—a man, that is, of mixed European and African descent, with features and skin-colour closer to the European—was safe. (Naipaul 1962:15)

The colored group is regarded by both the white group and itself as a separate socioracial category that may aspire to a social status and to economic positions traditionally closed to blacks; yet even whites of similar or lower economic or educational level insist upon maintaining social distance from them. Between these groups, there exists a discontinuity that contrasts with the (admittedly sometimes tenuous) continuity of racial groupings in the Hispanic countries. The colored group is, of course, internally differentiated, both economically and in terms of physical appearance. Those who form its lower ranks (in terms of jobs, income, etc.) do not close off access to upwardly mobile blacks, so that the socioracial structure is more continuous and solidary at the bottom than it is at the top. The whole racial power structure conspires to encourage the colored elite to emulate the white groups, both culturally and in physical appearance (fostering a desire for "whitening" or "improving the race"). The closure of the Creole white group in terms of private relations such as marriage (and for a long time certain public relations such as official receptions as well) places the intermediate group in a socially ambiguous position. Of course, intermediate positions suffer from ambiguity, almost by definition. Yet it seems plausible to assume that pent-up frustration tends to be greater in a situation where few bridging mechanisms exist between the intermediate and the upper group. Where slave revolts threatened or broke out, or where racial violence erupted, the intermediate group in the non-Hispanic societies sometimes was internally divided about what position to take and seemed to shift alliances more frequently than did the comparable group in the Hispanic area. Of course, such greater unpredictability should not be understood only in terms of the group's more frustrating situation. It was also often a matter of coolly assessing a specific conflict's probable outcome, in societies where whites—and coloreds—are numerically very weak indeed.

In its turn, the white group's intrinsic insecurity in such (frequent) times of crisis was aggravated by its nagging uncertainty about the intermediate group's course of action. Perhaps this is how we should understand the insistence of the white Creoles on maintaining as close an identification as possible, culturally as well as politically, with its only secure (if remote) ally—the metropolitan country. Even after generations in the colony, they preferred to see themselves as representing English, French, or Dutch civilization and their own institutions as extensions or copies of those in the mother country. Only the recent development of easier and more frequent communications has taught them that this was not so, that in the course of generations they had acquired different inflections, manners, and beliefs—in brief, that they too had been subject to a process of creolization. (See Brathwaite 1971 for a vivid description of this process in Jamaica.) Yet the need for identification with the mother country was there, and, creolization notwithstanding, white Creoles clung to their mother tongue (though they could speak in the local creole language if necessary) and to their metropolitan churches. Such adherence, amidst the religious and linguistic variety of the other classes, only served to emphasize the white group's boundaries and to increase its sense of isolation. Whereas the ambivalence of the intermediate group's self-image is between high and low social status, the native white's ambivalence is one between "here" and "there," between the urge to stay in their native country and the preparedness to withdraw in the face of decreasing power and influence, aggravated at times by the clear message that one's group is no longer perceived as native by the majority of the population, or that it is being isolated by some moral distinction. In Curaçao until recently all native Curaçaoans were called *yiu di Korsow* (children of Curaçao); lately a distinction is sometimes being made between *yiu di Korsow* and *bon yiu di Korsow* (good children of Curaçao), a term that excludes the native whites (Römer 1974:53).

Universal suffrage, political independence, and improved education have in most of these societies belatedly brought about a notable mobility of blacks and dark coloreds in the civil service, the educational system, and the higher echelons of police and army. These people were thus moving into positions previously often monopolized by native or metropolitan whites or by the old colored elite. (Curiously, the conversion of the French Antilles and French Guiana to *départements d'outre-mer* [overseas French departments] caused an influx of European French civil servants.) The decreasing political, and in some places social, importance of the native whites does not mean that the (fluid) line between blacks and coloreds is losing all of its former significance. On the contrary, we may observe how in some islands a core of well-established colored families succeed—by an intricate play of power and alliance both with the lower strata and with the black and colored middle classes, executed with all the self-assurance of a successor class—in occupying the crucial (if not always the most visible) positions in the political and social networks.

> Awareness of colour varies with class. The elite take for granted their own identity as whites; colour becomes an overt issue among them only in gross transgressions of the social code. Nor is colour *per se* a constant concern in peasant communities. But for the Caribbean middle class colour is the crucial determinant of status and suffuses most relationships. . . . Middle-class obsession with colour is exemplified in the legendary remark that at Government House one used to be sure of meeting no one darker than oneself. Now that blacks are not only guests but governors, some of the lighter skinned stay at home instead. (Lowenthal 1972:253–54)

Up to this point, we have hardly been specific but rather have presented a construct, a composite picture of some main traits of a "typical" three-tiered society in the non-Hispanic Caribbean. The variations on and exceptions to this general sketch are numerous. There were different proportions of whites, coloreds, and blacks in different societies and at different times; there were also different percentages of slaves and freedmen. Abolition laws were passed at quite different times: 1833 by the British, 1848 by the French, and 1863 by the Dutch. Islands are different in size and ecology; some countries (Suriname and Jamaica) were large and impenetrable enough for maroons to establish permanent settlements, while in the smaller islands, slaves could flee only by boat. Some plantation economies were run by private absentee proprietors or by metropolitan corporations; elsewhere, plantation owners lived on their estates. Some islands, such as Curaçao, St. Eustatius, and St. Thomas, were at different times more known for their commerce than for their crops. All such variables gave each society its particular character, with regard both to slavery and to race relations. The effect of the small scale of many societies has been summarized as follows: "Among the mass of the people as well, the small size of West Indian societies promotes a familiarity that makes it hard to sustain uncompromising hostility. West Indians who have to live in the same small island all their lives learn early how to get along with those from whom they differ" (Lowenthal 1972:141).

To formulate a more organized overview of present-day variety in this area, we might do well to follow the classification proposed by Lowenthal (1972:76–87). Four of his categories interest us here. First, there are "homogeneous societies" without much distinction as to class, color, or culture. Tiny islands such as Carriacou, Barbuda (black), and St. Barthélémy (white) are given by Lowenthal as examples; Bonaire (where people speak of themselves as "brown") might be added. Second, there are "societies differentiated by colour but not by class," such as Saba and Anguilla. Here, different racial or color groups live separately and have little contact, even though their style of life and economic position do not differ notably. Lowenthal's third category, "societies stratified by both class and colour," has already been discussed in general terms. Lowenthal points to Barbados and Martinique as having significant numbers of poor whites; whites number 4 percent in Barbados, only 1 percent in Martinique and in Jamaica. Other islands with small white elites are Trinidad, St. Kitts, Antigua, St. Vincent, Guadeloupe, and Curaçao. Finally, there is Lowenthal's fourth category: "societies lacking white Creole elites." Haiti and the U.S. Virgin Islands fall into this category, as do the Commonwealth Windward Islands of Grenada, St. Lucia, and Dominica. "Coloured Creoles, not whites, today comprise the Windward elite, such as it is; the saying that 'the only reason the coloreds got St. Lucia is that the whites didn't want it' expresses a typically rueful self-mockery. The closely interrelated, light-skinned upper class sharply distinguish themselves from all others of whatever shade" (Lowenthal 1972:85).

Let us turn briefly now to Jamaica, one of the larger islands under discussion. In a recent article, mostly devoted to Jamaican society (and characteristically entitled "Race and Class in the Post-Emancipation Caribbean") the social anthropologist R. T. Smith carefully tries to dissect the island's class system. His three-tiered class structure shows an upper class mostly of native whites (Smith writes, curiously, of "Creole Whites" and "Jews" as if the latter were neither white nor Creole) and a sprinkling of Syrians and Chinese; a middle class of colored merchants, bureaucrats, members of the intelligentsia, and an upwardly mobile group of blacks that only in the past half century increased markedly in number; and finally a lower class, overwhelmingly black. All three classes, of course, have a complex internal composition. Thus, though Smith set out "to describe groupings which seemed to emerge as identifiable elements either in the system of production, distribution and exchange or as politically conscious elements," the net result of his analysis *grosso modo* is not very different from the "tripartite class image . . . (White upper class, Coloured middle class, Black lower class)" that "writers on the Caribbean generally employ" (Smith 1982:104-5). He rightly observes that "even when . . . barriers to occupational mobility have been weakened or broken down, racial identification continues to cut across class and to distort incipient class solidarities" (Smith 1982:114). He also writes persuasively that "under these circumstances it is not surprising that, after the British departed, the emphasis of the independent [Commonwealth Caribbean] states on the equality of all racial groups in the building of the new nation soon came to be seen as a device to ensure the continuing hegemony of the Anglicised elite, and the economically privileged position of the local capitalist classes formed out of the light-coloured or white minorities" (Smith 1982:119).

H. HOETINK

Trinidad, Guyana, and Suriname

While there are communities of East Indians in many of the islands (e.g., Jamaica and Guadeloupe), it was only in three Caribbean societies that they came to form roughly half of the entire population. These are Trinidad (where modern plantations and massive importation of black slaves had started only in the early nineteenth century, after the colony had been taken over from Spain by Britain) and the vast but thinly populated plantation colonies of British Guiana (Guyana) and Dutch Guiana (Suriname). In Suriname, additional contract laborers were imported from Java in the Dutch East Indies. The general idea behind the immigration policy was, of course, to guarantee a sufficient supply of cheap labor after abolition.

Today, the descendants of these groups are still predominantly engaged in agriculture, either as cane cutters or as small and middle-size farmers; in Suriname, for example, rice cultivation in the western districts is mostly in the hands of these groups. While the Afro-American part of the population migrated increasingly from rural to urban areas, with the better educated among them moving (as we saw earlier) into the ranks of the civil service and the professions, the East Indians remained on the land, preserving their cohesive family organization, their language, and their religions. Cultural, "racial," and economic differences were thus accentuated by geographical separation. It was not until the 1940s that a slow process of urbanization got underway among the Asian groups. Their strong familial organization, their austere style of living, and a notable business acumen soon converted many of them into shopkeepers, some of whom succeeded in becoming the wealthy owners of wholesale enterprises. The children of these successful migrants produced a new and increasingly influential layer of university-trained professionals.

This increasing urbanization and mobility not only made for a greater visibility of this group in the mostly Afro-American (and white) higher urban strata; it also meant engaging East Indians in the competition for civil service and professional positions. The rural East Indians thus began to acquire a growing number of "representatives" and power brokers (economic, and eventually also political) in the urban area. The urban East Indians were, more than their rural brethren subject to cultural creolization, yet their ethnic allegiance remained strong, and they continued to be largely endogamous.

To a large extent, the political, religious, and educational organization of all three countries became centered on, and largely determined by, adherence to either of the two main competing groups. No longer is either contending section confined to one main economic activity or to one social class, as was the case in the past when the Afro-Creoles' pejorative stereotypes of the East Indians derogated their humble rural beginnings. Instead of a hierarchical ordering of the "racial" groups such as we find elsewhere in the Caribbean, we find here a vertical line of division, at each side of which people in comparable or equal class positions but of different "race" compete with one another.

The internal color and social differences of the Afro-American group remain intact, but these are overshadowed by the more central competitive struggle. The groups' political programs generally are universalistic in nature, yet they do not manage to attract more than a few voters of the contending racial segment. Thus in British Guiana, the East Indian Cheddi Jagan had his ethnic followers, spread over many economic classes, vote him into power in the early 1960s on a Marxist platform, the first—and so far the only—prime minister of East Indian descent in any of the three countries under discussion. During his government, just prior to independence, bloody riots between the two groups broke out, leading to British intervention and ultimately to the regaining of political power by the Afro-Guianese segment, which in turn was then led in a political direction not wholly dissimilar to that Jagan had advocated. In Trinidad (where the government has for many years been run by a predominantly Afro-Trinidadian party), in Suriname (where, prior to the 1980 military coup the East Indians' party participated in several coalition governments), and in the Republic of Guyana, the East Indians, in spite of their numerical strength and economic significance, still tend to be seen by the Afro-Americans as newcomers and outsiders. Thus, as Anthony Maingot points out in a review of the recently published selection of speeches by Trinidadian historian and Prime Minister Eric Williams, "to the very end he [Williams] spoke of Indian Trinidadians as if they were still an immigrant group" (Maingot 1983:94). And in Suriname (at least until very recently), the term *Surinamer* has implicitly referred to the non-Asian groups only, thus excluding both East Indians and Javanese. Every now and then small movements come to the fore, often led by young intellectuals educated elsewhere, that dismiss racial or ethnic allegiances with commendable idealism and strive truly to embrace the voting populace at large. So far, mutual suspicion, negative stereotyping, and a sense of identity nurtured by what is distinctive in each group rather than by what they have in common have proved hard to overcome.

> Matters are not helped by the fierce rivalry between Indians and Negroes as to who despises the other more. This particular rivalry is conducted by the liberal-minded, who will not be denied the pleasure of appealing to their group to show more tolerance towards the other group, and who are deeply annoyed when it is claimed by liberals of the other party that it is the other group which has to do the tolerating. . . . The Negro has a deep contempt, as has been said, for all that is not white. . . . The Indian despises the Negro for not being an Indian; he has, in addition, taken over all the white prejudices against the Negro. (Naipaul 1962:80)

MIGRATIONS

Up to this point, I have tried to paint, perhaps in overly broad strokes, a triptych of Caribbean race relations with one Hispanic panel and two panels devoted to the non-Hispanic Caribbean (divided between those societies with and without a large Asian population group). We should now try to make up for at least some of the imprecisions in this generalized scheme by drawing attention to the many movements of people within, toward, and away from the area.[4] Such movements attest to the connections between all parts of the Caribbean that we have so artificially separated; they make the social and ethnic fabric of the region more complicated and in some ways more unified; and they have in some instances profound influence on power, and hence racial, relations. Islands such as those in the Caribbean never have been entirely isolated but have continuously invited migration; their Robinson Crusoes have always had a chance to sight a ship.

Migrations within the Area

Successive waves of Amerindians who had migrated from the South American mainland were still at war when Columbus arrived; and at a time when few African slaves had reached their shores, the richer and larger Antilles imported Amerindian labor for their mines from the smaller *islas inútiles* (unusable islands). Later, fugitive slaves moved from Curaçao to Venezuela, from the Virgin Islands to Puerto Rico, from Saint-Domingue to Santo Domingo.

In the nineteenth century, Cuba's sugar boom first brought in Indians from Yucatán and later thousands of migrants from Haiti and various British West Indian islands. The Dominican Republic's sugar boom attracted both these and many Puerto Ricans. In the early twentieth century, Curaçaoans moved to work on a railway in Suriname, and Barbadians could be found in the rubber plantations of Peru. Tens of thousands of Jamaicans and other British West Indians went to work on the Panama Canal and on the banana and other fruit plantations along the Caribbean coast of Central America. (And "Black Caribs," originally deported by the English from some Eastern Caribbean islands, had long before settled in British Honduras [Belize].) In more recent times, many Dominicans moved to Puerto Rico; hundreds of British Windward islanders worked at the refineries of Aruba and Curaçao; some 40,000 Guyanese are reportedly now working in Suriname; Trinidad has absorbed thousands of immigrants from the Commonwealth's smaller Caribbean islands; and Haitians can be found in many other islands, such as Dutch St. Maarten, which is experiencing a tourist boom, and the French Antilles and French Guiana. The list is far from complete.

Not all intra-Caribbean migrations were of lower-class persons. Political and economic vicissitudes and chances for economic betterment were also the push and pull factors for migrants of higher status. Refugees from revolutionary Saint-Domingue fled to Louisiana and to the nearby Spanish colonies; French Creole colonists from Martinique moved to Trinidad; from annexed Louisiana and independent Venezuela went royalist *Criollos,* in the early nineteenth century, to the remaining Spanish colonies in the archipelago. The Haitian domination led some Dominican elite families to migrate to Cuba and Puerto Rico; in the 1860s sugar entrepreneurs fled from warring Cuba to Santo Domingo, where they were among the initiators of that country's modern sugar industry; Sephardic Jews from Curaçao spread to Cuba, Santo Domingo, St. Thomas, and Central America; fugitives from strife-ridden Venezuela and Colombia went to Curaçao. Upper-class girls from the Hispanic republics met each other in European-style boarding schools there, from which some of them returned with Dutch Antillean husbands. The small, commercially oriented islands of St. Thomas and Curaçao were, indeed, cosmopolitan nerve-knots in the nineteenth-century Caribbean. There, and especially on behalf of the independent republics of the area, foreign loans were arranged, products exchanged, and revolutions financed, and political refugees were kept abreast of developments in their countries. The largest Caribbean exodus of the present century, that of almost a million (mostly middle-class) Cubans leaving their island since the early 1960s, was mainly directed toward the United States, but Puerto Rico and (to a lesser extent) the Dominican Republic received their share as well.

Migrations to the Area

Migration from outside the Caribbean in the nineteenth century involved not only East Indians, Javanese, and Chinese, but many smaller groups as well, ranging from "free Africans" (contracted to work in Jamaica and the eastern British Caribbean) and Portuguese from Madeira (put to work in Trinidad and the Guianas) to a continuous trickle of Spaniards and Italians who sought their fortunes in the Hispanic islands. In the twentieth century many small groups were added to this mosaic. To cite just a few examples: the Hispanic islands benefited from an influx of Spanish intellectuals and artists who had fled the Spanish Civil War; and in the Dominican Republic German Jewish refugees established a modern dairy industry, a community of Japanese is engaged in horticulture, and a recent wave of Chinese from Hong Kong is investing heavily in tourism. During the 1930s and 1940s, some forty-odd nationalities (which included a substantial number of Madeirese) could be found in the oil-refining islands of Aruba and Curaçao. Nor do such migrants always remain in the first country of disembarkation. One may meet a Portuguese cabdriver in Caracas, an East Indian shopkeeper in St. Martin, or a Chinese businessman in Puerto Rico, whose personal or family history reveals a complicated itinerary from one Caribbean stepping stone to another.

While, as we saw, Cuba has a substantial Chinese community, smaller groups of Chinese descent are to be found in all other major Caribbean societies; most are still active in their traditional economic niche of laundries and restaurants, but there are also some larger entrepreneurs, and in the younger generation a university education is no longer rare. Both their economic fortune and their degree of assimilation vary considerably from one society to another (Patterson 1977:113–46). But it is perhaps more than a coincidence that in societies such as Trinidad, Guyana, and Suriname (where, as we have seen, two large "racial" segments are competing in economic and political life), a member of the small, socially discrete, "nonpartisan" Chinese group has more than once been invited to occupy a sensitive official position because the two contending parties found it impossible to agree on either of their own candidates. The first president of the Cooperative Republic of Guyana and the first native governor-general of Trinidad and Tobago both were Chinese; and in Suriname, when, after the 1980 coup, military and civilian authorities were still trying to achieve a certain balance in their relations, the physician Henk Chin A Sen was asked to assume the post of prime minister.

Another migrant stream remarkable for its mobility in many of the larger Caribbean islands (as well as in much of the South American mainland) is variously referred to as Turks, Arabs, Syrians, or Lebanese. These people first entered the Caribbean as citizens of the Ottoman Empire in the late nineteenth century. Starting out as peddlers, many of them eventually became prosperous merchants. While some members of subsequent generations stuck to the mercantile tradition, others entered the professions or started public careers, many of which were quite successful. Lebanese names such as Seaga (in Jamaica), Majluta (in the Dominican Republic), and Isa (in Curaçao) have at different times been political household words. In a comparison of the assimilation of Levantine groups in Haiti, Trinidad, and the Dominican Republic, Nicholls observes that the Lebanese community in the Dominican Republic has both the most active ethnic club and the highest degree of intermarriage and general acculturation (Nicholls 1981). One could argue that it was their speedy absorption into this Hispanic society (whose partly Mediterranean folkways and ethnic composition, especially of its middle and upper classes, were in many respects so akin to their area of origin) that made it particularly important for them to organize themselves (almost artificially) in order not to lose entirely their ethnic identity and cohesiveness. A greater social isolation of the Levantines in Haiti and Trinidad, caused partly by the social and "racial" structure of these societies, made the need for a special group organization there less imperative.

Permanent migrants should be distinguished, of course, from temporary residents; the French civil servant is in a very different position from the Martiniquan *béké* (Creole white), the Haitian seasonal worker from the native St. Maartener, and the expatriate tax-haven expert from the local Cayman islander. Yet the line of division is a tenuous one; some visitors remain longer than they first intended, and some temporary foreign enclaves end up providing a new creolized ingredient of the social patchwork.

Given the diversity of the cases, it would be imprudent to attempt to formulate general conclusions about the impact of these migrations on race relations for the Caribbean as a whole. Earlier we saw how relatively large additions to the black and white poles had important effects on the socioracial continuum in Cuba and the Dominican Republic after their sugar booms began. Massive East Indian migration to the Guianas and Trinidad did nothing less than change the character of these societies entirely. It is further obvious that in small communities the arrival of small numbers of migrants can have dramatic results; when, for example, the tiny white elite in the Dutch Windward Islands moved to the Leewards in the 1940s and 1950s, the entire socioracial structure of these islands was altered. In Curaçao, the riots and arson of May 1969 reflected the special ire against the most recently arrived yet already prosperous trading minorities, even though each of these minorities was small in absolute numbers. It may be that these middlemen migrants (whose commercial success is attributed by the colored and black strata as much to their allegedly preferential treatment by "white" banks and crass exploitation of lower-class personnel as to their habits of hard work and frugal living) tend to place themselves in a more socially precarious position than that of other newcomers. Yet here also, as our brief survey of Chinese and Levantine experiences indicates, the peculiar structure and culture of each host society has sufficiently profound effects on the role and behavior of its immigrants to preclude sweeping generalizations.

Migrations from the Area

Finally, it is important to say a word about migration away from the Caribbean. Here also, the present large-scale movements tend to overshadow in our minds the historical antecedents, such as the settling of Cuban migrants in Tampa and Key West, Florida, in the 1870s or the migration of members of the colored elites of Suriname and the British colonies to their respective metropolitan countries in the early twentieth century. In the latter half of the nineteenth century, of course, the New York area already had expatriate Hispanic colonies, which included exiled revolutionaries such as the Cuban José Martí and the Dominican Gregorio Luperón. It has been only in more recent decades that large numbers of Caribbean migrants, including more and more of low social status, have started to move to the United States, to Canada, and to Western Europe in search of better opportunities for themselves and their children; at times these people have been propelled by insecurities aroused by political instability, as their countries passed through processes of decolonization or revolutionary change.

As United States citizens, Puerto Ricans move back and forth to the mainland in large numbers; the rhythm of their movements is largely dictated by the ups and downs of the U.S. economy. Dominicans, free to leave their country after the fall of the Trujillo regime in 1961, now have a United States community estimated at some 300,000. The Cuban exodus dates from about the same time, and more recently the influx of Haitian "boat-people" to Florida has made headlines. Since the 1950s, there has been a steady stream from the British West Indies to Britain and North America, with the latter continent receiving relatively more, once Britain had adopted restrictive legislation. At times this stream accelerated, for example, when the worsening Jamaican political and economic situation in the late 1970s caused the departure of a significant number of that country's economic and professional elites.

The effects of such migrations on race relations are difficult to assess and have been researched very little. In societies where significant numbers from the middle or upper classes are leaving, their vacant positions may be taken by upwardly mobile blacks. And in societies (e.g., the Dominican Republic) where it is not the poorest group among the rural population that migrates but rather those who have a little land and some savings, there may be a "darkening" of the remaining population. Much more drastic changes take place in relatively small populations such as that of Suriname, of which one third (180,000) now lives in the Netherlands. The disproportionate numbers of Afro-Surinamers (as opposed to East Indian Surinamers) among the immigrants should render more precarious the traditional hold of the former over the latter in that country.

I would argue that the Caribbean migrations to Europe and to the United States, though caused by the same forces, are of a different order, both as an experience for the people involved and in their effects on the Caribbean region. While on both continents the immigrants tend, out of nostalgia, to idealize the country they left behind, to blur its once clear image, and to nurture less realistic views of its potential development, and while in both cases members of the second generation may suffer from cultural uprootedness and social rejection, their situation is aggravated in Europe by their awareness of the greater distance to the Caribbean. Travel between the Caribbean and the North American mainland is much more intense in both directions. Those who left and those who stayed behind remain better aware of each other's environment.

Further, the United States was already a multiracial society long before people began arriving from the Caribbean. In Europe, on the other hand, the prospect of becoming a multiracial society began to be faced only after these and other migrations had introduced the idea. In other words, in Western Europe (and to some extent in Canada as well), the Caribbean migrants together with other new minorities are involved in a slow process that will ultimately lead to some distinctive socioracial structure, but in the United

States they must find a niche in a preexisting multiracial structure that has an essentially twofold division between whites and blacks. Each group has, to be sure, a complex internal differentiation, but there is no socially recognized intermediate group of coloreds comparable to that in the Caribbean.

For those Caribbean migrants who are labeled unequivocally black or white in their country of origin, the U.S. dichotomy poses no problem; they become members of one or the other U.S. socioracial category, as they become less foreign in speech, dress, etc., and thus can be marked off and absorbed as "black" or "white" Americans. However, those from the non-Hispanic Caribbean who had belonged to the intermediate grouping of "coloreds" suddenly find themselves defined as "blacks" in their new country, and the same predicament befalls those from the Hispanic area who had occupied intermediate positions on the fluid socioracial scale there, or perhaps had even been defined as "whites" by social criteria not recognized in the United States. It should cause no surprise if this latter Hispanic group shows an active (and at times militant) interest in emphasizing and preserving its common cultural heritage, of which its socioracial labeling forms a part. By doing so they might well succeed in creating a new middle group of "Latins" (within which some internal ranking according to national origin and "color" would probably persist), located between the old "black" and "white" categories. This emphasis on the group's cultural origins rather than on "racial" labeling has made the "Hispanic" surname a main criterion of identification for purposes of social or political action.

The non-Hispanic coloreds in the United States, mostly English-speaking and by that fact alone more prone to cultural assimilation, have had to accommodate themselves within the group of U.S. blacks. Quite a few of them came from West Indian middle-class families and were well educated, which enabled them to move quickly toward the upper socioeconomic reaches of the black population in the United States. Such a combination of upward economic mobility and degradation in the socioracial structure may well have been one of the painful reasons why a significant number of black militants of the civil rights era—e.g., Malcolm X and Stokely Carmichael—had (British) Caribbean family connections. A similarly frustrating experience much earlier in this century may have led the Jamaican Marcus Garvey, now revered as a national hero in his country, to start a "Back to Africa" movement in the United States.

CONCLUSION

While it is tempting to make general statements on the plight and struggles of "the blacks" in the Western Hemisphere (statements, moreover, that are often both true and well justified), certain events and phenomena can be grasped only by keeping in mind the differences in the evolution of racial relations and structures in both Caribbean societies and those that host Caribbean migrants. An awareness of such differences helps explain, for example, the surprise of U.S. black visitors to Cuba in the early years of the revolution when they learned that an emancipatory struggle of blacks as a separate socioracial entity in North American terms fits neither with Cuba's ideological tenets nor with its much older and deeper-seated notions of a fluid socioracial continuum. And it helps us understand how the original Black Power ideology—based on the North American twofold division between black and white—met with resistance from those in the Caribbean who perceived themselves as colored and could in some cases accept the term only by redefining *black* as anyone, anywhere, who was being exploited by metropolitan or imperial policies and attitudes. In this redefined version, Fidel Castro could be called "black" and East Indians in the Guianas and Trinidad might, in the same vein, be invited to join the "other blacks" in a struggle for a more just society. Such "translations" may serve legitimate, perhaps even laudable, purposes, but in the process much of the original meaning of the term, and its validity in the context in which it operates, is lost.

This is perhaps the ultimate value of comparing race relations in different societies, an exercise to which the Caribbean region lends itself so well: it teaches us that the same word may have different meanings, and that *white, colored,* or *black* do not always mean what our own experience suggests they should.

NOTES

1. I take the word *creole* to mean the opposite of *foreign.* Thus *creole culture* refers to those aspects of culture that evolved or were adapted in the Western Hemisphere and became part of a New World society's distinctive heritage. In Latin America, the term *criollo,* when used in reference to people, was originally reserved for native whites. In the Hispanic Caribbean nowadays, it often includes all those born and bred in a particular society. Elsewhere, as in Suriname, the term may be used to denote long-established population groups, such as the Afro-Americans, as opposed to more recent immigrant groups.

2. The word *colored(s)* in this essay refers to persons of mixed African-European descent. Except in the United States, these persons tend to be perceived as a somewhat distinct socioracial category, with a position between "whites" and "blacks."

3. See also the conclusion of this essay.

4. This is perhaps the place to explain why, in this essay, I prefer not to distinguish rigidly between "racial "and "ethnic" groups. One and the same immigrant group may function as a cohesive and culturally distinct social grouping in one society, while in another its members may define themselves mainly or even exclusively in terms of one of the main socioracial categories. Conversely, in one society a long-established racial group may fully share the national culture, while in another it may have so many distinctive cultural traits as to be labeled an ethnic group. Elsewhere I have written:

If one defines an ethnic group as one in which the internal cohesion is based on ascriptive criteria, with the criteria seen intersubjectively as sufficiently crucial to generate a culture with comparatively clear boundaries (see Barth 1969), then it might be argued that each of the main socio-racial groups in the United States and the non-Iberian Caribbean deserves such a label. The reason that I have abstained from the use of the term "ethnic group" is that, as defined here, it easily suggests an absence of overlapping ascriptive loyalties and this does not occur in the structurally complex political units under discussion. Thus, in the United States, vis-à-vis the black population, the whites may be said to form an ethnic group; yet, this term is also commonly used for those white groups that entertain ascriptive loyalties based upon a common non-American origin and/or cultural background. Similarly, all ethnic groups in these [Caribbean] societies share, to a greater or lesser degree, feelings of identity with and loyalty toward their present nation or territory. Indeed, [under certain conditions] nations may also be defined as ethnic groups. . . . Thus, it would seem advisable not to subsume the manifold ascriptive loyalties which individuals from these societies may profess under the heading of so many "ethnic groups," but rather to analyze these loyalties in terms of their ascriptive content and in terms of their greater or lesser correlation. (Hoetink 1975:18-19)

REFERENCES

BARTH, FREDRIK
    1969 Introduction. *In* Fredrik Barth (ed.), *Ethnic Groups and Boundaries,* pp. 9–38. Oslo: Univ. Forlaget; London: George Allen & Unwin.

BRATHWAITE, EDWARD
    1971 *The Development of Creole Society in Jamaica 1770–1820.* Oxford: Clarendon Press.

HOETINK, H.
    1973 *Slavery and Race Relations in the Americas: An Inquiry into their Nature and Nexus.* New York: Harper & Row.
    1975 "Resource Competition, Monopoly and Socioracial Diversity." *In* Leo A. Despres (ed.), *Ethnicity and Resource Competition in Plural Societies,* pp. 9–27, The Hague & Paris: Mouton.
    1982 *The Dominican People 1850-1900: Notes for a Historical Sociology.* Translated from the Spanish by Stephen Ault. Johns Hopkins Studies in Atlantic History and Culture. Baltimore: Johns Hopkins University Press.

HOFFMAN, LÉON-FRANÇOIS
    1980 "Slavery and Race in Haitian Letters." *Caribbean Review* 9(2):28–32.

KNIGHT, FRANKLIN W.
    1970 *Slave Society in Cuba during the Nineteenth Century.* Madison: University of Wisconsin Press.

LEYBURN, JAMES G.
1966 *The Haitian People*. New Haven, Conn.: Yale University Press.

LOWENTHAL, DAVID
1972 *West Indian Societies*. London: Oxford University Press.

MAINGOT, ANTHONY P.
1983 Review of *Forged from the Love of Liberty: Selected Speeches of Dr. Eric Williams*, compiled and introduced by Paul K. Sutton (Port of Spain, Trinidad: Longman Caribbean, 1981). *New West Indian Guide* 57:89–97.

MINTZ, SIDNEY W.
1974 *Caribbean Transformations*. Chicago: Aldine. (Reprinted 1984. Baltimore: Johns Hopkins University Press.)

NAIPAUL, V. S.
1962 *The Middle Passage: The Caribbean Revisited*. London: André Deutsch.

NICHOLLS, DAVID
1981 "No Hawkers and Pedlars: Levantines in the Caribbean." *Ethnic and Racial Studies* 4:415–32.

PASTOR, ROBERT
1982 "Sinking in the Caribbean Basin." *Foreign Affairs* 60:1038–58.

PATTERSON, ORLANDO
1977 *Ethnic Chauvinism: The Reactionary Impulse*. New York: Stein & Day.

RÖMER, R. A.
1974 "Het "wij" van de Curaçaoenaar." *Kristof* (1/2):49–60.

SMITH, RAYMOND T.
1982 "Race and Class in the Post-Emancipation Caribbean." *In* Robert Ross (ed.), *Racism and Colonialism: Essays on Ideology and Social Structure*, pp. 93–119. Comparative Studies in Overseas History, Publications of the Leiden Centre for the History of European Expansion. The Hague: Martinus Nijhoff.

YARYURA, CAMILO
1983 El Santo Entierro. *Suplemento Listín Diario,* 4 June.

·3·

Sugar in the Caribbean:
Turning Sunshine into Money

G. B. HAGELBERG

Sugar cane has been grown in the Caribbean for nearly 500 years, introduced by Christopher Columbus himself on his second voyage to Hispaniola in 1493 (Deerr 1949–50, I:116–17). The first sugar mill of record in the New World, precursor of a vast industry that pervaded the archipelago as island after island was colonized, started grinding in about 1516 in what is now the Dominican Republic. Before the end of the 1500s, sugar was produced in Cuba, Jamaica, and Puerto Rico, the other Greater Antilles, all then under Spanish rule. In the course of the following century, British, French, Dutch, and Danish settlers planted cane and built sugar mills on more than a dozen islands of the Lesser Antilles. And 75 years later, Adam Smith, in his *Wealth of Nations,* was speaking in a single context of "our sugar colonies" and "our sugar islands" in the West Indies, the "corn provinces of North America" and "our tobacco colonies" in Virginia and Maryland.

The colonies as subject territories are gone and so is the sugar industry in some of them, but the Caribbean islands together produce more sugar now than ever. The question is often posed whether this is the most sensible thing to do, whether there is any future in it, whether they had not better turn to something else. Much of what happened in the centuries of growing and processing sugar cane in the Caribbean sheds light on the subject, and in answering the question we shall have to return to history. We shall also look at the part played by sugar in Caribbean economies today and why it continues to have a role. But first we must briefly introduce sugar itself and the ways in which it is produced and consumed. A notion of the technical peculiarities of this commodity will help to reveal certain connections.

SUGAR AND SUGAR CANE

Cane sugar is actually a member of a numerous family of sugars, called saccharides or carbohydrates. As the latter name suggests, sugars are composed of the elements carbon, hydrogen, and oxygen, with the hydrogen and oxygen usually present in the same ratio as in water. According to their complexity, carbohydrates are classified into three main groups: monosaccharides, oligosaccharides, and polysaccharides.

Monosaccharides are simple sugars, the most abundant being D-glucose, which has the empirical formula of $C_6H_{12}O_6$. Lehninger (1975:21) included D-glucose in the set of primordial biomolecules that may be regarded as the ancestors from which all other organic biomolecules have been derived in the course of biochemical evolution. Its universality is evidenced by its common names of grape sugar, corn sugar, and blood sugar. D-glucose is the major fuel for most organisms—it is, for example, the only fuel of the brain under normal conditions—and the building block of such widespread polysaccharides as starch and cellulose, which are nothing other than long chains of D-glucose units (Lehninger 1975:249, 838).

Cane sugar, technically known as sucrose, is an oligosaccharide, more precisely a disaccharide, i.e., a union of two monosaccharides, in this case of glucose and fructose (also called fruit sugar, which has the same elemental composition as glucose but with a different arrangement of the atoms). The empirical formula of sucrose is $C_{12}H_{22}O_{11}$. Other common disaccharides are lactose, the sugar found in milk, and maltose or malt sugar.

Sucrose is easily hydrolyzed by acid or enzyme to equimolar amounts of glucose and fructose, and the mixture is then called invert sugar. Starch is similarly hydrolyzed to glucose and to maltose which is in turn hydrolyzed to glucose. In order to produce ethanol by alcoholic fermentation for drinking (e.g., rum) or other purposes (e.g., automobile fuel), sucrose, starch, and similar more complex carbohydrates must first be hydrolyzed to simple sugars.

A family trait of many mono- and disaccharides germane to this discussion is their sweet taste. Relative sweetness depends on concentration, temperature, pH, and the presence of other components that may affect the physiology of taste. Approximate figures for the relative sweetness of some common sugars are:

Fructose	1.1	Glucose	0.7
Sucrose	1.0	Maltose	0.4
Invert sugar	0.9	Lactose	0.4
(Irvine 1977b)			

It is particularly the presence of fructose, glucose, and sucrose in different amounts and proportions that gives a sweet taste to fruits, young vegetables, maple and sorghum syrups, the juice of certain palm species, and honey.

The two main commercial sources of sucrose are sugar cane and sugar beet. Both plants produce large quantities of sucrose in their leaves by the process of photosynthesis. In a complicated series of reactions, solar light energy is converted into chemical energy, which is then used to bring about the reduction of carbon dioxide to form carbohydrates and other products. Sucrose is transported from the leaves to the stalk of sugar cane and to the root of sugar beet to fulfill a storage function analogous to that of starch in other plants.

Ordinary refined or white table sugar is at least 99.7 percent sucrose and nothing but a stored form of energy. In extracting sucrose from sugar beet and cane we are doing basically the same thing as our primitive ancestors who robbed wild bees of their honey, insofar as we are taking easily assimilable energy from the environment, because as heterotrophs or feeders on others, we cannot fix carbon dioxide from the air but must obtain our carbon in a fancier form (Lehninger 1975:363f.). Nowadays, sugar cane and sugar beet, in a ratio of about 60 to 40, supply every inhabitant of the globe on the average with slightly more than 50 grams of sucrose per day in the form of centrifugal sugar, equivalent to perhaps 8 percent of the total food energy intake.[1]

Globally, some 34 million acres of sugar cane and 23 million acres of sugar beet—together slightly more than the area occupied by the states of Delaware, Pennsylvania, and Ohio—were harvested in 1981 (Food and Agriculture Organization 1971–). These plants would not be cultivated on such a large scale and sucrose would not play such an important dietary role if it were not sweet. Without sweetness, centrifugal sugar would indeed be mere "empty calories," to echo the inane cliché of food writers (e.g., Rombauer and Becker 1980:6). The fact that sugar tends to be one of the most economical sources of dietary energy would not, by itself, enable it to compete against starchy foods (even if these did not, in addition to energy, provide minor quantities of other nutrients). What has made sucrose the only chemical substance to be consumed in practically pure form as a staple food is that it enhances the beverages and other foods in which it is ingested. Sucrose cannot be consumed by itself in significant volume. One can eat a plateful of boiled potatoes or rice without anything else; it would be difficult to take in the caloric equivalent of granulated sugar without at least dissolving it in water. Sugar is a piggyback food consumed in large quantities because it is sweet in a not very intense way and makes its carriers more palatable.

Conversely, sugar that did not give energy would be empty sweetness. By definition, a condiment or flavoring agent does not lead an independent existence. It has to flavor something. Although it may be important in various ways, it is not required in large quantities unless it also has some other use. Per capita consumption in the United States in 1982 of saccharin, the noncaloric artificial sweetener discovered over a century ago, was no more than 7.3 pounds (sugar sweetness equivalent), against an estimated 124.8 pounds of caloric sweeteners (U.S. Department of Agriculture 1979–).

The symbiotic nature of sucrose, revealed in the way it plays its roles as an energy source and sweetener, is confirmed by its further functions as a preservative, flavor enhancer, bulking agent, and stabilizer. It is this capacity to serve several ends at once that has supported the evolution of cane and beet sugar from a luxury to a regular part of the diet in one country after another. And so far the only serious competition to sucrose has come from related substances with a similar set of properties.[2]

Sugar cane, the major source of processed sucrose, is a perennial giant grass belonging to the same tribe as corn (maize) and sorghum. Modern cane varieties are generally derived from hybrids of two or more of the six species of the genus *Saccharum* which are thought to have originated in southern Asia, the islands of southeast Indonesia, and the New Guinea area (Irvine 1977a). The accepted view is that sugar cane was first cultivated thousands of years ago as a garden plant for chewing. It seems to have been grown as a field crop in India several centuries before the Christian era; the first definite mention of sugar in the Punjab dates from 325 B.C. (Deerr 1949–50,1:15, 40–41).

Unlike maize, sugar cane is grown from seed pieces (cuttings) obtained from parent plants. Depending on cropping system and location, the time between planting and harvest ranges from less than 10 months to over two years. In common with other grass species, sugar cane offers the possibility of successive stubble (or ratoon) harvests from the same planting. In the Caribbean it was not unusual to find fields from which 10 or more crops had been taken before low yields made further ratooning uneconomic, but usually a plant cane and up to five ratoon crops are followed by reconditioning of the fields and replanting.

Harvesting is the most difficult operation in the cane production cycle. Ideally, the raw material sent to the factory for processing should consist of freshly cut, clean stalks of mature cane, and deliveries should be sufficient to allow the mill to operate continuously throughout the harvest, stopping only for cleaning, repairs, and scheduled holidays. These requirements can be met as long as field labor is abundantly available at a favorable wage rate / sugar price ratio. Up to about 1960, all but a small fraction of the sugar cane produced in the Caribbean was cut "green" (i.e., unburned) with a broad, heavy knife, the leafy tops severed, and the dry trash removed from the millable stalks, which were then loaded manually onto vehicles for transport to the factory or railroad siding. Except for changes in the means of transport, the system had remained essentially unchanged for hundreds of years, only expanding in size.

This time-honored routine was shattered when labor became scarce at the going rates during harvest time (the period of peak demand), first in Puerto Rico in the 1950s and subsequently in most of the other Caribbean cane-growing areas. Sugar cane is a high-volume crop of low unit value—even at today's prices, gross returns to the growers work out to less than two cents a pound—and harvesting the cane at a tolerable cost became the crucial challenge of sugar production in the Caribbean. Setting fire to the cane fields just prior to cutting was a partial answer, since it eliminated most of the trash and increased the productivity of both manual cane cutters and mechanical harvesting equipment. But loss of the trash cover as a result of burning meant higher expenditures for weed control later on, and on certain soils and in low-rainfall areas burning could have a disastrous effect on subsequent ratoon yields. Moreover, unplanned cane fires could disrupt harvesting schedules so that cane could not be cut before it spoiled.

The need to introduce machines to harvest the cane arose in the Caribbean at a time when there was still relatively little international experience in the mechanized handling of this crop and a dearth of suitable equipment (Hagelberg 1974:93–97). Mechanical loading of hand-cut cane commenced in Puerto Rico in the 1950s, and by 1964 more than half the crop was handled in this way, but even then the teething pains were still great and the gain in efficiency minor.

Yet the problems encountered in the switch from manual to mechanical loading, such as an increase of extraneous matter in the cane delivered to the factory, were child's play compared to those posed by mechanical cutting. This entailed a revolution of the entire production process, beginning with changes in field layout to convert small, irregular plots into large rectangular areas with long rows in order to minimize time lost in turning, the creation of headlands (strips left unplowed at the ends of fields), reform of drainage and irrigation systems, removal of tree stumps and other obstacles, land leveling, and different planting practices (e.g., row spacing). It took at least five years to adapt fully a cane farm with a cycle of one plant cane and three ratoon crops to mechanical reaping. If combine harvesters that cut, chopped and loaded in a continuous operation were chosen in preference to whole-stalk cutters that simply deposited the cut cane in lines on the ground, it further required changes in the transport system and in the reception facilities. Operators had to be trained, and support services capable of maintaining sophisticated machinery had to be created. Most importantly, cost-effective utilization of expensive mechanical equipment presupposed very different management attitudes and skills from those that had been developed to supervise large numbers of manual field workers.

This technological upheaval has to a greater or lesser extent affected the performance of most Caribbean sugar industries since the 1960s; the notable exception to this generalization is the Dominican Republic, where in the second half of the 1970s nearly all the cane was still cut and loaded manually, mainly by Haitian workers, many of whom had become permanent residents in the country. In Guyana, too, all cane in the mid-1970s was still cut and loaded by hand, mainly into punts, for transportation by water to the factories. Mechanical cutting equipment, although much improved, is still not perfect, particularly for harvesting unburned cane. For those that initiated mechanical reaping earlier, inadequate infrastructures, the deficiencies of the available equipment, and belated recognition of the fact that efficient mechanical harvesting depended as much on the establishment of propitious field and organizational conditions as on the development of suitable machines all meant a costly learning process. The ambiguousness of the employment situation, reflected in the appearance of labor shortages in economies characterized, at least seasonally, by high unemployment, the incomprehension of trade union and political leaders, and doubts concerning the long-term viability of Caribbean sugar industries added to the difficulties of the transition.

Roughly three-fourths of the weight of clean cane stalks is water; the rest is composed of fiber and soluble solids. About four-fifths of the solids dissolved in the juice is sucrose, which is accompanied by small amounts of glucose and fructose, soluble polysaccharides, minerals, organic acids, and colorants. Although we speak of sugar "factories," what actually takes place there is not a manufacturing process, in the sense of a transformation such as that taking place in a shoe factory, but rather a series of liquid-solid separations to extract and purify the sucrose made in the cane and to transfer it from the solution to the solid phase.

Sugar cane is unique among crops in the extent to which it furnishes its own processing energy. By rule of thumb, one tonne (see note 1) of wet bagasse (the fibrous residue from juice extraction) is equivalent to a barrel of fuel oil. In theory, a modern raw cane sugar factory should be self-sufficient in energy under normal conditions and even produce a surplus. A growing number do, and these enjoy an increasing advantage in an era of rising energy costs. Steam and electricity produced from excess bagasse are often fed to attached refineries and distilleries, and some cane sugar factories deliver power to the public grid. A plant producing furfural (an intermediate organic chemical) from bagasse has been in operation in the Dominican Republic since 1954, and Cuba has several factories that manufacture bagasse board and paper.

Bagasse has only fairly recently become a significant by-product of sugar cane processing as a result of a trend toward more fibrous cane varieties and greater thermal efficiency in the factories, and fuller exploitation of its potential lies in the future. The more familiar by-product of the sugar industry, going back hundreds of years, is final or blackstrap molasses. "I know not why we should blush to confess that molasses was an essential ingredient in American independence," wrote John Adams in 1775, referring to the role of West Indian molasses in the New England distilling and shipping industries. "Many great events have proceeded from much smaller causes" (quoted in Sheridan 1974:339). In modern practice, blackstrap molasses is the heavy, viscous liquid separated from the final low-grade massecuite (mixture of mother liquor and sugar crystals produced in the boiling process) from which no further sugar can be crystallized by the usual methods. Roughly 0.3 tonne of final molasses is produced for each tonne of raw cane sugar, containing approximately one-third sucrose, one-fifth reducing sugars (mainly glucose and fructose), and the remainder ash, organic nonsugars, and water. It is mainly used for the manufacture of ethanol, rum, and yeast, and as an ingredient in animal feed.

Together, sugar, bagasse, and molasses are the tangible evidence of the productivity of sugar cane as a converter of solar energy. The highest yield of yearly, averaged photosynthesis (Calvin 1974) means that sugar cane as a rule produces larger quantities of utilizable organic matter per land unit in a given time than any other crop in the tropics and subtropics. Even where this does not at a particular moment return the greatest amount of money, it is something to be kept in mind when thinking about the rational allocation and utilization of resources for the long run.

CARIBBEAN SUGAR PRODUCERS

Like the Caribbean islands themselves, the sugar industries of the region defy generalization. While abstraction from the specific circumstances surrounding sugar production in each locality in the end becomes unavoidable, and while some conclusions may actually hold fairly widely, a brief survey such as this must carry Patrick Leigh Fermor's (1950) prefatory warning: "Each island is a distinct and idiosyncratic entity, a civilization, or the reverse, fortuitous in its origins and empirical in its development. There is no rule that holds good beyond the shores of each one unless the prevalence of oddity, the unvarying need to make exceptions to any known rule, can be considered a unifying principle."

The following thumbnail sketches will intimate the diversity of the Caribbean sugar industries.[3] As is usual in discussions of Caribbean sugar, I exclude the Central and South American producers that border on the Caribbean Sea but include Guyana in the company otherwise composed exclusively of islands. Guyana's long association with the British West Indies lives on in its membership in the Sugar Association of the Caribbean, a consultative industry grouping (of which the other members are Barbados, Jamaica, St. Kitts–Nevis–Anguilla, and Trinidad and Tobago). Another reason for including Guyana is that its sugar-producing region—the narrow strip of rich alluvial soil along the coast, on which almost all of Guyana's population is concentrated—forms virtually an island, bordered by the sea on one side and the largely uninhabited and undeveloped interior on the other. Production figures for the territories covered are summarized in Table 1.

Barbados

An exception to the rule that Caribbean islands are the summits of a submerged volcanic mountain range, Barbados is a coral island of comparatively flat contours. It is the most densely populated of the Caribbean sugar producers and one of the smallest in area; more than a quarter of a million people

TABLE 1.

Centrifugal Sugar Production: Annual Averages for Selected Five-year
Periods (000 tonnes, *tel quel* or raw value)[a]

Territory	1934/35–1938/39	1951–55	1956–60	1961–65	1966–70	1971–75	1976–80
Barbados	123	176	172	178	173	118	117
Cuba	2,741	5,512	5,604	5,215	5,902	5,675	7,074
Dominican Republic	445	613	875	798	817	1,177	1,191
Guadeloupe	52	100	137	181	161	122	96
Guyana	192	242	299	312	344	335	308
Haiti	39	55	54	68	62	67	58
Jamaica	104	330	376	472	443	376	299
Leeward and Windward Islands[b]	63	89	88	68	40	26	39
Martinique	57	61	79	79	41	23	13
Puerto Rico	839	1,118	942	905	594	266	207
Trinidad and Tobago	140	162	186	234	227	199	158
U.S. Virgin Islands[c]	4	10	10	11	1	—	—
Caribbean producers	4,799	8,467	8,822	8,521	8,805	8,384	9,560
World cane	14,525	22,091	27,200	32,464	38,753	45,121	53,343
World beet and cane	24,580	36,900	46,702	56,811	67,952	76,128	87,439

Sources: International Sugar Council 1963, 2; International Sugar Council/Organization 1963–;
Food and Agriculture Organization 1971–; F. O. Licht 1980–, 1983b.

[a] Includes fancy but not high-test molasses.
[b] St. Kitts–Nevis–Anguilla, plus Antigua up to the end of the 1971 crop; St. Lucia up to the end
of 1963; St. Vincent up to the end of 1962; Grenada up to the end of 1961.
[c] Ceased production in 1966.

live on just over 100,000 acres. Sugar cane occupies about 44 percent of the
national territory and is the main crop.

On the agricultural side, the Barbados sugar industry is composed of some
130 so-called estates with an average of close to 300 acres, which produce
85–90 percent of the cane, plus several thousand small holders. Three companies—two public, the shares of which are quite widely held, and one private—
and their subsidiaries control approximately one-fifth of the estate cane lands.
Private ownership predominates; government-owned farms contribute only
about 5 percent of the total cane supply. Although all but a few estates are
locally owned, not many are owner-operated. The attorney system—a legacy
of the days of absentee ownership—remains a prominent feature of the management structure.[4] Barbados is relatively advanced in field mechanization
and is a leader in cane technology research and development, the fruits of
which are also exported to other countries.

On the processing side, the number of factories was down to six in 1983
from 34 in 1950, but their average output has tripled. A new mill, replacing
three closed plants, was inaugurated in 1982. Factory capacities are still rather

small compared with many other producers, however.[5] As this has to do with the road system, further consolidation is highly problematical. All six factories are operated by one company, in which the shares (tied to ownership of cane land) are held by the growers and the government, both in its own right as a landowner and on behalf of the smallholders.

Production reached a peak of 212,000 tonnes in 1967 but in the last three years has averaged less than 100,000, the worst performance since 1929–31. This decline is partly due to a secular reduction in the area devoted to cane, which is not offset by increased yields. To a considerable extent, however, it can be attributed to passing problems amenable to solution (especially the resort to burning) which are in turn partly a reflection of labor shortages and the initial difficulties of harvest mechanization. For reasons that will be discussed later, the government has taken various steps to encourage the industry to return to a level of around 150,000 tonnes—a difficult but not impossible target.

Cuba

In the alphabetical list of Caribbean sugar producers, Cuba follows Barbados, and there could be no better illustration of the magnitude of Antillean contrasts. Cuba, the giant of the Caribbean, is 266 times the size of Barbados (while, by way of comparison, the United States is only 82 times the size of Cuba), has 37 times the population, and averaged 60 times the sugar production in 1976–80.

The Cuban sugar industry is governed by its own government department, which controls nearly 400 enterprises engaged in the growing and processing of cane, by-product exploitation, engineering and construction, research and development, and the operation of sugar, molasses, and alcohol terminals. Close to 450,000 persons are employed in these activities, 300,000 of them in the agricultural sector.

About 4.2 million acres were planted with sugar cane in 1980, two-thirds of the total arable land. Approximately 620,000 acres were in the hands of 35,000 small growers; the rest was in state farms, the management of which is increasingly being merged with that of the factories into mill-plantation complexes.

The processing sector is composed of 154 factories with daily grinding capacities ranging from 800 to 14,000 tonnes of cane. Four of these are new plants designed to mill 7,000 tonnes of cane per day, the first sugar factories built in Cuba since the 1920s. Four more mills with the same capacity are under construction, and it seems that the Cubans have developed a standard factory layout of this size.

Sugar production in 1976–80 represented an increase of about 20 percent over 1956–60, taking into account the sugar equivalent of high-test molasses and invert syrups produced in the earlier period (cf. Hagelberg 1974:132–134). There is no reason to doubt that the technical and organizational difficulties that dogged the Cuban sugar industry in the 1960s and early 1970s have been largely overcome and that in the process a technological revolution has been accomplished in Cuban cane agriculture.

What started off as a poorly thought out and very expensive crash program of harvest mechanization, precipitously launched in response to the sudden and unexpected appearance of labor shortages in the early 1960s, evidently reached the pay-off stage in less than 20 years. By 1979, nearly all cane was being mechanically loaded and roughly 40 percent was being mechanically cut by a fleet of 2,300 combine harvesters, composed of some 1,730 machines of Cuban-Soviet design and manufacture (the KTP-1) and 560-odd Australian Massey Ferguson and West German Claas Libertadora units. Given the size of the Cuban crop, this meant that more cane was mechanically cut in Cuba than in any other one country. Since 1977, the KTP-1 has been assembled / built in Cuba in a factory with a capacity of 600 units a year. Specialists agree that the KTP-1 is not the world's most elegant piece of cane harvester engineering. But it must work well enough with green cane in local field conditions to have allowed the Cubans to abandon the practice of burning. And it has an obvious economic advantage. While local assembly / manufacture no doubt relies on quite a few components imported from the Soviet Union, the cost is in rubles (the currency of Cuba's preferential sugar market) and value-added Cuban pesos, not convertible currency. It seems quite possible that in real terms Cuba has become again a relatively low-cost sugar producer, as it was before the 1959 revolution.

Dominican Republic

The Dominican sugar industry, now the second largest in the Caribbean after Cuba's, is regulated by the Dominican Sugar Institute, which sets production targets, assigns export quotas, and directs product and market research. Of the 16 mill-plantation complexes in the country, 12, accounting for nearly two-thirds of the sugar produced, have belonged to the state since 1962, when the assets of ex-President Trujillo were nationalized following his assassination; three belong to the Vicini Group, a Dominican family company; and one, the largest, is owned by Gulf & Western Americas Corporation. Factory capacities range from 500 to 13,500 tonnes of cane per day. There has been a marked shift since the late 1960s from growing cane on land under direct factory management toward contracting with outgrowers (*colonos*). As mentioned earlier, among Caribbean producers the Dominican Republic is a latecomer to harvest mechanization. Up to the latter part of the 1970s, only one Vicini-owned plantation was using mechanical harvesters in a minor way, and much of the short-haul transport was still by oxcart. However, since 1980 there have been reports of shortages of the Haitian cane cutters who have provided much of the labor in Dominican cane fields. The financial problems encountered particularly by the state sector in 1982, as rising production costs collided with low world market prices, indicate the beginning of a difficult period of compulsory technological changes for the Dominican industry comparable with the earlier experience of other Caribbean producers.

French Overseas Departments

Sugar production in Guadeloupe and Martinique continues to decline and in 1982/83 was expected not to exceed 68,000 tonnes (white value). The number of sugar factories in Guadeloupe has fallen since 1952 from 12 to four, and only one sugar mill is left in Martinique. During the 1970s Guadeloupe developed aubergines as an export crop, and there was also a marked increase in animal production. In Martinique, land has been switched from cane to bananas and pineapples, two products in which growers can achieve high quality and for which there is a guaranteed market in France. The Martiniquan sugar industry has been strictly regulated by the French authorities in recent years with a view to reducing sugar production to the level of local requirements and eliminating exports. Cane production has not shrunk quite to the same extent, however, since Martiniquan distilleries make rum from cane juice rather than from final molasses, the more usual raw material.

Guyana

Cane agriculture in Guyana has two peculiarities: it is an amphibious operation starting with flood fallowing and ending with harvest transport, and there are two harvest seasons each year as the local climate has two wet and two dry periods. The cane is grown on land evolved from the sea and from swamps, which requires for its maintenance an intricate and costly system of sea walls, dams, irrigation and drainage canals, sluices, and pumps.

The state-owned Guyana Sugar Corporation, set up in 1976 when the previously British-owned mill-plantation complexes were nationalized, controls all aspects of sugar production. There are 10 factories with capacities ranging from 1,700 to 4,400 tonnes of cane per day. Small growers now contribute about 10 percent of the cane supply. Despite grave problems, Guyana is the only anglophone Caribbean sugar producer to have maintained a reasonably stable volume of production, not falling below the level of the 1950s, although government targets have not been met. Declining cane and sugar yields have been offset by expanding the area under cane, which obviously increases costs. The industry has suffered alternately from heavy rains, smut disease, labor disputes, and spare parts shortages engendered by the scarcity of foreign exchange. The hurdle of harvest mechanization has yet to be tackled in what are unique ecological conditions.

Haiti

Within a hundred years of Spanish recognition of French claims to the western portion of Hispaniola in 1697, Saint Domingue, as it was then called, had become the foremost sugar producer and exporter in the world, according to the records, and like Jamaica a byword for planter opulence. On the eve of the slave insurrection in 1791, reported output reached nearly 80,000 tonnes, a colossal amount for the production methods of that time. Following the rebellion that gave rise to the Republic of Haiti, the sugar industry virtually disappeared, and was not resurrected until the 1920s, a hundred years later (Deerr 1949–50, 1:238–40). Today Haiti is a net importer of sugar, although in addition to the 65,000 tonnes of centrifugal sugar estimated by the International Sugar Organization to have been produced there in 1980, another 80,000 tonnes of noncentrifugal sugar are believed to have been made (Food and Agriculture Organization 1971–). The formal sector of the industry is composed of four factories, the largest of which has a throughput of 3,600 tonnes of cane per day. One of the factories is a new mill put into operation in 1982, and the government intends to make the country self-sufficient in sugar.

Jamaica

For the second year running, Jamaica was expected to produce under 200,000 tonnes of sugar in 1983, and the government reiterated its desire to withdraw from ownership in the sugar industry by divesting state-owned factories to the private sector. The government owns 8 of the 11 remaining sugar factories on the island and operates 7 of them. Earlier the government dissolved 23 bankrupt cane-growing cooperatives that had been established on state-owned estates by the previous administration and sharply increased domestic sugar prices in order to reduce the industry's deficit.

The process of indigenization of foreign landholdings and eventual nationalization of the mills that was begun in 1970 has been marred by policy differences over the future direction of the industry, poor management, and difficulties in obtaining foreign exchange to purchase vital inputs, a spillover from the general economic state of the country. Labor disputes have disrupted field preparation and harvesting. In addition, the Jamaican industry, like other Caribbean producers, has been plagued by adverse weather and cane diseases. The effect has been a progressive decline in the area harvested as well as in yields. Harvest mechanization has not advanced much beyond mechanical loading. The future of the Jamaican sugar industry is clouded and will remain so until the government arrives at a coherent long-term sugar policy.

Puerto Rico

The Puerto Rican sugar industry, in the 1950s still the second largest in the Caribbean, has plunged from 34 factories and 1.2 million tonnes of sugar in 1952 to 5 factories and perhaps 100,000 tonnes of sugar in 1983. Some 390,000 acres of cane were harvested for sugar in 1952; in 1983, it was around 55,000 acres. In fact, the sugar cane acreage harvested 30 years ago was more than twice as large as the total area under temporary crops on the island today. Puerto Rico's sugar industry did not shrink this much because farmers found better things to grow. Nor did it shrink because the market disappeared. Within the domestic cane sugar producing areas of the United States, Puerto Rico's loss has been Florida's gain in strikingly similar proportions. Between 1952 and 1983, Florida's harvested sugar cane acreage expanded from 43,000 to 353,000 acres, while sugar production grew from 140,000 to 1.0 million tonnes.

Initially, Puerto Rico's difficulties in maintaining its competitive position on the U.S. sugar market stemmed largely from the labor intensiveness of its production methods and increasingly disparate labor costs. Not that labor productivity in the island's cane fields did not improve substantially over time; field worker requirements per short ton (2,000 pounds) of raw sugar fell from about 133 man-hours in 1946–50 to 70 man-hours in 1966–70. But in Florida, they were 54 and 16 man-hours, respectively. So while the absolute difference between Puerto Rico and Florida was reduced, in round numbers, from 78 to 54 man-hours, in relative terms the gap actually widened. In the immediate post-World War II period it took 2.4 times as much field labor in Puerto Rico as in Florida to produce 2,000 pounds of sugar; 20 years later it took 4.4 times as much. The upshot was that whereas in Florida the average farm labor costs per short ton of raw sugar declined from $35.58 in 1946–50 to $29.84 in 1966–70, in Puerto Rico they rose from $42.49 to $55.20 (Hagelberg 1974:120, 149).

The competitive position has been made worse by a deterioration in physical performance. While Florida has more or less held earlier yield levels (stagnating yields have been a general problem in sugar cane), Puerto Rico now obtains only about 2 short tons of sugar per acre, compared with over 3 tons in the 1950s and early 1960s, primarily because of a marked fall in the percentage of sugar recovered from the cane. This is the cumulative result of various problems: lack of effective means to combat white grubs (a pest that attacks sugar cane roots) following prohibition by the Environmental Protection Agency of the use in cane of Aldrin, a pesticide previously applied to keep the grubs in check; overage ratoons, kept because of the high cost of replanting; adverse weather; delays in the start of the harvest due to labor disputes; and cane fires. The Puerto Rican government began to acquire combine harvesters in the late 1970s, but in 1980 still less than half the crop was cut mechanically.

St. Kitts

This is the only remaining export sugar industry in the Leeward and Windward islands (that is, the string of islands stretching from Anguilla and St. Martin through Grenada). There is one factory, now owned by the government, which through another company also manages the former cane estates.

Although it ceased to figure in the statistics of the International Sugar Organization in 1961, Grenada continued to produce sugar for domestic consumption and is credited by the Food and Agriculture Organization with 1,000 tonnes in 1980. Two other islands, Antigua and St. Vincent, are in the process of resuming sugar production for internal use.

Trinidad and Tobago

The industry is reduced to four factories, now owned by the state. Production has fallen from 205,000 tonnes in 1976 to about 81,000 tonnes in 1983, reflecting poor weather and the disruptive effect of labor disputes and unplanned cane fires. The industry has registered large financial losses for a number of years and has survived on the basis of heavy subsidies, granted primarily out of consideration for the employment it still gives to thousands of workers and small cane farmers. A series of reports and recommendations have addressed themselves to ways of making sugar production profitable, including further mill closures, sales of land for housing, and greater exploitation of by-products, and there have been repeated proposals to phase out sugar exports. Like the Jamaican government, the Trinidadian authorities have not made up their minds on a long-term sugar policy.

Taking the Caribbean region as a whole, centrifugal sugar production in 1976–80 was twice what it had been before World War II but only 13 percent more than in 1951–55. Growth since the first half of the 1950s has been at a cumulative rate of under 0.5 percent per year, whereas world cane and beet sugar production has grown at an annual rate of 3.5 percent. As a result, the region's share in the total supply has fallen from 23 percent to 11 percent (see Table 2). However, as we shall see, surplus Caribbean sugar still plays a major role in satisfying world requirements.

Within the Caribbean, Cuba is clearly in a class by itself, accounting in 1976–80 for nearly three-quarters of regional production, up from 65 percent in 1951–55. During this period, Cuban production grew on average by 1 percent a year. Its share in global output declined from nearly 15 percent to 8 percent, and Brazil took its place as the largest centrifugal cane sugar producer in the world. But Cuba still produces about 800 kilograms (nine-tenths of a short ton) per inhabitant, and in terms of exportable surplus it remains the nearest thing to the sugar bowl of the world.

Although a far smaller producer than Cuba, the Dominican sugar industry

TABLE 2.
Percentage Shares of Caribbean Sugar Industries in World and Regional Production

Territory	1934/35–1938/39	1951–55	1956–60	1961–65	1966–70	1971–75	1976–80
Caribbean percentage of world cane sugar	33.0	38.3	32.4	26.2	22.7	18.6	17.9
Caribbean percentage of world beet and cane sugar	19.5	22.9	18.9	15.0	13.0	11.0	10.9
Cuba percentage of Caribbean	57.1	65.1	63.5	61.2	67.0	67.7	74.0
Dominican Republic percentage of Caribbean	9.3	7.2	9.9	9.4	9.3	14.0	12.5
Cuba percentage of world beet and cane sugar	11.2	14.9	12.0	9.2	8.7	7.5	8.1

Source: Calculated from Table 1.

actually grew more rapidly between 1951–55 and 1976–80, expanding at an average rate of 2.7 percent a year. As a result its share in the region went from 7 to 12.5 percent, and it remains one of the largest sugar exporters in the world.

The relative stability exhibited by the Dominican sugar industry for several decades is indeed remarkable. At least as common in the world sugar economy is the kind of violent fluctuation of which Jamaica is an example. Seventh among Caribbean producers just before World War II, the Jamaican industry tripled its output in the course of the next 15 years, advancing to fourth place in the region. At its peak in 1966, Jamaica produced slightly over half a million tonnes of sugar—to tumble back to little more than 200,000 tonnes 15 years later. Nor is this the first time that Jamaica has performed such a Yo-Yo act. In 1805, following the collapse of the industry in Saint-Domingue, Jamaica was the largest individual exporter of sugar in the world, with a production of about 100,000 tonnes (Deerr 1949–50, 1:177, 198), but after the emancipation of the slaves the business went into a long decline until in 1913 production had fallen to 5,000 tonnes. The 1805 level was not regained until 1936 under the policy of imperial preference.

History teaches that the sharp decreases in sugar production observed in several Caribbean territories in recent years cannot be looked upon as irreversible without closer examination. Of course, it is highly unlikely that places such as Dominica, Grenada, Montserrat, Nevis, St. Croix, St. John, St. Thomas, St. Vincent, and Tobago (all Caribbean islands that at one time or

another produced and exported sugar) will reappear on the world stage—certainly not with quantities significant in relation even to their small economies. Many of them are suited by their physical formation to produce at most enough sugar to satisfy their own requirements.

But territories that in the past have grown large quantities of sugar cane could obviously do so again, unless the land has been permanently lost to agriculture or is unsuited to mechanization. They have shown that they can turn sunshine into money, which in the end is what sugar cane growing is all about.

THE MARKETS FOR CARIBBEAN SUGAR

Historically and now, the fortunes of the Caribbean sugar industries have been influenced by the sugar policies of their principal foreign buyers. Six Caribbean sugar producers—Barbados, Cuba, the Dominican Republic, Guadeloupe, Guyana, and St. Kitts—are still heavily export-oriented, with domestic consumption absorbing less than 20 percent of their output (Table 3). Two more—Jamaica and Trinidad and Tobago—as recently as 1981 exported a substantial part of their crops but covered domestic consumption to some extent by imports. Haiti, Martinique, and Puerto Rico have become net importers, as are all other Caribbean territories that at some point in the past produced sugar. Together, the eight net exporters supplied 8.5 million tonnes of sugar to other countries in 1981, equal to one-third of world net exports. The Caribbean remains by a wide margin the foremost surplus sugar region supplying the rest of the world.

Table 3 shows the main foreign outlets of the Caribbean sugar industries in 1981. It will be seen at once that over half the exports went to three markets—the European Economic Community (EEC), the Soviet Union, and the United States—reflecting political links and the existence of preferential trading arrangements.

A large part of the international sugar trade has been compartmentalized for many years into various preferential marketing arrangements, which grew out of the historical associations that were forged when great chunks of the Caribbean sugar industries were foreign-owned, principally by British and U.S. companies. The so-called free world market comprises less than one-fifth of the total amount of sugar produced and consumed and for most producers constitutes a residual outlet after domestic requirements and exports to preferential markets are met.

For 40 years, one major trading area outside the free world market was defined by the U.S. Sugar Acts, in force from 1934 until 1974. These divided the U.S. sugar market between domestic and designated foreign suppliers by assigning quotas expressed in tons or as percentages of consumption require-

TABLE 3.

Caribbean Sugar Industries: Production, Domestic Consumption, Net Exports, and Main Foreign Markets, 1981
(000 tonnes, raw value)[a]

Country	Production	Domestic Consumption	Net Exports	Main Foreign Markets		
				First	Second	Third
Barbados	97	16	64	EEC: 45	USA: 12	Canada: 5
Cuba	7,926	552	7,071	USSR: 3,204	China: 573	Canada: 376
Dominican Republic	1,108	206	864	USA: 711	Venezuela: 119	Algeria: 21
Guadeloupe	98	10	56	n.a.	n.a.	n.a.
Guyana	320	37	282	EEC: 201	USA: 68	Canada: 11
Jamaica	204	100	95[b]	EEC: 125	—	—
St. Kitts–Nevis–Anguilla	33	2	30	EEC: 16	USA: 14	Caribbean islands: 0.4
Trinidad and Tobago	93	39	48[c]	EEC: 67	—	—

Sources: International Sugar Council/Organization 1963–; F. O. Licht 1983b (for Guadeloupe production and consumption); Food and Agriculture Organization 1981 (for Guadeloupe net exports).

[a] Centrifugal sugar, including fancy molasses.
[b] Gross exports of 124,512 tonnes minus imports of 29,167 tonnes (8,052 from Brazil; 8,259 from Cuba; 12,856 from U.S.A.).
[c] Gross exports of 67,333 tonnes minus imports of 19,577 tonnes (all from U.S.A.).

ments, and geared to achieve a price objective (Ballinger 1971). Control of the volume of sugar coming onto the U.S. market acted as a price support. Foreign quota holders received the domestic price less import duty.

Both prior to and during the life of the U.S. Sugar Acts, other legislation conferred special concessions on certain suppliers. Puerto Rican sugars have been admitted free of duty since 1901. Virgin Island sugars had duty-free access from 1917. The duty on Cuban sugars was reduced by 20 percent in 1903 in accordance with the Reciprocity Act and stayed at various levels below the full rate until the suspension of the Cuban quota in 1960 (U.S. Department of Agriculture 1975:118–19). Up to then, Cuba had the largest quota of any foreign country in the U.S. market and in 1955–59 furnished on average 3,146,000 short tons (raw value) annually, or over 70 percent of the receipts from all foreign suppliers (U.S. Department of Agriculture 1975:7).

Following expiration of the Sugar Act at the end of 1974, U.S. sugar imports became part of the free world market, but the Generalized System of Preferences (GSP) established under Title V of the Trade Act of 1974 has since the beginning of 1976 provided duty-free treatment for sugar imports from designated developing countries under certain conditions.[6] The value of this concession varies with the level of the sugar tariff, which stood at the statutory minimum of 0.625 cents per pound (raw value, 96 degrees) from February 1980 to December 1981, when it was raised to the legal maximum of 2.8125 cents per pound (raw value). Caribbean sugar exporters eligible for GSP duty-free treatment as of 31 March 1983 were Barbados, Guyana, Haiti, Jamaica, St. Kitts, and Trinidad and Tobago. Implementation of the Caribbean Basin Initiative will also exempt from duty the Dominican Republic's sugar shipments up to 860,000 short tons.

On 5 May 1982, President Reagan reestablished the system of specific country import quotas. Initially operated on a quarterly basis, the system returned to annual quotas as of 1 October 1982. Caribbean suppliers received the following percentage allocations, which applied to an overall import quota of 2.8 million short tons (raw value) in 1982/83:

Dominican Republic	17.6	Guyana	1.2
Jamaica	1.1	Barbados	0.7
	Trinidad and Tobago	0.7	

Haiti and St. Kitts shared with four other countries a combined percentage of 0.3 but, in order to provide at least one economically feasible shipment, were allowed access for 16,500 short tons each. The effect of the reimposition of country-by-country quotas and the accompanying phasing out of the import fee previously levied in addition to duty was to make the U.S. market once again a remunerative preferential outlet.[7]

Another large bloc was marked off from the free world market by the

Commonwealth Sugar Agreement (CSA) of 1951. This initially provided the British West Indies and British Guiana, as they were then, with a guaranteed outlet in the United Kingdom for 640,000 long tons of sugar *tel quel* (see note 1) at a negotiated price "reasonably remunerative to efficient producers" of £30.50 per long ton c.i.f. (cost, insurance, and freight). Quantities and prices increased during the life of the agreement until at the end in 1974 the Commonwealth Caribbean members had access for 725,000 long tons at £83 per long ton f.o.b. (free on board), raised in September of that year to £140 per long ton. The negotiated price quotas formed part of so-called overall agreement quotas, of which 951,000 long tons eventually corresponded to the West Indies and Guyana. Whereas the negotiated price quotas established the quantities the exporters were obliged to sell and the United Kingdom was obliged to buy, the overall agreement quotas fixed an upper limit on exports to markets available for the entry of Commonwealth sugars on a preferential tariff basis, i.e., mainly the United Kingdom and Canada.

As a result of the United Kingdom's entry into the EEC, which made the British sugar market subject to the community's Common Agricultural Policy, the CSA was superseded in 1975 by the sugar provisions of the Lomé Convention and associated agreements between the EEC and a number of African, Caribbean, and Pacific (ACP) countries. These guaranteed annual purchases by the EEC of 409,100 tonnes of sugar (white value) from the West Indies and Guyana, divided as follows:

Barbados	49,300	Guyana	157,700
Jamaica	118,300	St. Kitts–Nevis–	
		Anguilla	14,800
	Trinidad and Tobago	69,000	

Compared with the negotiated price quotas of the CSA, the Lomé convention quotas represented a contraction of about 40 percent in the guaranteed outlets of the West Indies and Guyana, traceable to the nonfulfillment of their CSA obligations in 1974 and their decision at that time to opt for smaller EEC quotas in order to take advantage of what were expected to be more favorable world market prices. By contrast, Belize, Fiji, Mauritius, and Swaziland obtained EEC quotas substantially higher than those previously held under the CSA.

Most of the sugar granted preferential access to the EEC under the Lomé Convention and related agreements is refined and sold in the United Kingdom. The EEC, however, not only recognized a right of access but also guaranteed ACP suppliers that if the quantities covered by the quotas were not bought by European refiners under normal commercial arrangements, the community's intervention authorities would accept the sugar at the intervention price. The EEC's purchasing commitment is explicitly for an indefinite period, which means that even if the rest of the Lomé Convention were to lapse, the sugar provisions would remain in force. Prices are negotiated annually between the ACP countries and the EEC within the price range obtaining in the Community for beet sugar producers. Like U.S. domestic sugar prices, EEC prices are normally higher than those on the free world market.[8]

The third major special arrangement comprises the sugar exports by Cuba to designated European and Asian socialist countries (Article 31 of the International Sugar Agreement of 1977). It can be traced back to 1960, when the Soviet Union, China and several East European countries in effect substituted for the American market following the cessation of the sugar trade between Cuba and the United States (Hagelberg 1979a). In a long-term agreement concluded with Cuba in 1964, the Soviet Union promised to admit 24.1 million tonnes of sugar in the period 1965–70 at a price equivalent to about 6 U.S. cents a pound. In the event, Cuba delivered just over 13 million tonnes because of production difficulties. Since then, purchase commitments do not appear to have been fixed in advance. Cuban exports to the Soviet Union in the period 1971–82 fluctuated widely between 1.1 million tonnes in 1972 and 4.4 million in 1982, according to the statistics of the International Sugar Organization.

Table 4 shows the average prices paid by the Soviet Union for Cuban sugar in the last 10 years as given in a recent official Cuban publication (Banco Nacional de Cuba 1982).

Banco Nacional de Cuba (1982:14) explained that "the price of sugar exported to the USSR was linked and varied in proportion to the prices that Cuba had to pay for imports from that country, including oil" and that after 1976 this form of indexing was also adopted by other trading partners belonging to the Council for Mutual Economic Assistance (Comecon). This broadly confirmed previous analysis of Cuban trade statistics (Hagelberg 1979b), which, however, had shown that Eastern European countries followed the Soviet lead in raising the price paid for Cuban sugar from the level of just over 6 U.S. cents a pound, beginning with Bulgaria as early as 1973. Banco Nacional de Cuba (1982:21) also confirmed previous indications that a part of Cuban sugar sales to socialist countries was paid for in convertible currency,

TABLE 4.

Average Prices Paid By the USSR for Cuban Sugar (rubles per tonne)

Year	Rubles/Tonne	U.S. Dollar/Ruble[a]	U.S. Cents/Pound
1972	121.23	1.206	6.63
1973–75	341.67	1.321–1.386	20.47–21.48
1976–80	615.61	1.326–1.547	37.03–43.20
1981–82	660.00	1.380 (1981)	41.31

Source: Banco Nacional de Cuba 1982.
[a] Food and Agriculture Organization 1981.

although it did not reveal whether only the Soviet Union or also other socialist trading partners were involved. The following convertible currency returns from sugar exports to socialist countries were reported for the period from 1975 through the first half of 1982. (Values are given in millions of pesos; the official exchange rate of the Cuban peso was U.S.$1.1977 in August 1982.)

1975	1976	1977	1978	1979	1980	1981	First half 1982
350.1	130.1	177.2	104.7	99.6	–	180.8	303.9

The omission of convertible currency payments in 1980 is probably explained by the high free world market prices in that year, which boosted Cuban earnings from sugar exports to market economy countries; but there is no obvious pattern in the fluctuations.

So much for the preferential markets. Sugar in excess of domestic requirements and special trade arrangements is sold on the free world market, subject to the regulations of the International Sugar Agreement. Largely because of the residual character of the free world market, its prices are notoriously volatile. A British parliamentary investigation of commodity prices ranked sugar first in price instability by a wide margin among 13 major primary commodities in the years 1950–75 (House of Lords 1977). Annual averages of the International Sugar Agreement daily price fluctuated between 7.81 and 29.66 cents per pound in current dollars in the period 1974–81, and in constant dollars the spread was even greater. International Sugar Agreements past and present have not been very effective in dealing with this problem, and it remains to be seen whether the new agreement currently being negotiated will do better.

From 1975 until the restoration of country-by-country quotas by the United States in 1982, the Dominican Republic was the only Caribbean sugar exporter of consequence that was entirely dependent on the free world market. Dominican shipments to free market destinations totalled 864,000 tonnes in 1981, equivalent to 78 percent of production. Cuba in the same year sold over 2.2 million tonnes on the free market, but this was less than one-third of all Cuban sugar exports and only 28 percent of production. Barbados, Guyana, and St. Kitts were the other Caribbean free market exporters in 1981, and the extent of their future exposure will depend on the amount of sugar they have to sell above their EEC commitments and on the size of their U.S. quotas.

PROBLEMS AND UNCERTAINTIES

By and large, preferential trading arrangements such as the sugar provisions of the Lomé Convention and the U.S. quota regulations offer producers a considerable measure of security with respect to both the volume and the value of sugar exports. But they do not invite complacent disregard of chang-

ing political, economic, and technological circumstances, and they have their negative aspects.

Obviously the EEC's sugar regime and the U.S. sugar program were framed in the first instance not for the sake of peripheral suppliers, no matter how important, but rather for the benefit of domestic interest groups. The priorities were clearly stated by the secretary of agriculture in a comment on the first U.S. Sugar Act, the Jones-Costigan Act of 1934. "The program as outlined in the President's message and implemented by pending legislation recognizes a duty to stabilize the price and production of sugar for the benefit of the continental producers and the industry of the insular possessions. It also takes into account the obligations of the United States towards Cuba as implied by the Monroe Doctrine and specified in the Platt Amendment" (quoted in Ballinger 1971:40).

Protective mechanisms such as these, then, may well impede the operation of the classical international trade theory of comparative advantage. They may well distort but do not completely exclude competition within the protected area. And, like any drug, they may well have harmful side effects.

This point is illustrated in various ways. The burden of adjusting to market changes in the United States, for example, has been borne mainly by foreign suppliers, not domestic beet and cane growers and processors. Continental beet and cane sugar production and receipts from domestic offshore areas increased from 5.0 million tonnes (raw value) per year in 1960–64 to 5.4 million in 1978–82, whereas receipts from foreign sources remained stationary at 4.0 million tonnes (U.S. Department of Agriculture 1975, 1979–). Because of the growth of population this meant that U.S. per capita consumption of home-grown beet and cane sugar dropped by 10 percent from 54.9 pounds per year in 1960–64 to 49.6 pounds in 1978–82, while that of imported sugar fell by 20 percent from 42.6 pounds to 34.2 pounds. Because of increased usage of corn sweeteners, particularly high fructose corn syrup, the share of home-grown sucrose in total U.S. caloric sweetener consumption declined from 48.8 percent in 1960–64 to 39.4 percent in 1978–82, but the share of imported sucrose diminished from 37.9 to 27.2 percent.

The EEC sugar regime has operated in such a way that sugar production in the eight producing member countries (excluding Greece but including French overseas departments) increased from 9.5 million tonnes (white value) in 1973/74 to 14.7 million in 1981/82 (Bartens/Mosolff 1977/78–). The EEC's consumption amounted to 10.3 million tonnes (white value) in 1973/74, but only 9.3 million in 1981/82 (again excluding Greece).[9] A small deficit was converted into a huge surplus.

Because of the link between the United Kingdom's entry into the EEC and the sugar provisions of the Lomé Convention,[10] the evolution of the British market is of particular interest. The British Sugar Corporation, the domestic beet sugar processor, was encouraged to expand production from a level of

960,000 tonnes (white value) in the final years of the Commonwealth Sugar Agreement to a target output of 1.25 million (Monopolies and Mergers Commission 1981:9), which was actually exceeded in 1982/83. It can be argued that some expansion was economically justified by the improvements in British beet sugar technology (Harris 1973:46). The trouble is that British sugar demand has fallen from somewhat over 2.6 million tonnes (white value) in the days of the CSA to little more than 2.2 million, thus reducing the gap to be filled by ACP sugar from Africa, the Caribbean, and the Pacific. More white beet sugar and lower consumption resulted in excess refining capacity in the United Kingdom, forcing a rationalization that has reduced the number of British sugar refineries since 1972 from six, with a capacity of 2 million tonnes, to two, barely adequate to handle the ACP imports.

There can be little doubt that the former British sugar regime provided a more congenial atmosphere for Commonwealth suppliers than its EEC successor. The failure of West Indian exporters to fulfill their CSA quotas in 1974 led to the inclusion of more stringent provisions in the Lomé sugar protocol governing the treatment of shortfalls (Harris and Hagelberg 1975). The CSA price-fixing procedure, which took into account changes in the production costs of the Commonwealth suppliers (Hagelberg 1974:32), was at least in theory more accommodating to the problems experienced by overseas cane sugar producers than the Lomé formula, which links the price for ACP sugar to the range obtaining for domestic beet sugar producers, although initially the latter did give ACP suppliers much higher unit returns than they had received under the CSA (McGregor 1978:105, 259). Hence containment of production costs, which in the second half of the 1960s had begun to rise sharply in the Caribbean (Smith 1976; Hagelberg 1974:64–66), became much more critical under Lomé than it had been under the CSA. Just as the price objective of the U.S. Sugar Acts could not prevent the contraction of an increasingly uncompetitive Puerto Rican industry, so the Lomé price guarantee is small comfort to cane sugar producers who cannot match the efficiency of Western European beet sugar industries. The conflict between the desire of the EEC, with a sugar mountain of its own, to whittle down its Lomé commitments and the need of ACP suppliers to stretch them to offset higher rates of cost inflation provides a fertile soil for differences of interpretation of the letter and spirit of the provisions.

The existence of preferential trade arrangements aggravates the residual character of the free world market and contributes to its price instability. Moreover, it tends to depress the general level of free market prices. Sugar production is a high fixed cost operation. If the overheads are covered by the quantity sold at the high protected price, additional amounts can be profitably disposed of at a free market price barely above the variable costs. Producer price protection then subsidizes surplus disposal. The EEC's sugar regime, which has promoted the expansion of production in the community far beyond the level of self-sufficiency, has had precisely this result. Its unsettling and, on balance, depressing effect on free market prices is well established (Koester and Schmitz 1982; Harris 1981; McGregor 1978). This is why it is non-sense to refer only to the benefits derived from special arrangement sugar prices—be they American, Russian, or Western European—in relation to the free market price.[11] The losses on world market sales at lower prices must be offset against the special arrangement gains. As far as the Caribbean sugar industries are concerned, Cuba and the Dominican Republic are obviously the most adversely affected by the EEC sugar regime: they obtain no benefit and are large free market exporters. It is no consolation to them that low free market prices may boost sugar consumption in poor developing sugar-importing countries on the other side of the world.

Quite unexpectedly, a number of ACP sugar exporters have seen the benefits of the Lomé sugar protocol eroded in still another way. The certainty of a guaranteed price gradually rising in line with the price range obtaining in the EEC has been shattered by exchange rate fluctuations. The currencies of all the Caribbean Lomé Convention subscribers are linked to the U.S. dollar. EEC sugar prices, however, are couched in European Currency Units, a basket of currencies in which the dollar plays no part, while actual sales to the United Kingdom refiner are transacted in pounds sterling. As a result of the weakness of the EEC currencies with respect to the dollar in recent years, the take-home return on sales to the Community has been substantially reduced, and a notionally stable trade arrangement has been destabilized, at least for the time being.

From a longer-term viewpoint, there is much anxiety among Caribbean cane sugar producers about the inroads made into sucrose markets by substitutes, especially high fructose corn syrup. This is only in part a new development. Commercial grape sugar production began in Europe shortly after the German chemist Konstantin Kirchhof observed the transformation of starch into glucose by acid hydrolysis in 1811. This itself was only a few years after the establishment at the beginning of the nineteenth century of the first beet sugar factory, forerunner of the European beet sugar industry, which has been described as "the earliest example of the market for an important tropical product being seriously eroded by the application of modern scientific methods in relatively advanced countries" (Timoshenko and Swerling 1957:235).

Starch sweeteners have been produced in the United States since before the Civil War. Output of corn syrup in 1927, the earliest date for which figures are available, amounted to 427,000 short tons, and that of dextrose (crystallized glucose) to 412,000 short tons (both dry weight), which represented about 11 percent of the combined sucrose, corn syrup, and dextrose consumption in the United States that year (Ballinger 1971:8, 15, 37). These figures indicate that starch sweeteners were already then of competitive significance to beet and cane sugar producers, although not as much as today.

Saccharin, a nonnutritive toluene-based compound considered to be about 300 times as sweet as cane sugar, was discovered at the Johns Hopkins University in 1879. Commercial production in the United States began in 1901 and reached its first peak in 1918 and 1919 during the sugar shortage caused by World War I, when it started to be used not only by diabetics and others who could not tolerate sugar, but also as a direct replacement for sugar. According to the U.S. Tariff Commission, nearly 548,000 pounds of saccharin were produced in 1919, equivalent in sweetness to about 82,000 short tons of sugar, or 1.7 percent of U.S. sugar consumption that year (Keim 1979; Ballinger 1971:22, 39).

Leaving aside the distortion of consumption patterns during World War II, when beet and cane sugar were scarce, it is only since 1957 that the use of starch sweeteners in the United States has consistently grown more rapidly than that of sucrose. The opportunity was there because of the displacement of home-prepared foods by processed foods, since starch sweeteners so far are generally suitable only for industrial use, and the opening of a considerable price advantage provided the economic motive. Relative to the New York City wholesale price of refined cane sugar, the price of corn syrup, dry basis, dropped from a base of 100 in 1957 to 77 in 1963 and, with interim fluctuations, further to 51 in 1979 (Ballinger 1971:106–114; U.S. Department of Agriculture 1979–).

The raw material for starch sweeteners in the United States is corn (maize), but they can also be made from potatoes, sweet potatoes, rice, tapioca (starch from cassava or manioc), wheat, or sorghum. (For a useful overview of the techniques and economics of starch sugar manufacture, see Keim 1979.) Each has its peculiarities. One important difference between the corn sweetener and the beet and cane sugar industries is that corn is storable and traded internationally, whereas beets can be kept only a short time, cane must be processed within days of harvesting, and neither one figures in international trade. Another difference is that beet and cane are grown almost exclusively for sugar, but only a small proportion of the corn crop is used for sweetener production. As in the beet sugar industry, by-products play an important role in the economics of corn sweetener manufacture.

Stimulated by relatively high sucrose prices, research and development in the field of alternative products in the 1950s and 1960s led to the appearance of high fructose corn syrup (HFCS), which is produced by the enzymatic isomerization of glucose to fructose. (From the summary of the nature of sugars at the beginning of this essay it will be recalled that glucose and fructose have the same chemical formula, but that their atoms are arranged differently in space; that is, they are isomers of each other. An enzyme called glucose isomerase changes the atomic arrangement of glucose into that of fructose.) The advantage of equilibrium high fructose syrup over glucose syrups, which are less sweet than sucrose, is that the former is equal in all respects to invert syrup made from sucrose. This opened up various new applications for starch sweeteners in industries, such as soft drinks, that had been major users of sucrose. In the second half of the 1970s a whole new line of sweeter syrups came on the market with fructose contents of up to 90 percent. These have the further advantage of providing high-intensity sweetness with fewer calories. In 1981, HFCS for the first time made up more than half the total corn sweetener use in the United States.

Total corn sweetener consumption in the United States reached 5.6 million short tons (dry basis) in 1982, which compares with 8.7 million short tons of beet and cane sugar (U.S. Department of Agriculture 1979–). HFCS use increased to 3.1 million short tons, of which 58 percent went into soft drinks. The application in soft drinks will rise further following the decision of the Coca-Cola Company and PepsiCo to permit greater amounts of HFCS in their major cola products. In the first quarter of 1983, the price of 55-percent HFCS, used in beverages, was 40 percent below that of beet sugar in the Chicago-West market.

Preliminary figures for 1982 show that the average American consumed 75.2 pounds of beet and cane sugar, down from a peak of slightly over 100 pounds in 1969–73; 48.2 pounds of corn sweeteners (dry basis), more than twice as much as in 1969–73; 1.4 pounds of honey and edible syrups, virtually the same as in 1969–73; and 7.3 pounds (sugar sweetness equivalent) of saccharin, less than the total amount of noncaloric sweeteners used in 1969, the last year that cyclamates were allowed in food, but more than in subsequent years.

Information on starch sweetener consumption in other countries is less complete. Over the period 1960–79, the demand for glucose syrups and isoglucose (as HFCS is called in Europe) in the United Kingdom increased from 163,000 tonnes to 475,000 tonnes, dry weight (Monopolies and Mergers Commission 1981:15). Current EEC sugar market regulations, in force until 30 June 1986, establish production quotas for isoglucose, corresponding to the A and B quotas for beet and cane sugar, totalling just over 198,000 tonnes (dry basis) per year for the whole Community. Anything above that level must be exported, effectively putting a ceiling on isoglucose consumption in the EEC, which is fairly insignificant compared with a sucrose consumption on the order of 9.6 million tonnes. Japan's HFCS supply in the year ending 30 September 1983 is estimated at 607,000 tonnes in terms of dry matter content of standard 55-percent HFCS, while the projected beet and cane sugar consumption is 2.5 million tonnes, white value (F. O. Licht's International Sugar Report 115: 402, 28 July 1983). Canadian HFCS use in 1982 is believed to have been of the order of 157,000 tonnes (sucrose sweetness equivalent) or 14 percent of a total sweetener consumption of 1.1 million tonnes (F. O. Licht's International Sugar Report 115: 317, 10 June 1983).

The United States, Japan, the EEC, and Canada are the major HFCS producers, and from the figures cited it is safe to conclude that total world availabilities of HFCS in 1983 do not exceed 4.4 million tonnes (dry basis). This must be set against an estimated world offtake of 93.7 million tonnes (raw value) of centrifugal beet and cane sugar in the year ending 31 August 1983. The HFCS invasion is actually no more than a beachhead at this point. Its market effect is enhanced, however, because it is concentrated in three major sucrose importers.

For a realistic assessment of the prospects, several points should be kept in mind. First, the rate of increase of per capita sugar consumption falls as higher consumption levels are reached. Obviously there is a limit to the amount of sugar that people can or desire to eat. Average per capita caloric sweetener consumption in Europe, the Americas, and Oceania exceeds 4 ounces a day or 90 pounds a year and in a number of countries has reached the saturation point. Where this is so, the increase in total offtake is reduced to the rate of population growth. That part of the additional demand for sugar that is generated by the catching-up process is concentrated more and more in Asia and Africa.

Second, elderly persons and white-collar workers require less food energy than young persons and manual workers. Aging populations and sedentary occupations tend to reduce the overall food energy requirements in developed countries.

Third, rising per capita incomes are accompanied by a change in consumer habits from home-prepared to processed foods. This has two consequences for sucrose consumption. It provides more opportunities for replacement, since most bulk caloric substitutes are so far available only in forms suitable for industrial use; and it shifts control over how much sucrose is eaten from the ultimate consumers to the food manufacturers, who may be motivated by different considerations, with the consumers often not even knowing how much and what kind of sugar is contained in the product they buy. (This does not necessarily militate against sucrose consumption, which may, indeed, rise with increased purchases of certain products, such as soft drinks.)

Fourth, high prices and periods of scarcity put a damper on the consumption of sucrose and encourage its replacement. The impulses in favor of substitutes that were provided by the sugar price booms of 1963/64, 1974/75, and 1980/81 are recorded in U.S. sweetener consumption statistics like earthquakes on a seismogram. Sucrose consumption is also restrained and substitution stimulated (unless itself administratively curbed, as in the EEC) by producer support policies that put the price of sucrose to the consumer higher than it would be otherwise. "You can't have it both ways" is unquestionably one of the more frustrating injunctions against human nature; but even where the price elasticity of the demand for sucrose is extremely low, as it tends to be in developed countries, beet and cane sugar producers cannot enjoy high prices and expect to sell exactly the same quantities that they would at lower prices, particularly when cheaper substitutes are available.

Fifth, the competitive position of sucrose relative to possible substitutes is affected by government in various other ways. Behind the ability of the U.S. corn wet-milling industry to produce low-cost sweeteners lie not only its technical competence but also Washington's grain programs. The reluctant acquiescence of Brussels to the disposal of large quantities of by-product corn gluten feed in the EEC has also helped. In Japan, HFCS manufacture has been influenced by protectionist measures in favor of domestic potato and sweet potato producers, the different tariff treatment of corn and raw sugar, and the unequal imposition of excise tax.

Sixth, the combination of circumstances that has favored the growth of corn sweeteners in the United States—high ratio of industrial to household sweetener usage, profitable by-product outlets, abundant supply of cheap, home-grown feedstock, and huge market only partly covered by domestically produced beet and cane sugar—does not exist to the same extent elsewhere.

Seventh, the rapid advance of starch sweeteners at the expense of sucrose in the United States will slow down unless a product suitable for household use is developed. As Hannah (1982) put it, people do not fancy pouring high fructose syrup on their cornflakes. Theoretically, high fructose syrups could replace sucrose in all industrial uses except where a dry product is required. This means that sucrose could potentially lose 100 percent of its markets in beverages and canned foods, 70 percent in ice cream and dairy products, 50 percent in baking and miscellaneous foods, and 20 percent in confectionery (Keim 1979). Some of these limits are being approached as far as formulation problems will allow. Department of Agriculture forecasts of U.S. caloric sweetener consumption in 1985 predict a rise of HFCS use to 4.3 million short tons (dry basis), a glucose syrup and dextrose offtake of 2.6 million (little changed from the present), and a further decline in beet and cane sugar consumption to about 7.9 million tons. Total caloric sweetener consumption, including honey and edible syrups, in 1985 is put at 15 million short tons, an increase of half a million tons over 1982.

Fears of a shrinking U.S. sweetener market appear premature. The division of the market is another matter—and, at least in the short run, as much a matter of politics as of economics.

THE POLITICAL ECONOMY OF CARIBBEAN SUGAR

Few commodities raise as many complex economic, political, and social issues as sugar. None, probably, is as fraught with ideological baggage.

"Little, if any, mention has been made of the deep emotions which sugar excites in the Barbadian heart, the irrational fears and responses," Senator John Wickham commented after the passage through the Barbadian parliament of legislation concerning the sugar industry in 1982.

> We are bonded to sugar in our imagination as surely as we were in our bodies 200 years ago.. . . I am as much enslaved to the idea of sugar as anyone else. My eyes have become so accustomed to the sight of cane fields that even when I shut them far away from Barbados, I can still see the arrows in the wind and the stretch of what has been called the impersonation of wheat between the hedgerows. I carry around the whole arrangement of plantations on the landscape, the tenantries, the aroma of boiling juice and even the memory of the mule sweat and leader boys of my youth as part of my emotional equipment. (*Sunday Sun,* Bridgetown, 10 October 1982, p. 7)

In the Caribbean, sugar is difficult to divorce from a history of colonialism, slavery, indentured labor, and plantation agriculture, which bequeathed racially mixed societies retaining traces of former occupational structures, social relationships, and mental attitudes, although power is no longer held by plantocrats and imperial administrators.

Elsewhere, sugar has less profound but equally influential connotations: sugar trust, sugar barons, sugar lobby, rotting teeth, bulging waistlines, depending on the turn of mind. Who today would write, "Sugar and spice and all things nice, / And such are young women made of"? Eating spinach or carrots is virtuous; sugar is sweet, and fudge cake desirable, but nobody nowadays thinks them wholesome.[12] The belief that sugar is not good for us disposes toward the conclusion that it really is not so essential. Surely one can do with much less. Why worry about Caribbean sugar? The region should be encouraged to produce something else. This would also eliminate some vexing trade problems.

"Because of its past associations with slavery and the discriminatory control of the plantocracy, the sugar industry is a fertile field for ideological rhetoric and political posturing," editorialized the *Advocate-News,* a Barbadian newspaper, on 2 October 1982. Apart from the rhetoric and posturing, however, policy makers in the Caribbean as well as in Europe and North America are genuinely concerned about the viability of the Caribbean sugar industries, the future of their markets, the possibilities of agricultural and industrial diversification, the costs and benefits of sugar production and of potential alternative economic activities, the consequent priorities of resource allocation, and the choice of development strategies.

Although from a distance the Caribbean may be seen as an entity and a single problem, and although the islands share certain characteristics that bear on these questions, the circumstances of, say, Barbados and Trinidad, not to mention the Greater Antilles, are far too diverse for a uniform set of answers.

This is perhaps a reason why the broad plantation and dependency theories propounded by a prominent school of academics in the West Indies and elsewhere, however revealing in their analysis of the causes of economic underdevelopment, are not very relevant to the practical task of formulating an operational model of economic development, as the governor of the Central Bank of Barbados has repeatedly pointed out (Blackman 1979, 1980). Or as another critic realistically observed, "Third World countries are confronted not only with centuries but also with years and decades, and the hope of a socialist millennium does not help market a sugar crop or protect fledgling textile mills from more efficient competition" (Mahler 1981). While it is too much to hope that concepts such as diversification, import substitution, export concentration, instability, and cost competitiveness will cease to become degraded by familiarity into little more than buzzwords, a check list of some caveats and reservations, with the usual proviso, "Strike out where not applicable," may be useful.

Take the question of agricultural diversification and import substitution. Wide stretches of prime land are occupied by sugar cane in the Caribbean. Sugar and molasses still constitute a considerable proportion of agricultural and total merchandise exports (see Table 5), although in several cases their share has fallen considerably from earlier levels. On the other hand, food imports consume large and growing amounts of scarce foreign currency. Instead of producing so much sugar for export, why not grow more food and save on imports?

Now we know that sugar cane was brought to the Caribbean, so it cannot be said that the region was predestined by nature to produce sugar. Moreover, in

TABLE 5.

Percentage Shares of Exports of Sugar and Molasses[a] in Total Merchandise Exports and Exports of Agricultural Products, 1978–80

| | Percentage Shares of Sugar and Molasses | |
Territory	Merchandise Exports	Agricultural Exports
Barbados	23.2	79.3
Cuba	86.1	95.6
Dominican Republic	27.6	46.5
Guadeloupe	33.6	36.4
Guyana	37.0	72.7
Jamaica	7.2	45.4
St. Kitts[b]	n.a.	98.1
Trinidad and Tobago	1.1	45.2

Source: Food and Agriculture Organization 1981.

[a] Standard International Trade Classification Section 06, including negligible amounts of natural honey.
[b] 1979–81, sugar only.

the English and French colonies there was a presugar stage of development during which small farmers grew tobacco, cotton, annatto, indigo, and ginger, together with food crops such as cassava, plantains, beans, and corn. This stage ended with the appearance of the capitalist planter and the introduction of slave labor (Deerr 1949–50, 1:160, 168, 228; 2:289). But, as Mahler (1981) has remarked, there are reasons why sugar cane is grown in the Caribbean that are not wholly the product of history.

At least since the inquiry of the West India Royal Commission in 1938–39, it has been recognized that sugar cane is the best (or even the only) suitable crop in many parts of the Caribbean, since it can survive hurricanes, floods, and drought, and is moreover relatively resistant to pests and diseases (Hagelberg 1974:15f.). "No other crop plant is so adapted to the ecological requirements of a humid tropical environment," confirms a geographer (Smith 1975). "Sugar cane as a crop steals least, despite man's greed, from the environment and habitat which cradle its agricultural success." The insight has not remained buried in official reports and academic journals. "Sugar cane is the single agricultural crop that can ensure that Barbados remains a farming country—or in fact a country with a viable environmental future," reiterates an editorial in the *Advocate-News* of 2 October 1982.

The ecological suitability and yield capability of sugar cane are not disputed. But there is a curious reluctance to think out the implications. Tropical and subtropical Caribbean countries do not grow bread grains, the yields of corn and sorghum are so far very much inferior, and rice requires irrigation, which in many places is not available. If sugar cane in these conditions is the "impersonation of wheat," i.e., the staff of life, it is difficult to conceive of a better use of the land except in isolated and special cases. Would diversification be recommendable for the Corn Belt or the Canadian prairie provinces?

Sir Arthur Lewis thought that temperate countries might have the real competitive advantage in agriculture, since their climate is more favorable to the retention of soil fertility than the harsher climate of the tropics (Lewis 1965). If sugar cane is the exception because it is better adapted to tropical climates and soils, other crop plants are ipso facto relatively less so. To borrow from Joan Robinson, the misery of growing sugar cane is nothing compared to the misery of growing other crops.[13] As Mahler (1981) reminds us, "the one Caribbean country that is largely comprised of peasant proprietors producing their own food is Haiti, the poorest country by far in the western hemisphere and one of the poorest in the world."

Small wonder, then, that giving up sugar cane does not automatically lead to the production of other crops on the vacated land. More often the land returns to bush. This is shown by the land use statistics of Puerto Rico (Table 6), which indicate that a decline in the harvested area of sugar cane of nearly 90,000 hectares (217,000 acres) between 1961–65 and 1980 was accompanied by a contraction of close to 150,000 hectares (365,000 acres) in the total

TABLE 6.

Land Use, Cuba and Puerto Rico, 1961–65 and 1980 (000 hectares)

	Cuba		Puerto Rico	
	1961–65	1980	1961–65	1980
Total area	11,452	11,452	890	890
Land area	11,452	11,452	886	886
Arable and permanent crops	1,790	3,200[a]	287	139
Arable land	1,616	2,525[a]	192	77[b]
Permanent crops	174	675[a]	96	62[b]
Permanent pasture	2,349	2,523[b]	310	336
Forest and woodland	1,616	1,900[a]	118	178
Other land[c]	5,697	3,829	171	233
Sugar cane (area harvested)	1,108	1,400[a]	120	32[a]

Source: Food and Agriculture Organization 1971–.

[a] FAO estimate.
[b] Unofficial figure.
[c] Other land includes unused but potentially productive land, built-on areas, wasteland, parks, ornamental gardens, roads, lanes, barren land, and any other land not otherwise listed.

area under arable and permanent crops. As a result, per capita agricultural output in Puerto Rico in 1980 was little more than half of what it had been in 1961–65. It may make commercial sense to grow sugar cane in Florida rather than Puerto Rico, let agriculture on the island decline, and distribute food stamps to the population to buy imported products; but this merely demonstrates what can happen when market prices are the sole criterion governing the administration of natural resources. Other Caribbean territories in which a decline in sugar cane production has had a marked effect on per capita agricultural output are Barbados, Guadeloupe, Martinique, and Trinidad and Tobago. In contrast, Cuban land use and output statistics point to an improved resource utilization.

Upon reflection, it is again not surprising that land taken out of sugar cane is prone to become less rather than more productive. (We are talking about large-scale, unirrigated crop husbandry, not market gardening.) Given the natural advantages of sugar cane over other field crops, a country that by the usual commercial standards is a relatively high-cost cane producer is hardly likely to be a relatively low-cost and more competitive producer of another crop. A few visits over a period of 12 months to Barbadian supermarkets will confirm that on average imported potatoes are a better buy than local root crops, as far as price is concerned, and that macaroni made from imported wheat is a cheaper carbohydrate than home-grown products except sugar. This is nothing new. Nearly 40 years ago, Simey (1946:141) stated, "Land and labor put into the sugar industry produce much higher returns in the way of salt fish and flour than the same amount of land and labor put into the growing of yams and beef." For the same reason, Eric Williams, later to become prime minister of Trinidad and Tobago, wrote in 1944 that the pressure of population on the soil necessitated the maximum utilization of all available resources and ruled out self-sufficiency as an attainable ideal (Williams 1944).

It is true, of course, that until fairly recently agricultural research in the Caribbean and in the tropics generally was concentrated on the export crops to the neglect of those destined for home consumption. Yields and costs of nonsugar agricultural products would probably compare more favorably had they received more attention. But this bias was due to problems of scale as well as economic considerations, and it is open to doubt whether the very great lead of sugar cane would have been wiped out (Hagelberg 1974:16f.).

It must not be forgotten that we are dealing here with small, in some cases very small, countries that by their nature are open economies, extremely dependent on the outside world. Of the eight Caribbean net sugar exporters listed in Tables 3 and 5, four (Barbados, Guadeloupe, Guyana, and St. Kitts) have populations of less than one million, one (Trinidad and Tobago) has just over one million, another (Jamaica) a little more than two million, and the remaining two (Cuba and the Dominican Republic) have between six and ten million. The size of each domestic market is thus more or less severely limited. Its absorptive capacity is moreover affected by the tastes and preferences of the population. For example, high per capita incomes may increase the demand for fruits and green vegetables but have a negative impact on the demand for locally grown root crops.

Smallness is not wholly a disadvantage, in that a palpable improvement in the degree of self-sufficiency in a given product can be quickly achieved. But it presents special problems. The effect of seasonality, for instance, is greatly exaggerated. While the total annual supply may fall short of the total annual demand, the periodicity of harvesting, inadequate quality control, and insufficient storage facilities make for a succession of gluts and shortages. "Glut seems to be becoming the most popular word in Barbados these days," complained a columnist in the *Sunday Sun* of 17 April 1983. "When there is not a chicken glut, there is a potato glut, an onion glut, a yam glut, a vegetable glut of one kind or another and so on. Because of these gluts hardly a month passes without newspaper pages being plastered with stories and pictures of this vegetable or that ground provision having to be ploughed back into the ground or having to rot in the storehouses. Only recently because of glut, we saw farmers having to give away acres and acres of sweet potatoes while even more acres had to be ploughed back in."

Within the confines of a very small island market like the Barbadian one, the vegetable production of a single farm occupying less than a hundred acres can affect market prices. This is in contrast to the island's role on the international sugar stage, where as a small producer it is a price taker. The conventional economic wisdom that an individual grower's decision to expand production does not influence the price (or, as economists would say, that he faces an infinitely elastic demand curve) does not apply to a country of a quarter of a million inhabitants. Given the limited size of the domestic market, increased production in certain lines can be disposed of profitably only by export or by improving agricultural and marketing techniques to reduce the problem of seasonality and achieve a better adjustment of supply to demand. This requires a continual balancing act on the part of producers and marketing institutions (a feat not made any easier by the large annual crop fluctuations induced not so much by growers' decisions as by the weather) and subjects them to a much greater burden and risk than they would face in a larger market. A report to the Barbados government (McGregor et al. 1979:77) concluded that, as far as domestic requirements were concerned, only a small portion of the land under cane could be usefully devoted to horticultural crops.

This illustrates the point that in a small economy the limits of successful import substitution are reached as quickly in agriculture as in manufacturing, and there are the same dangers of spreading the available resources too thinly over numerous small ventures and of attempting to produce things for which the environment is not favorable. So we are back to exporting, only this time something other than sugar. This, of course, is not impossible. St. Lucia, for example, switched from sugar cane to bananas because the hilly topography of the island and prevalence of small farms made sugar production unprofitable. But experience has shown the banana business to be just as risky as the sugar business, if not more so, because of droughts and hurricanes, and just as subject to the vagaries of the international marketplace with its tariffs and trade barriers. It goes without saying that each commodity presupposes the creation and maintenance of the appropriate institutions and infrastructure, overheads that can be borne only if production attains a certain scale.

The continued existence of several Caribbean sugar industries, at least on the scale of production obtaining at this time, is occasionally questioned from another angle. With a finger pointed at their high production costs, observers suggest that output be stabilized at a lower and less costly level by closure of what are considered uneconomic mills and abandonment of purportedly marginal cane land. Such proposals are usually coupled with calls for factory modernization, greater field mechanization, improved transport, and more research, at first sight a very attractive package. Some of the assumptions, however, deserve a closer look.

In the first place, the realness of the production costs needs to be examined. Not that the costs are fictitious—competent auditors certify that the money has been spent. Nevertheless, without entering into an extended discussion of accounting practices, methods of depreciation, overhead allocation, and the difference between financial and economic costs, one can think of several reasons why the reported production costs may mislead. In times of high inflation, for instance, the difference between nominal and real interest rates can become quite substantial. Then there are various kinds of transfers working both ways. A sugar producer shows a rise in costs and a balance sheet loss as a result of price increases on purchased goods and services, the suppliers of which may well show higher profits.[14] Conversely, concessional haulage rates reduce the cost of transporting sugar cane and sugar. Then again, there is an implicit assumption that all sugar producers seek to minimize their production costs. However, not only may they be prevented from doing so by, say, labor legislation on out-of-crop employment, which has the effect of increasing the wage bill and of hindering the adoption of cost-saving technology; but they themselves may have other objectives. A centuries-old industry like the sugar industry is more than a branch of manufacturing like the garment or electronics industry. It is also a social institution. In various situations, enterprise behavior may not be governed by any minimizing or maximizing principle, but rather by what in economists' jargon is called a satisficing objective function (Scott 1978). In thinking out the possible consequences of this, it has also to be remembered that whether or not a piece of cane land is marginal depends not only on such things as soil and rainfall but also on the system of production employed.

Secondly, in an industry characterized by high overheads, the effect of contraction on the marginal costs and overall economic viability of the industry has to be considered. All too often there has been a failure to recognize the implications of cutting into the critical mass of the sugar industry by successive amputations. Because of the fixed costs (including such items as an adequate level of research and development), production cutbacks increase the unit cost of the remaining output, other things staying equal. With the weather contributing wide fluctuations in yield per acre, the emasculated sugar industry is soon incapable of satisfying even preferential markets. (The latest example is Trinidad's shortfall on its U.S. quota.)

Discussions on the future of the Caribbean sugar industries reflect the broad issues of Caribbean development strategy. That the Caribbean economies are small, open, dependent, and fragmented is well known, as Prime Minister Adams of Barbados reminded the Fifth Annual Conference on Caribbean Trade, Investment and Development held in Miami in December 1982 (*Advocate-News,* 9 and 10 December 1982). It is also well known that in spite of a diversity of resource endowments, they are resource poor in relation to their populations (with limited arable acreage, for example), competitive rather than complementary, historically inclined to overdependence on a single sector, and beset by high rates of unemployment, even in periods of rapid growth. Hence the long-term objective of Caribbean development is the restructuring of the economies, while the immediate problem is to cope with the inevitable need for imports and to service an already burdensome debt.

Looking at the pros and cons of an export-led versus an import-substitution strategy of development for the Caribbean economies, Mr. Adams argued that this dichotomy is as ill founded as other development dichotomies that have been fashionable from time to time (e.g., growth versus social equity or private sector versus government ownership). Of course, opportunities for import substitution should be exploited to the benefit of the development process. But to rely on import substitution as a long-term solution to the problem of economic restructuring when the rest of the world is becoming more integrated and dependent on trade is to swim against the tide. As far as the problems of import capacity and debt servicing are concerned, no amount of import substitution can by itself provide an adequate answer. Unless commitments to continued growth and improvement of the standard of living are to be abandoned, the Caribbean countries must import. In order to import, they have to export, and in view of the limits of even an integrated Caribbean market, this means exports to markets outside the region.

Traditional export agriculture continues to play an important role in Caribbean economies. As Mr. Adams pointed out, the receipts from exports of traditional agricultural products represent an important source of foreign exchange (a point that will be confirmed by a glance at Table 5), not only in absolute terms, but also in terms of the relatively high value added of such activities. Abandonment of traditional export agriculture raises the problem of the alternative use of the factors of production (especially land and labor) now employed in the sector. Moreover, it would in almost all cases adversely affect the viability of other agricultural activities (another point confirmed by experience, as we have seen).

It is perhaps partly due to the ideological taint attached to sugar that it is not credited with the same potential to contribute to economic development as, say, the traditional agricultural exports of New Zealand. Another reason could be a lack of confidence that developed countries will provide the necessary outlets by not favoring their own sugar industries. Be that as it may, no other Caribbean country continues to rely on sugar to advance its economic development as much as Cuba, which has had considerable success in developing linkages that are both backward (manufacture of agricultural machinery and sugar factory equipment) and forward (by-product utilization). It would be odd indeed if history were to record that a centrally planned economy took advantage of the sun to produce food and other essential goods, while market economies were increasingly reduced to using sunshine to tan the skins of tourists.

NOTES

1. This refers only to centrifugal sugar, as defined in the International Sugar Agreement, which means sugar in any of its recognized commercial forms derived from sugar cane or sugar beet, including edible and fancy molasses, syrups, and other forms of liquid sugar used for human consumption, and excluding final molasses, low-grade types of noncentrifugal sugar produced by primitive methods, and sugar destined for uses other than human consumption as food. This is not the place to dispute this definition (Hagelberg 1978). Suffice it to say that inclusion of so-called

noncentrifugal sugars, some of which are in fact centrifugal, would shift the ratio of cane to beet sugar closer to 65 to 35 and would increase the per capita supply by about 10 percent. International sugar statistics are expressed in white value, raw value (raw sugar testing 96 sugar degrees by the polariscope, which for practical purposes is taken to mean a sucrose content of 96 percent on a dry-weight basis; the factor to convert white value to raw value is 1.087), or *tel quel* (as it comes). Quantities are expressed in tonnes (metric ton = 1,000 kilograms = 1.1023 short ton = 0.9842 long ton = 2,204.6 pounds), long tons (2,240 pounds), short tons (2,000 pounds), and pounds (453.6 grams). Pertinent area measures are the acre (0.4047 hectare) and the hectare (2.471 acres).

2. I am indebted to Mintz (1985) for suggesting the need to emphasize the properties of sucrose and how they relate to the growth of sugar consumption.

3. The number of sources from which information has been taken for this section would make references tedious. Two major sources were International Sugar Organization 1982 and F. O. Licht 1983a. Some of the material on Barbados comes from McGregor et al. 1979. Recent information on the Cuban sugar industry was found in Torralbas González 1983, David 1983, Edquist 1982, and Pollitt 1981. Scott 1978 was a source for the Dominican Republic, and U.S. Department of Agriculture 1979– was consulted on Puerto Rico. The risk of errors in compiling details of this kind is high, and I can only hope that there are not too many.

4. An attorney represents the interests of the owners and controls the expenditures. Under him there is a manager responsible for the day-to-day running of the estate. An attorney is likely to have charge of more than one estate. In fact, four attorneys controlled 34 estates with a total of 16,000 arable acres in Barbados in 1979. When the Jamaican industry was in desperate straits in 1848, Lord John Russell complained in Parliament, "Attorney's cook, attorney's groom, attorney's servant, attorney's washerwoman, attorney's maid, attorney's pigs, picking grass for attorney, besides which there are manager's servants and overseer's servants" (quoted in Deerr 1949–50, 2:356). Although many latter-day attorneys are able agriculturalists and their fees are modest, it is debatable whether such a hierarchical management system is the most appropriate for modern mechanized farming. In any event, here is an example of a particular institution not replicated in many other places, the sort of national circumstance that makes international comparisons so hazardous.

5. Again there are historical roots. Deerr (1949–50, 1:166) noted as a remarkable and unique feature of the Barbados sugar industry that while in its early days the factories were of the then normal size, it did not participate in the movement toward larger factories, the use of steam, and vacuum boiling. It became a colony of self-contained properties and individual proprietors but nevertheless maintained a substantial degree of prosperity. In 1911 there were still 329 sugar-works on the island, of which 220 used windmills and 109 employed steam power, with an average output of 100–150 tonnes of sugar.

6. Otherwise eligible beneficiary countries are excluded if the U.S. import value of a commodity (such as sugar) from a country in the previous year equals or exceeds 50 percent of all U.S. imports of that commodity, or if U.S. imports exceed a specified value that is fixed each year in relation to the U.S. gross national product. This "competitive need" criterion was $53.3 million for 1982. The only Caribbean sugar exporter affected by this limitation in recent years has been the Dominican Republic.

7. U.S. Department of Agriculture (1979–) provides a running account of U.S. sugar market developments and regulatory actions.

8. Sugar production in the French overseas departments of Guadeloupe and Martinique, like that of metropolitan France, is protected by the Common Agricultural Policy sugar regime.

9. EEC consumption—statistical disappearance would be a better term—was unusually high in 1973/74. A more normal level for the first half of the 1970s would have been about 9.7 million tonnes. The decline is therefore somewhat overstated.

10. As an official report (Monopolies and Mergers Commission 1981:7) recently put it, "as part of the terms of the United Kingdom's entry into the EEC, guarantees were sought to ensure

that a reasonable level of United Kingdom cane refining capacity would remain after entry and that those developing countries whose economies depended on sugar cane [*sic*] exports had right of access to the Community market on reasonable terms."

11. A better base would be the weighted average of prices received from all markets or an estimated equilibrium price. It may be impossible to locate the latter exactly, but one can have a rough idea. As the head of the Economics and Statistics Division of the International Sugar Organization observed recently:

> Much has been written about the equilibrium price of sugar. But if it is accepted that the supply of sugar runs ahead of demand except for the temporary shortages occurring every 5–7 years, it follows that there has never been an equilibrium price of sugar in the normally accepted sense of a price which roughly equates the quantity supplied with the quantity demanded. Either the price is depressed by excess supply or forced too high by competition for "scarce" supplies. We can only speculate, therefore, on the possible level of an equilibrium price for sugar, knowing only that it is not below 10 cents per pound or above 35 cents per pound. My guess is that it is somewhere in the region of 20–25 cents per pound in current dollars. (Hannah 1982)

Hannah noted that the midpoint of the price range of the 1977 International Sugar Agreement, adjusted for inflation by the International Monetary Fund world consumer price index, was 27 cents per pound.

12. Cane sugar producers missed a chance when they failed to call their product something like NutraSweet, the trade name given by a United States drug manufacturer to the protein-derived aspartame, a new competitor for saccharin 200 times as sweet as sucrose and hardly nutritive in the concentrations used. They could reasonably claim that the name fits sucrose better.

13. "The misery of being exploited by capitalists is nothing compared to the misery of not being exploited at all" (Robinson 1964:46).

14. This is after all one of the ways in which the sugar industry has contributed to economic development throughout its history. In the seventeenth and eighteenth centuries, it was not only the trade in sugar that was of value; the cycle of trade that developed out of the sugar industry was of greater value still. Ships left England for West Africa with trade goods that were bartered for slaves as well as gold, ivory, and pepper. The slaves were in turn exchanged in the West Indies for sugar, which with molasses and rum formed the homeward freight. The same cycle appeared in the New England economies, with the sugar and slave trade even more closely linked. The route was outward bound with rum to the slave coast, transatlantic with a human cargo to the West Indies, and then homeward bound with molasses to make more rum. The planters and the sugar industry did not have the greatest share of the profits in this triangular business, though they formed its cornerstone and bore the risk of drought, hurricanes, pests, and diseases (Deerr 1949–50, 2:290–91).

REFERENCES

BALLINGER, ROY A.

1971 *A History of Sugar Marketing*. Agricultural Economic Report No. 197. Washington, D.C.: U.S. Department of Agriculture, Economic Research Service.

BANCO NACIONAL DE CUBA
1982 *Economic Report.* .

BARTENS / MOSOLFF
1977/78– *Zuckerwirtschaftliches Taschenbuch.* Berlin-Nikolassee: Verlag Dr. Albert Bartens.

BLACKMAN, COURTNEY N.
1979 *The Balance of Payments in the Caribbean: Which Way Out?* interdisciplinary seminar, University of the West Indies, Cave Hill, Barbados.
1980 "Ideology and the New World economists." Speech at Chancellor Hall, University of the West Indies, Mona, Jamaica, 14 March 1980. *Reprinted in* Courtney N. Blackman, *The Practice of Persuasion,* pp. 1–8. Bridgetown: Cedar Press, 1982.

CALVIN, MELVIN
1974 "Solar Energy by Photosynthesis." *Science* 184, 4134:375–81.

DAVID, EDUARDO
1983 "Sugar Production in Cuba." *Sugar y Azúcar* 78, 2:100–108.

DEERR, NOEL
1949–50 *The History of Sugar,* 2 vols. London: Chapman & Hall.

EDQUIST, CHARLES
1982 *Technical Change in Sugar Cane Harvesting: A Comparison of Cuba and Jamaica, 1958–1980.* World Employment Programme Research Working Papers, Technology and Employment Programme, WEP 2–22/WP.96. Geneva: International Labour Office.

FERMOR, PATRICK LEIGH
1950 *The Traveller's Tree: A Journey through the Caribbean Islands.* London: John Murray.

F. O. LICHT
1980– *Sugar Supply and Distribution Statistics.* Ratzeburg: F. O. Licht.
1983a "New Processing Capacities in the World Sweetener Industry." Part 2: Sucrose. *F. O. Licht's International Sugar Report.*
1983b "World Sugar Balances." *F. O. Licht's International Sugar Report.*

FOOD AND AGRICULTURE ORGANIZATION
1971– *Production Yearbook.* Rome: Food & Agriculture Organization.
1981 *Trade Yearbook.* Rome: Food & Agriculture Organization. .

HAGELBERG, G. B.
1974 *The Caribbean Sugar Industries: Constraints and Opportunities.* New Haven, Conn.: Yale University, Antilles Research Program.
1978 "The Statistical Treatment of Artisan Sugars." *Zuckerindustrie* 103:140–43.
1979a "Cuba's Sugar Policy." *In* Martin Weinstein (ed.), *Revolutionary Cuba in the World Arena,* pp. 31–50. Philadelphia: Institute for the Study of Human Issues.

1979b "Sugar and the Cuban economy." *In* Helmut Ahlfeld (ed.), *F. O. Licht's International Sugar Economic Year Book and Directory,* pp. E5–E9. Ratzeburg: F. O. Licht.

HANNAH, A. C.

1982 "Imbalance in the World Sugar Economy: Some Ideas about Causes and Remedies in the Context of a New International Sugar Agreement." *F. O. Licht's International Sugar Report* 114:581–89.

HARRIS, SIMON

1973 "British Sugar Market in an International Context." *In* Simon Harris and Ian Smith, *World Sugar Markets in a State of Flux.* London: Trade Policy Research Centre.

1981 *Recent Trends in Protectionism in the World Sugar Market.* Group of Latin American and Caribbean Sugar Exporting Countries (GEPLACEA) Secretariat Market Report No. 94.

HARRIS, SIMON, AND G. B. HAGELBERG

1975 "Effects of the Lomé Convention on the World's Cane Sugar Producers." *ODI Review* 2–1975: 38–52.

HOUSE OF LORDS

1977 *Select Committee on Commodity Prices. Vol. 1: Report of the Committee.* London: Her Majesty's Stationery Office.

INTERNATIONAL SUGAR COUNCIL

1963 *The World Sugar Economy: Structure and Policies. Vol. 1: National Sugar Economies and Policies;* vol. 2: *The World Picture.* London: International Sugar Council.

INTERNATIONAL SUGAR COUNCIL / ORGANIZATION

1963– *Sugar Yearbook.* London: International Sugar Council / Organization.

INTERNATIONAL SUGAR ORGANIZATION

1982 *The World Sugar Economy: Structure and Policies. Vol. 1: Central and South America.* London: International Sugar Organization.

IRVINE, JAMES E.

1977a "Sugar Cane." *In Meade-Chen Cane Sugar Handbook,* 10th ed., pp. 3–13. New York: John Wiley & Sons.

1977b "Economic Aspects of the Sugar Industry." *In Meade-Chen Cane Sugar Handbook,* 10th ed., pp. 30–39. New York: John Wiley & Sons.

KEIM, CARROLL R.

1979 "Competitive Sweeteners." *In Sugar y Azúcar Yearbook,* vol. 47, pp. 101–20. New York: Palmer Publications.

KOESTER, ULRICH, AND PETER MICHAEL SCHMITZ

1982 "The EC Sugar Market Policy and Developing Countries." *European Review of Agricultural Economics* 9:183–204.

LEHNINGER, ALBERT L.
1975 *Biochemistry,* 2nd ed. New York: Worth Publishers.

LEWIS, W. ARTHUR
1965 "A Review of Economic Development." *American Economic Review, Papers and Proceedings* 55, 2:1–16.

MAHLER, VINCENT A.
1981 "Britain, the European Community, and the Developing Commonwealth: Dependence, Interdependence, and the Political Economy of Sugar." *International Organization* 35:467–92.

MCGREGOR, ANDREW
1978 "The Lomé Convention and the ACP sugar exporters: The political economy of conflicting policies." Ph.D. thesis, Cornell University.

MCGREGOR, ANDREW, S.W.D. BAXTER, G. B. HAGELBERG, AND MALCOLM MCGREGOR
1979 *The Barbados Sugar Industry: Problems and Perspectives.* Report to the Director of Finance and Planning, Government of Barbados..

MINTZ, SIDNEY W.
1985 *Sweetness and Power: The Place of Sugar in Modern History.* New York: Viking Press.

MONOPOLIES & MERGERS COMMISSION
1981 *S & W Berisford Limited and British Sugar Corporation Limited. Report on the Proposed Merger.* London: Her Majesty's Stationery Office.

POLLITT, BRIAN H.
1981 *Revolution and the Mode of Production in the Sugar Cane Sector of the Cuban Economy, 1959–1980: Some Preliminary Findings.* University of Glasgow, Institute of Latin American Studies, Occasional Paper No. 35.

ROBINSON, JOAN
1964 *Economic Philosophy.* Harmondsworth, Middlesex: Penguin Books.

ROMBAUER, IRMA S., AND MARION ROMBAUER BECKER
1980 *Joy of Cooking,* 5th ed. London: J. M. Dent & Sons.

SCOTT, C. D.
1978 *Technology, Employment and Income Distribution in the Sugar Industry of the Dominican Republic.* Regional Employment Programme for Latin America and the Caribbean, PREALC/158. Geneva: International Labour Office.

SHERIDAN, R. B.
1974 *Sugar and Slavery: An Economic History of the British West Indies, 1623–1775.* Bridgetown, Barbados: Caribbean Universities Press.

SIMEY, T. S.
1946 *Welfare and Planning in the West Indies.* Oxford: Clarendon Press.

SMITH, IAN
1976 "Can the West Indies' Sugar Industry Survive?" *Oxford Bulletin of Economics and Statistics* 38:125–40.

SMITH, S. IVAN
1975 "Functional Ecology of Sugar Cane in the American Tropics." *Caribbean Studies* 15, 3:57–77.

TIMOSHENKO, V. P., AND B. C. SWERLING
1957 *The World's Sugar: Progress and Policy.* Stanford, Calif.: Stanford University Press.

TORRALBAS GONZÁLEZ, DIOCLES
1983 "The Development and Prospects for Cuban Sugar Production." *Sugar y Azúcar* 78, 2:95–97.

U.S. DEPARTMENT OF AGRICULTURE
1975 *Sugar Statistics and Related Data Compiled in the Administration of the U.S. Sugar Acts.* Vol. 1 (revised). Statistical Bulletin No. 293. Washington, D.C.: U.S. Department of Agriculture, Agricultural Stabilization and Conservation Service.
1979– *Sugar and Sweetener Outlook and Situation* (supersedes *Sugar and Sweetener Report*). Washington, D.C.: U.S. Department of Agriculture.

WILLIAMS, ERIC
1944 "The Economic Development of the Caribbean up to the Present." *In* E. Franklin Frazier and Eric Williams (eds.), *The Economic Future of the Caribbean.* pp. 19–24. Washington, D.C.: Howard University Press.

·4·

From Plantations to Peasantries in the Caribbean

SIDNEY W. MINTZ

THE BACKGROUND TO PEASANT FORMATION

Because it has been a history without royalty, without a feudal past, and without the dissolution of older empires into new sorts of states, the history of the Americas since Columbus has been different from that of most other large world areas. The aboriginal peoples of the hemisphere (some of whom *did* have royalty, and even empires) were destroyed by war and disease or were increasingly confined within narrow areas chosen by their conquerors. Those who were able to remain relatively unchanged over the centuries could do so only by retreating—into jungles, deserts, or polar wastes. This whole half of the world was violently remade with the coming of the Europeans. Such a radical transformation was perhaps even truer of the Caribbean islands than it was of most other New World regions (such as Mexico and the Andes), where large native populations were at least able to survive, even though dwindling after impact to a fraction of their former numbers.

In the Caribbean region, the Europeans settled early—within a year of Columbus's arrival—and they have stayed there as long as anywhere else in the hemisphere. A good example is Barbados; the English took the island in the 1620s, but independence did not come until the 1960s. As another example, the French *départements* of French Guiana, Martinique, and Guadeloupe have had nearly as long a colonial history, but they are now considered integral parts of France itself, never having been granted independence. Finally, there is the case of Puerto Rico, settled by the Spaniards in the 1500s, which remains to this day a dependent, colonial possession, though of the United States, not of Spain.

But it was not only by coming early and staying long that the Europeans in the Caribbean region made their occupation somewhat different from what it was, say, in the Andes or highland Central America and Mexico. The populations of the islands, though substantial, were unable to withstand the effects of the conquest, and their numbers were reduced at horrifying rates by disease, war, and maltreatment. Whereas the peoples of the Andes and of Mesoamerica are at last reaching again their probable numbers at the time of conquest, those of the Caribbean islands were either absorbed genetically by settler populations or else completely annihilated. Only one group of island aboriginal people preserving in any degree the cultural forms of their ancestors may be said to survive—the so-called Island Carib of Dominica. In this way, too, the European presence came to dominate more fully than in most other portions of the hemisphere.

In sum, the Caribbean islands and certain parts of the surrounding mainland, such as the Guianas, have been subject to longer, more persistent, and more complete European influence (and often, rule) than nearly any other part of the New World. Even so, that influence has not always taken the form of majority European settlement. Indeed, it is striking that in much of the hemisphere on the Atlantic side of the continents, and from Brazil to the U.S. South, European power was exercised over centuries through the importation of non-European peoples—Asians, Native Americans from Central America, and Africans, but principally Africans—rather than through the settlement of Europeans in order to carry out European projects of development and change.

Such projects took many forms: mining, agriculture, commerce, and even manufacture. But for that same region most typified by the importation of Africans rather than peoples from elsewhere, the major undertaking was agriculture, and it had a particular and characteristic form: the so-called plantation system. Though it changed greatly over the centuries, from about the middle of the sixteenth century until nearly the end of the nineteenth the plantation system had several characteristics that typified it.

1. It was based on large estates, mostly acquired by mere occupation (or the forcible ejection and destruction of native populations).

2. The estates produced single items—such as tobacco, cotton, indigo for dyes, or sugar—to be sent, usually in some partly finished form, to the European countries that ruled the Caribbean, for consumption overseas.

3. The labor for the estates was almost all forced labor, and principally enslaved labor. Though some forced (and indentured or contracted) laborers at certain periods and in certain circumstances came from Europe, Asia, or elsewhere, nearly all of those who were enslaved came from Africa or were the descendants of Africans—so-called Creole (New World–born) people of Old World origins.

Beyond these features, the colonial societies in which the plantation system flourished were also typified by certain traits connected to (and to some degree, at least, determined by) the plantation system. Though somewhat more variable than the diagnostic features of the plantation itself, these characteristics have had an even longer-term effect on the economic, political, and cultural development of the Caribbean societies themselves.

1. The division into a small group of European leaders and masters on the one hand and a large group of mainly non-European forced laborers on the other produced a deeply divided social structure in each colony, only partly leavened over time by the growth of intermediate social groupings and, eventually, by the decline of slavery itself.
2. The domination of the plantation system left little or no room for the growth of alternative economic activities, or for the rise of substantial middle classes.
3. The colonial system, which traditionally limited trade and commerce to the colony and its "mother country," produced a narrow range of interests among the rulers of the colony, largely confined to their economic stakes in a system that had little long-term capacity for growth or improvement.
4. The political and cultural life of each such society was constrained by slavery, which prevented any kind of democratic participation and was, moreover, constantly threatened by the possibility of revolt and revolution.

Though these were generalized features of Caribbean societies over the course of several centuries, they did not typify all of the islands and the colonies on their surrounding shores during this entire lengthy period. For a variety of reasons, having to do in part with local environmental conditions (soil fertility, rainfall, topography, etc.) and in part with the struggle of the Europeans for political control over the region, the various Caribbean colonies did not develop in exactly the same way or at the same pace.

Moreover, certain parts of the region were ill fitted to plantation development and remained peripheral to the "big push" by which, from the early sixteenth century until the late nineteenth, island after island was launched successively upon a plantation career. Because of this uneven development, the role of slavery and forced labor in local economic life varied greatly from one island to another, as well as from one time period to another. For instance, the hispanophone (Spanish-speaking) Caribbean societies, which remained under Spain's control from the conquest until the nineteenth century—Puerto Rico (1898), Cuba (1898) and Santo Domingo (1844)—were the earliest Caribbean slave plantation sugar colonies, but their momentum withered before the end of the sixteenth century, largely because of lack of encouragement from Spain itself. A colonial backwater for nearly two centuries, these possessions entered again into the plantation picture only toward the very end of the eighteenth century. Hence their economic, social, political, and demographic development over time was radically different from that of the French, Dutch, British and other sugar colonies, and their character as societies was also noticeably different.

After the end of slavery—by revolution in French Saint-Domingue in 1804; and by law, in the respective colonies, in 1833 (Britain), 1848 (France and Denmark), 1863 (Netherlands), 1873 (Puerto Rico), and 1886 (Cuba)—the problem of the plantation economies became, even more than ever before, one of labor supply. To a large extent, this problem was solved by the importation of contracted labor from Africa, Outer Asia, India, and even southern Europe, and by the gradual modernization of plantation production. The planters themselves were caught between two millstones, one political and the other technical. On the one hand, they needed to obtain labor—labor willing to work at derisory wages under terrible conditions and without genuine political rights—at a time when a trend toward permitting greater social justice in the colonies was growing in the mother countries. On the other, if they could not get labor, the planters needed to modernize (by mechanizing) their industries, which meant obtaining substantial capital loans during a period when such capital for investment in tropical colonies was not easily gotten.

Even though there would come about a vast reexpansion of plantation production in the closing decades of the nineteenth century, there was already visible on the horizon a somewhat different future for the Caribbean colonies. This was portended by the development of plantation production elsewhere in the world; by the continuing strength of beet sugar production in temperate climes after the middle of the century; by the beginning development of sweetener substitutes; and by the gradual decline of interest among the European powers in their Caribbean colonies. What the Caribbean future would be was by no means clear; but as early as the second or third decade of this century—and even while plantation production was still on the upswing in many places—it was becoming more and more apparent that the region could not subsist forever by serving as the sugar bowl, tobacco pouch, coffee shop, and rum supplier of the world. It is in the context of this kind of past, of a present that is increasingly difficult and contradictory, and of a future that still remains shrouded in uncertainties, that the story of the Caribbean peasantries must be told.

WHAT IS MEANT BY "CARIBBEAN PEASANTRY"

The words *peasant* and *peasantry* ring strangely in American ears. The United States has had farmers, plantation laborers, migrant fruit pickers, stoop laborers, sharecroppers, slaves, squatters, and "Okies" in its history, but it never had any peasants. The word is one we connect particularly with Europe and other Old World areas, where primarily agrarian societies, ruled from the center and with a strong hand, rested on the backs of vast numbers of small-scale cultivators, who were engaged principally in the production of some basic complex carbohydrate (wheat, millet, rice, buckwheat, barley, etc.), who were usually organized socially and religiously through some local village structure, and who traditionally used mostly family labor to wring their livelihood from the soil. Our sense of it is that such communities of cultivators, producing most of their food by their own families' labor, were, if not self-sufficient, at least capable of obtaining nearly everything that they needed by exchange; and that most of their economic activities were bound up with people like themselves, forming a vast "horizontal" network of village communities, spreading more or less continuously across the countryside. This kind of collectivistic image is what is likely to come to our minds if we think about China, say, or India—or, for that matter, of Japan, Viet Nam, or even the Soviet Union. In other words, we can imagine such structures largely without reference to the overarching political systems within which such local, rural agrarian systems function; and to a large extent, our imaginings are not too wrong. It does not matter for the moment, perhaps, in what ways they *are* wrong. More important is the question, Can we think similarly when we consider the Caribbean region?

Even a moment's reflection, taking into account what has been said about the Caribbean past (the importance of slavery and forced labor, and the part played by European conquest and the plantation system) will probably suggest that Caribbean peasantries, if they exist at all, must be very different from those elsewhere. In fact, there are peasants, and the part they play in Caribbean life is important. But they are, indeed, very different from most of the world's peasantries, for reasons that are not difficult to pin down. The fact is that Caribbean peasantries, practically without exception, have always grown in the crevices of their societies—before slavery, or after slavery, or in places where the plantations failed, or in places where the plantation never came. Such crevices have been both historical and ecological: *time periods* when European control faltered or was relaxed, when the political future was clouded, or when runaways and squatters were able to establish themselves "outside"; *geographical spaces* where the plantation could not work because of soil or slope or aridity or distance from the sea or some other such reason. Even where and when plantation and peasantry flourished together, they usually seemed to remain locked in some odd struggle with each other, at once interdependent (as when peasants both farmed their own plots and sold their labor during the cane harvests) yet in conflict (as when the plantation sought to acquire peasant landholdings for its own use by seizure, legal maneuver, or the use of governmental pressure).

Like blades of grass pushing up between the bricks, the peasants of the Caribbean have been embattled since their beginnings; and in the historical record one can easily find embryonic peasantries that were snuffed out before they could establish themselves firmly. Traditionally, any kind of agricultural or infrastructural improvement—in roadways, marketing facilities, agricultural extension and credit, crop varieties, etc.—went to the plantation sector rather than the peasant sector. But these embattled cultivators, like those blades of grass, have also been tougher. Perhaps the most unusual thing about Caribbean peasantries is that any of them survived at all; but so they have.

One way to look at Caribbean peasantries would be to try to classify them, and it would be possible to enumerate as many as a dozen "types." This might be done historically, according to the ways in which they came into existence, for example. In the fledgling colony of Barbados, to take one case, the first cultivation by European settlers, at first completely without any slave labor, was carried out on small farms. Though these farmers grew a variety of crops, the principal item soon came to be tobacco, then enjoying its first vogue in England. This flourishing colonial horticulture could be properly described as a peasant development. The farms were small enough to be cultivated without hired labor, for the most part; usually, families worked the land. Though a large part of subsistence was produced, the cash crop was tobacco, for export; this peasantry, like all peasantries, had to produce a saleable commodity to get the cash needed to buy those goods they could not make for themselves or obtain locally.

But within a couple of decades the plantation system, linked to the cultivation of sugar cane instead of tobacco, and stimulated by foreign (Dutch) know-how, capital, and encouragement, began to grow. In no time at all, the Barbadian peasant farms were swallowed up by the plantation system, producing sugar cane and making sugar in small grinding mills and boiling houses, using ever larger quantities of slave labor and land. This early peasantry was soon driven out as the plantations bought up the land; there was no way for independent small-scale peasants to compete with the plantations, or to sell their labor to the planters. All that remains of these very early peasants today, more than three centuries later, are the so-called redlegs of Barbados, a handful of impoverished rural folk of European ancestry.

Another quite different example of an early peasantry is provided by the runaway slave communities that grew up in nearly every slaveholding colony in the Americas south of the United States. Good historical cases are known for Jamaica, Spanish Santo Domingo, Suriname, and Brazil among many others. In each case, the runaways (maroons) were primarily agricultural. But in no case were these people able to produce everything they needed, such as iron tools, guns and powder, or cloth. Hence circuits of trade, often illicit, inevitably grew up between the maroon communities and the outside world. Again it is defensible to call these folk peasants, though they fall outside most conventional definitions of the peasantry (among other things, since they lay outside the political control of the state). One may ask, confronted with this example, why people who had escaped from the system in the first place would still feel the need to obtain items such as cloth and iron, at some risk to their freedom and independence, instead of seeking to develop usable substitutes. In the solution to that puzzle there lies an important aspect of the peasant adaptation everywhere: the solidification of the conventional consumption patterns that make up cultural norms in any society.

All Caribbean peoples, the slaves included, were newcomers from other regions whose ways of life were completely remade in the new settings. Though enslaved Africans were often cruelly treated in the Caribbean, they too adapted to the harsh new conditions, acquiring new knowledge and new tastes. Whether freedom came by escape (as in Suriname), by revolution (as in Haiti), or by emancipation (as in most of the Caribbean), the free people had meanwhile developed notions of the good and proper in consumption and were not ready to forgo those notions easily. Hence it is not really mysterious that the maroons (descendants of runaway slaves, who inhabit interior Suriname) to this day value outside goods and either sell some items to get the cash they need, or migrate to sell their labor, thereafter returning to their natal villages.

A final and perhaps most important example, since it applies to so many Caribbean peoples today, has to do with those many cases in which the slaves were enabled, by a combination of coercion and inducement on the part of the masters, to produce some major part of their own subsistence, growing it on land supplied by the plantations but not in those areas where the main plantation crops were produced. In many of these societies slaves were given time off from plantation labor to produce foodstuffs; in many instances, they soon were able to carry their surpluses to local markets, and to use the profits of their effort to buy their selection of luxuries—in some rare cases, even to amass enough wealth to buy their own freedom. These people, too, deserve the name *peasant*, though elsewhere I have argued for calling them a proto-peasantry (since they were still enslaved).

THE SOCIAL AND CULTURAL IMPORTANCE OF CARIBBEAN PEASANTRIES

To this list could be added still other categories. But the point should be clear already. In both the past and the present, the Caribbean is typified by peasantries, though they are very different in character from the peasantries of other world areas. These differences inhere in many conditioning regional factors: the historical importance of slavery and the plantation; the complete population replacement represented by European conquest; the lack of traditional village, or religious, or kinship structures; and lengthy colonial control. To a substantial extent, such factors obstructed or slowed the emergence of Caribbean peasantries or limited their spread. But it is vital, in assessing the character and importance of Caribbean peasants, to notice that they did come into being, and that they have survived, in spite of such difficulties. Often characterized as backward, dormant, or dead (in assessments reminiscent of the news story of Mark Twain's death, which he described as "vastly exaggerated"), Caribbean peasants have survived even the condolences of their supposed friends.

Because of the overpowering importance of the plantation system through time, friends of the plantation (and even some of its enemies) have underestimated the role of the peasantries in Caribbean life. By stressing one kind of economics over politics and culture, they have been prone to describe the peasantry as no more than a castoff social product of the plantation, rather than as an adaptation in its own right. That this view has little to recommend it can be demonstrated by describing two peasant types that, while they might be called products of the plantation, nonetheless show the creative and resistant character of the peasant adaptation.

The first such peasant type is the proto-peasantry, to which I have already referred. It arose in plantation societies from Brazil to the U.S. South; Jamaica is a particularly well-documented case. Long before the end of the period of apprenticeship (1838), Jamaican slaves were producing not only most of their own subsistence but also an astoundingly large surplus of foods, the bigger part of which ended up on the tables of free people, including the planters themselves. In effect, what had begun as a technique for saving the planters the costs of supplying their slaves with food had then become an essential basis for the food supply of the nonslave population. Were it not such a deplorable comment on slavery itself, it would be funny to realize that the British garrisons maintained in Jamaica before emancipation "to keep order" were almost entirely provisioned by the slaves, working on their own time. One writer, an enthusiastic supporter of slavery at that, concluded that perhaps as much as 20 percent of the metallic currency in Jamaica at the end of the eighteenth century was in the hands of the slaves. Not only had the production of foodstuffs on plantation land allocated to the slaves become a major feature of Jamaican life, but the free population was also now dependent upon it—and this in a society where, to all intents and purposes, there were no free agricultural workers of any kind.

This picture was replicated (though with tremendous variation) in societies stretching from the southern United States to Brazil. Such developments are a powerful critical comment on the notions that slaves were enslaved "for their own good," and that work had to be both brutal and simple for slaves to be able to understand it. On the one day per week that slaves were grudgingly given for themselves, their behavior on their little garden plots completely contradicted the planters' insistent claims that "stupid, lazy savages" were incapable of working intelligently for themselves. These, then, were the proto-peasants: enslaved Africans and their descendants, becoming Americans (or better said, perhaps, Afro-Americans) under the lash, yet asserting their own essential humanity, initiative, and intelligence, in the face of every cruel limitation.

The significance of such people for the story of Caribbean peasantries is that, in every society in which this development was permitted, slaves were able to learn much of what they would need to survive in freedom, even while still enslaved. Though the consequences of such learning were not every-where the same, the possibilities embodied in the proto-peasant adaptation were of many sorts. In Haiti, where freedom came by revolution (1791–1804), the postrevolutionary economy was built upon the activities of former slaves whose cultivating skills had been principally learned before freedom. In Jamaica, the peasant economy after emancipation in 1838 involved plants, planting methods, processing, and marketing techniques mastered by the slaves before abolition. It was as slaves that these Caribbean peoples learned to budget their own time, to judge soil quality, to select seed, to cultivate and harvest, to prepare foods for sale, and otherwise to make the proto-peasant sector successful. They managed their family labor, learned to store and conserve seed, saved their earnings, acquired new habits of consumption, raised animals for sale and food—all the while being subjected to the prevailing view that their capacities as individuals were too limited to enable them to survive as free persons.

The second such type of peasantry, very different in character but also developed in the face of both negative opinion and difficult circumstances, belongs with the postslavery periods, when newly imported laborers were brought to the region by the planters, exploiting contract arrangements that were deeply prejudicial to the laborers' own interests. Among these contracted laborers were half a million Indians, brought principally to the British West Indian possessions, but also imported to the Dutch and French Caribbean. One such migrant group consisted of some 239,000 Indians who reached the colony of British Guiana between 1838 and 1917. These people were imported to work on the sugar cane plantations, and most did. But even as plantation laborers, many of the newcomers were able to develop a peasantlike adaptation of considerable economic and political importance, based on small-scale rice cultivation. This innovation was achieved in spite of great obstacles; it is worth noting that it probably improved, rather than hurt, the productivity of the sugar cane plantation sector. In 1962, more than 28,000 tons of rice they grew themselves was exported by the peasants of Guyana (former British Guiana) to Cuba; not only did this activity greatly benefit the trade balance of the nation, but it also implies that great quantities of rice were consumed locally, further benefiting the economy.

These examples by no means exhaust the variety of peasant adaptations, but they do suggest their importance. Nor should it be thought that it is only as economic adaptations that peasant patterns matter, for these forms give free rein to the abilities of the individual in ways that plantation labor does not. They require more self-reliance and more planning and call for more individual responsibility than does plantation wage labor. Not surprisingly, peasantries also evince somewhat different political attitudes from rural proletarians, doubtless because access to land and family budgeting balanced against family resources are a vital feature of the peasant mode of livelihood. Where people both carry on independent cultivation on small holdings and sell their labor to the plantations, as is common in Caribbean life, their political perspective is likely to be influenced by both commitments, sometimes making them seem more peasantlike and other times more proletarian in their values, aspirations, and preferences.

The peasant adaptation, as we have seen, never grew naturally from the Amerindian past of the region. The early destruction of local populations and the swift replacement of local ways of life with European transplants prevented such continuities. And yet a good deal of the aboriginal cultural past was perpetuated in the Caribbean, particularly within peasant forms of adjustment. Slash-and-burn horticulture, hearkening back to Amerindian traditions (and perhaps influenced by other traditions as well), survived on some islands until the relatively recent past. The crop repertory of contemporary Caribbean peasants includes a large number of items derived from the Amerindian past, including such well-known foods as Indian corn, cassava, sweet potatoes, a local variety of squash (*Sechium edule*), the so-called hot pepper, numerous beans, and many fruits. After the conquest, aboriginal foods from the American mainland were added, including the true potato (*Solanum tuberosum*), the tomato, the peanut, the papaya, cacao, and the avocado. The Europeans brought many of the so-called fresh or green vegetables, such as onions, leeks, carrots, cabbages, asparagus, and artichokes, that flourished in the islands. From Oceania there came taro, breadfruit (carried to Jamaica by the infamous Captain Bligh on his second, successful voyage), and mangoes; from Africa, there came watermelon, millet, okra, ackee, bananas, and plantains. Spices, which burgeoned marvelously in the islands, came from India and Indonesia; but at least two important spices, allspice (pimento) and annatto, were native to the Caribbean. The New World root food called arrowroot spread from one Caribbean island to the others after the conquest; Old World spices, such as nutmeg (with its vivid scarlet covering, mace), did so well in the Caribbean that their production shifted largely from the Old World to the New. Though corn (maize) and millet were both popular with Caribbean slaves, rice gradually won out as the favorite island carbohydrate. Beans were transformed into a sauce base in nearly all of the islands; and hot peppers became important in some (though not all) island cuisines (e.g., that of Trinidad).

In short, the Caribbean was an arena for the encounter of different foods, as it was for the encounter of different peoples; over time, new cuisines emerged, now typically Caribbean, though wearing older pedigrees. In food, as in all else, the islands took on their distinctive individual character—part African, part Asian, part Amerindian, part European. Though it may all seem quite remote from the emergence of peasant adaptations, this matter of crops, tastes, dishes, and cuisines is intimately tied to the growth of peasantries. In this world area, cuisine was not so much a matter of the food of the elite classes percolating downward, but rather of the choicest plates of the poor becoming the quaint and colorful fare of the privileged. Much as happened with other aspects of culture in this region, "refinement" began with imitation, more than with innovation, at the top. The role of slave cooks in creating fine cuisine was as important in the Caribbean as in Brazil and the U.S. South. The planters' main contribution was their appetite.

In good measure, of course, what was favored as food was linked to what could be caught, grown, processed, and preserved in the islands. Such delicacies as turtle steak and land crab, the great conch (*Strombus gigas* L.) and the flesh of the sea cow, or manatee, were gradually given status as preferred foods. Such local cultivated plant foods as ackee and okra (which came from Africa), the native Caribbean squash, *Sechium edule* (called by many different names on different islands), the Caribbean species of *Amaranthus* (the *calalu* or *calalou* of the British and French Caribbean—though there are edible amaranths nearly everywhere in the world), the odd little pubescent herb *Calathea allouia* (called *llerén* in Puerto Rico, and *topinambour*, *topitambour*, or *pititambou* in the Lesser Antilles), and many other unusual items were combined with such unlikely ingredients as dried salted codfish, corned beef, and herrings in the gradual evolution of distinctive island cuisines and tastes. Peasantries figured importantly as the producers and gatherers of "native" foods now essential to local preparations; to a large extent, it was in peasant homes that such food preferences and taste patterns were shaped and stabilized. In the processing of manioc flour and the pepper-pot base (cassareep) made from the boiled residue, the extraction of color flavor from the saffron substitute annatto (also called *achiote* or *roucou*, and once used by local Indians to paint themselves), the grinding of cornmeal for *akasan* or *funche*, the mashing of bananas and plantains to make *fufu* or *pasteles* and other cakes or fritters (which are then wrapped, steamed, boiled or deepfried), Caribbean peasantries were both perpetuating older traditions and creating new ones.

But it was probably in their role in maintaining social and economic stability in the large, nonplantation rural areas that peasantries have been most important in Caribbean history. In societies such as Santo Domingo, Haiti, Jamaica, Puerto Rico, and Cuba, small-scale local cultivators produced items both for sale and for subsistence, using their own family labor to eke out their livelihoods, and selling their own labor locally or abroad when necessary. These peasants obtained much of the cash they needed by preparing and selling for export a few particular items (such as coffee, tobacco, or even sugar cane, but often including such seemingly improbable items as fustic, logwood, shrub, goats' horns, goatskins, essential oil grasses, bitter-orange peels, and pimento). They were the real backbone of rural life, even if the plantations were conveniently viewed by most local leaders as the real source of great wealth and favored by them economically and politically. Peasant adaptations helped to sustain families that could not have survived on plantation wages alone. They provided stability and order to family life and to the round of the seasons and the years. And even when large numbers of local people (principally males) had to migrate to seek more money, work patterns at home were traditionally maintained, awaiting their return.

It is in this regard that the last half century has witnessed a radical change in the nature of Caribbean societies and in the fate and status of their peasantries. The vast upswing in migration, particularly during the last decade but prefigured by the movement of Puerto Rican citizens from their island home to the metropolises of the North American mainland and of Jamaicans and other British West Indians to London and the port cities of the United Kingdom, has been based upon contracting economic opportunities at home, the sharp decline in the relative cost of air travel, and the growth of job opportunities for unskilled labor in the metropolitan cities.

These changes have been paralleled by the movements of south European, North American, and Middle Eastern migrants from their homelands to Western Europe. Yet they are different in certain regards. For the United States, Caribbean migrants represent the first substantial movements of nonwhite peoples to this country since the end of the slave trade. They are proportionally more important for their countries of origin as well, since these are small countries, and the migrations are relatively massive. But doubtless most important of all is the fact that the migrants are moving out of homeland situations to which they are less and less likely to return, particularly since they are now more inclined to move their families with them, or soon after their settlement. Thus the older pattern, anchoring the cultural continuity in those who maintained the peasant adaptation at home, is crumbling. It is doing so, among other things, because of the continuous deterioration of the peasant position—economic, social, political—in the homeland. We will need to return to that deterioration presently.

PROBLEMS OF THE PRESENT

We have seen how Caribbean peasantries appeared and sometimes flourished, particularly when they successfully replaced earlier economic adaptations based upon large-estate agriculture. Because almost all areas of the Caribbean region were developed in terms of the economic objectives of outsiders, agriculture devoted to satisfying local subsistence needs never took precedence over export-oriented production. But in any case, a subsistence agriculture aimed only at subsistence or self-sufficiency would never have been able to provide the foreign exchange any modern society requires. For this reason, even in instances where a reconstituted peasantry did successfully supplant plantation agriculture, as in the case of Haiti, for instance, small-scale cultivators were soon producing large quantities of exportable items. It was this production that brought them the cash income to satisfy their own culturally defined needs, meanwhile enriching exporters, commission merchants, importers, and the state itself.

Hence the notion that peasants are self-sufficient producers who either provide for all of their own needs locally, or exist independent of the state apparatus, is misleading. Only on the rarest occasions have Caribbean local agricultural producers been able to escape entirely from the control of the state, as in eighteenth-century highland Puerto Rico. The price for such independence was always near complete isolation from sources of needed materials (such as iron tools or cloth) or services (such as medical care or schools)—an isolation that peasantries can ill afford and none really desire.

The Caribbean peasantries that evolved during the nineteenth century, then, did not consist of people aiming to cut themselves off economically from the outside world, but rather of people who intended to be a free and active part of it. Through possession of land they hoped to escape from the stigma of slavery and from the drudgery of plantation wage labor on the land of others. But because of a combination of factors—official favoritism toward the plantations, limited technical and financial assistance through extension (such as credit, tools, and seed), regressive taxation, and inability to influence agricultural developments elsewhere—Caribbean peasantries have usually been unable to become independent of the local plantation economy or of the commercial and financial sectors outside the plantation system. More serious, those segments of the peasantry that can subsist without selling their own or their families' labor off the farm have always been tiny minorities in Caribbean history.

In these societies, where the overwhelming majority of the population is agrarian and where agriculture is the biggest foreign exchange earner, most of that agriculture is likely to be plantation based. In the exceptional cases where peasant production is of equal (or greater) importance, only a modest minority of peasant families are likely to live entirely from the income of their own agricultural property. The point is that no peasant society is economically homogeneous. In any peasant society, the poorest relatives of the poorest peasants probably own no land at all, often work for their richer relatives, and may sell their labor to the estates or the state as well. They are, in short, rural proletarians, even though their proletarian status may be concealed by the familial networks within which they carry on much of their work for wages. In contrast, the richest peasants own more land than they can work by themselves with the help of their families; hence they hire labor for wages, and they probably also engage in other, nonagricultural pursuits (such as money-lending, renting out processing machinery, or buying crops on commission).

SIDNEY W. MINTZ

In none of these ways are Caribbean peasantries unique or even very unusual; but the patterns of differentiation within peasant classes have been worked out in characteristically Caribbean ways—as, for instance, in the link between seasonal plantation labor and the maintenance of peasant holdings.

Today, Caribbean peasantries usually produce more than one item for sale; but the market for their products is likely to be divided. Such peasants typically concentrate their productivity on one major crop, to which the others are supplementary. The list of such crops is a long one, however: in Jamaica, bananas, citrus, pimento, and a small quantity of coffee; in Haiti, coffee, sisal, and essential oil plants; in Guyana and Suriname, rice; in the Dominican Republic, coffee and bananas; in Trinidad, cacao; in Grenada, nutmeg, mace, and bananas; and so on. In each society with a peasant population, one or two crops become stabilized as peasant products; but the details are usually quite complex, and Caribbean history shows that some crops may be substituted, one for another, with surprising rapidity in some instances.

Though it is not likely that Caribbean peasants base many conscious production decisions on careful cost accounting procedures, they have to think in terms of producing items to be sold for export, items for local sale, and items for their families' consumption. The items themselves need not be entirely different, of course; Haitian peasants eat the bananas and drink the coffee and cacao that they also cultivate for export. (Typically, the quality of the crops consumed is inferior to the quality of those sold; but they are often the same crops.) In most cases, the exported items have substantial foreign markets, as in the case of bananas, coffee, and cacao. Some are highly specialized, as in the case of arrowroot starch, pimento (allspice), nutmegs, and mace, or essential oils (for perfumes). Yet items produced for local markets generally overlap heavily with peasant foodstuffs: tubers and rhizomes such as sweet potatoes, yams, "sweet" cassava, taro; fresh vegetables, such as carrots, salad greens, and scallions; fruits; and poultry and dairy products. Most Caribbean peasants prefer to sell locally, if they can, the more costly and delicate items they cultivate (eggs, the best poultry, tomatoes, the sweetest fruit), rather than to consume them, in order to buy coarser and cheaper foodstuffs, or items deemed more desirable than food, with the proceeds. Thus the best products of the countryside tend to flow either to the wealthier urban classes, to the tourist hotels, or abroad, while the cheap bulk items tend to remain in the countryside. Often, deluxe local products (such as Jamaican Blue Mountain coffee) are sold as exports, while their producers consume cheaper imports (such as instant coffee). Everywhere complex carbohydrates—potatoes, maize, millet, rice, etc.—form the bulk of the diet; the consumption of protein-rich foods, particularly eggs, meat, and fish, has always been meager.

Caribbean peasants (much like peasantries elsewhere) are accustomed to confine their own consumption in order to stretch their resources, and to work

long, hard hours to protect their property in, or access to, the land. By
working part of the time for wages for others, by selling the labor of family
members, by confining their own consumption, and by working long hours,
peasants may maintain the economic viability of patterns otherwise in decline.
But even the restriction of consumption and the increased output of their own
labor may not be enough when labor resources are contracting in absolute
terms while population continues to grow. Haiti, the most extreme Caribbean
example, now has a population in excess of five million but began this century
with only slightly more than a million. Under these circumstances, unless
productivity grows at the high rates insured only by capital inputs to technological improvement, or unless outside sources of income are greatly
enlarged, the ability of the peasantry to maintain itself economically is
gravely compromised. One obvious answer for the Caribbean peasantry has
been migration; but this is not, as many people believe, a new answer.
Caribbean people have been emigrating for nearly a century in search of
work, and in some societies, migration long ago became an institutionalized,
cyclical phenomenon, with a large number of each generation of males emigrating in turn. Many of these emigrants returned, however; few migrated
with their spouses or families; and most maintained at least some lifelong
contact with their natal communities. In recent years, these patterns have also
begun to change, with unpredictable long-term consequences.

CARIBBEAN PEASANTRIES: SOME EXAMPLES

Any thorough examination of the position of the peasantry in each Caribbean society would be impractical in an essay of this length. Not only are
there many different societies involved, each with many local variations, but
also the data are not easy to interpret even when obtainable. In size, scale, and
topography, Caribbean societies vary widely. If we include the mainland
portions that belong with the insular Caribbean on economic and historical
grounds, such as Belize and the Guianas, the lands involved range from tiny
insular dots (such as Dutch Saba, with five square miles of area and two
thousand people) to large independent countries (such as Cuba, with 44,000
square miles and perhaps ten million people, and Guyana, with more than
83,000 square miles but less than one million people). Large and small,
densely populated and sparsely populated, jungle and mountain—the physical
contexts for Caribbean peasantries are so varied that even a superficial overview of all fifty or so societies would overflow an introduction of this sort
before it was properly begun. Moreover, because the local situation of the
peasantry is an ongoing series of problems and adjustments, most of the
generalizations one can offer about Caribbean peasants are either obvious or
plagued by exceptions. Even what seems to North Americans to be a relatively simple statistical matter—knowing how much land is farmed, on what

numbers of properties, of what differing sizes—is often very inexactly reported or, as in the case of Haiti, where there has never been a cadastral survey, simply unknown. Not surprisingly, in the absence of solid factual information, opinions vary widely. In the case of Haitian peasant farming, for instance, there are those who argue that nearly all Haitian rural people own or have access to some land, while others lay stress on the degree to which wealthy and powerful coffee producers and middlemen now dominate the land use picture. Under such circumstances, it may be more useful to discuss a few specific cases in detail, in order to give some idea of the variety of adaptations, than to try to provide thorough coverage.

In some Caribbean cases, such as the Dominican Republic or Jamaica, we see substantial countries with considerable variation in land forms, vegetation, rainfall, and soils; peasant adaptations can persist in these countries, even in the face of drastic economic and political changes, and despite the importance of the plantation economy, tourism, and increasing emigration. In smaller societies, such as St. Lucia or Guadeloupe, peasantries are likely to be interdependent with other rural adaptations. The fate of the peasantry is more closely linked to that of other groups, and sweeping changes in the countryside can alter or even undermine the peasant sector. Because each case is in some ways unique, however, it is not possible to look at every one. In St. Vincent and St. Lucia, we have two small-island economies in which peasants played a vital economic role after emancipation, and particularly during the nineteenth century. Today, however, the part played by the peasantry is losing some of its importance, emigration continues to be important, and land has acquired new (and, in terms of the long-term economic future, somewhat questionable) value. In Haiti, the most thoroughgoing peasant society in the region is being transformed, both internally by demographic and ecological forces and externally by emigration, small-scale manufacture, and increasing dependence on food imports. In Cuba, a socialist regime rather unfriendly to private enterprise of all sorts has whittled away at the peasantry over time, even though many landless Cubans benefited greatly at first from the revolution. These four cases, then, while they by no means afford us a sense of the complete range of variability of Caribbean peasant life, can serve to give us some feeling for variant possibilities in the peasant sector. What follows is a necessarily brief sketch of the peasant pattern in each of these four societies.

St. Vincent

In a thoughtful analysis of peasant farming in a small St. Vincent community, Rubenstein (1977) has shown how an early plantation pattern was eventually replaced by a peasantry, subsequently sustained in large measure by emigration, which kept population at levels that did not overtax local agricultural resources. St. Vincent is a good example of a small Caribbean society where plantation production of sugar was becoming less profitable, even while the opportunities for a more labor-intensive, peasant agriculture were improving. First settled by French colonists from Martinique in 1719, St. Vincent developed a substantial peasant class during its first half century of settlement; tobacco, cacao, and coffee were produced for export to France on holdings that "rarely exceeded 100 acres" (Rubenstein 1977:22). In 1762, St. Vincent was ceded to Great Britain by the Treaty of Paris, whereupon it was transformed into a sugar colony, with large plantations and enslaved African labor. Overproduction and emancipation brought about an economic decline into the 1830s, and the introduction of indentured labor failed to solve the labor needs of the cane industry during the second half of the nineteenth century.

But while sugar was declining in St. Vincent, a somewhat unexpected substitute commodity, this one raised principally by small-scale cultivators, was taking its place. Arrowroot, a starchy tuber or rhizome native to the Lesser Antilles, is the source of the finest cooking starch in the world and has nutritive and pharmaceutical uses as well (Rochin and Nuckton 1980). By 1847 St. Vincent arrowroot was outranked only by sugar in export value. Yet before the end of the century, arrowroot also suffered from declining demand. Nonetheless, the peasant agricultural sector managed to expand from the end of slavery onward. The export commodities changed over time: arrowroot and cotton vied for first place during the first half of this century, while bananas have outstripped both since about 1950. These are export commodities whose markets have always been uncertain, because of the inability of small-scale local producers to affect developments in other tropical colonial areas. The rise and fall of such exports, when not protected by quotas, is an old and often repeated story. But they have always been grown alongside large quantities of foods destined for consumption by peasant families, by the nonagricultural classes, and by landless laborers. Caribbean peasants typically balance their production of export items against food products that may either be consumed by the producers or sold through internal markets. Not surprisingly, a recent trend in peasant agriculture, especially in the Lesser Antilles, has been the growing exportation of these crops as well, usually to neighboring islands, in effect shifting large quantities of subsistence items into the export commodity category. Thus, for instance, the marketplaces of Point-à-Pitre, Guadeloupe, are full of produce from Dominica, and many of the hucksters, now resident in Guadeloupe, are either Haitian or Dominican female migrants.

St. Vincent export value figures for 1981 show bananas accounting for more than 72 percent of the total value of export commodities, coconuts and plantains for about 6.3 percent, and other products for 22 percent. But the category of "other products" breaks down into mangoes, tobacco, arrowroot, carrots, nutmeg, peanuts, ginger, sweet potatoes, yams, tannias, eddoes, dasheens, and breadfruit. (In fact, the variety is doubtless even greater than this list suggests and has probably never been entirely described.) In view of this variety, all produced by small-scale cultivators, it is important to note that *half* of St. Vincent's arable land is held by the forty largest estates, which are mostly in banana cultivation; while of the reported 6,700 acres of usable land that is not cultivated, most of it is on these estates. At the same time, St. Vincent has 7,100 farms, most of them of less than five acres each. Accordingly, most of the 12,000 full-time farmers—whom I would label peasants— must work with less land than they can profitably cultivate, while most of the land they do work is held in small, scattered, multiple plots. Yet another 12,000 part-time farmers probably combine work on their own or rented land with wage labor on larger holdings or elsewhere. Put differently, forty farms in St. Vincent control 54 percent of all of the land while 3,000 farms control only 4 percent of the land.

Those 3,000 who farm less than one acre cannot possibly sustain themselves on their holdings and must also sell their labor or obtain some income otherwise. But 44 percent of St. Vincent's 7,000 farms are only from one to five acres; the most successful of the peasants who farm them may have to sell little or none of their labor for wages (though they may indeed sell the labor of family members). Such cultivators must nonetheless cultivate for more than subsistence if they are to survive. The most important current cash crop is bananas though, as we have seen, many Vincentian peasants produce other crops as well, which are sold for local consumption or marketed on neighboring islands. According to Rubenstein, peasant farmers—small holders producing both subsistence and cash commodities, mainly with family labor—were producing 80 percent of the banana crop in the 1960s. It was only in this century "that a full-blown, land owning peasantry developed in the valley" Rubenstein studied (1977:34). Yet by the time he was doing his fieldwork in the early 1970s, he reported that "the agricultural stagnation characteristic of large valley estates is also evident on many peasant holdings, and a large portion of them are uncultivated and most of the rest of them significantly under-cultivated" (1977:35).

Thus the growth of peasant agriculture in this case shows a steadily changing responsiveness to alternate opportunities: first in regard to the crops grown, then in regard to alternative uses for labor locally, and finally in regard to competing opportunities elsewhere. While emigration serves to support local patterns that might otherwise become completely impractical financially, both by siphoning off surplus labor and by returns of cash sent home by the emigrants, it may also eventually eat away at the peasant adaptation itself. This is probably particularly true when, as noted earlier, emigrants begin moving spouses and families permanently, thereby undercutting the continuity that had formerly been provided by the families that stayed behind.

St. Lucia

Similar patterns are to be found in certain other islands. St. Lucia, for example, is similar in some regards to St. Vincent. There as in St. Vincent, the flourishing sugar plantation economy grew weaker after emancipation; but sugar cane continued to be the main crop thereafter and is now produced through various sharecropping arrangements, as well as on small estates. Crichlow (n.d.) points out that a nearly complete changeover was made around 1963, when bananas emerged as the premier cash crop, a position they have not since relinquished. Other major export items include cacao, spices, fruits, vegetables, and unrefined coconut oil. But particularly noteworthy in this case, as in that of St. Vincent, are the bipolar distribution of farms by size and the role of small-scale cultivators in the economy. Whereas sugar cane production is usually dominated by large-scale producers, bananas are a highly suitable small-cultivator item, and the risks of production then fall upon the peasant farmer, rather than upon the estate owner or manager. The land ownership pattern demonstrates how peasant production here operates within an unusual land concentration setting. The 1973–74 census of land-holdings reveals that 47 percent of the agricultural land in St. Lucia was held by 17 persons, while 4,700 small cultivators had less than an acre each—thus paralleling the St. Vincent picture, though being even more extreme. Large landowners, many of them foreign, are more interested in speculating in land than in producing on it. Even so, a substantial part of the production of bananas and other "peasant crops" is also produced on these larger holdings.

Crichlow argues that in St. Lucia small holders with less than an acre must sell their labor and perhaps also cultivate some subsistence; that those with upward of five acres may actually produce a major portion of their own subsistence, as well as bananas for export; and that those with more than five acres may be able to minimize the sale of their own and their families' labor. Again we see a peasantry integrated into arrangements including large estates and an agro-proletariat on the one hand, and a wide range of peasant cultivators at different levels of operation on the other. Yet cultivators owning less than ten acres of land were producing 70 percent of the banana crop (Meliczek 1975), and more than 80 percent of major arable crops comes from small holdings (LeFranc 1978), which suggests the continuing success and importance of the peasantry. These small holders, according to Crichlow, use more family labor, mostly unpaid—even though the costs of banana production on islands such as St. Vincent and St. Lucia far exceed those in mainland countries such as Colombia, Ecuador, and Costa Rica. Not enough is known to explain the persistence of high production costs. (Ecuador, for example, produces 12.5 tons per hectare at $16.90 per ton; the Windward Islands, including both St. Vincent and St. Lucia, produce 9.5 tons per hectare at $37.10 per ton.) Because items such as bananas and sugar are sold both on the world market and within specified quota arrangements, world market prices often differ from quota prices, which may enable high-cost producers to continue producing. This is certainly the case with much agricultural production in the Caribbean region and must be taken into account in any discussion of the future of its peasantries.

If we turn from smaller islands such as St. Lucia and St. Vincent to the Greater Antilles, a wider variety of peasantry forms confronts us. As I have already suggested, the situation is further complicated by the fact that the socialist economy of Cuba has left some segments of small-scale agriculture more or less intact, and by the relatively greater significance for peasant adaptations of large, interior mountainous areas on the big islands. Haiti and Cuba, along with Jamaica, Puerto Rico, and the Dominican Republic have been peasant-based coffee producers in greater or lesser degree. And while the major Caribbean agro-social basis for coffee production has been the large estate, coffee is an ideal crop for small-scale peasant producers. The capital outlays required for tools and processing equipment are modest; family labor can be readily employed (and labor-intensive production can result in a higher-quality coffee); small holdings are not an obstacle to production; and peasants can usually market their crops in modest quantities, and without outside help, if permitted to do so by the state.

To this day coffee is grown by small holders in all five of these countries, though under varying conditions. But in spite of coffee's virtues as a peasant crop, the last half-century has witnessed a general contraction of coffee production in the islands and an increase in the importation of cheaper non-Caribbean coffees by the large Western consuming countries such as the United States. Caribbean coffees tend to be mild and of excellent quality, and they have traditionally been mixed with other, stronger-tasting coffees to make special blends in Western Europe. The decline in coffee production in the Caribbean region has been a function of the competition of cheaper coffees on the world market, rising labor costs locally (paralleling the increased emigration of local labor), and a reduction in standards of taste among coffee drinkers in the last half century. Puerto Rico has become a coffee importer, and countries such as Haiti, for which coffee continues to be a big foreign exchange earner, face future difficulties as cheaper coffees continue to invade their markets. Specialty coffees, such as Jamaican Blue Mountain, cannot be mass produced and have little future if they give up their specialty character; but the elite market for high-cost coffees is small and plagued by fashion. There are other difficulties connected with coffee. The plants require from four to seven years' care before they bear a marketable crop, and so they represent a long-term investment of wealth, land, and labor, often beyond the means of the peasant cultivator. Nonetheless, coffee continues to be an important peasant crop.

Haiti

In Haiti, coffee became an important export before the revolution, growing to rival even sugar in the last twenty-five years of the *ancien régime* (Trouillot 1982). Once the revolution was won and the peasant adaptation began to spread in independent Haiti, coffee bloomed while sugar withered. A peasant pattern was created upon the ruins of the colonial slave plantation economy, and ever since, coffee has been Haiti's premier peasant crop.

Today, Haiti earns about half of its foreign exchange from agriculture, and most of that comes from coffee—about 80 percent by value of all agricultural exports. Most of the coffee is produced on small holdings—though how many, and of what average size, is moot. Girault (n.d.:92), probably the most authoritative student of the modern coffee situation, estimates some 180,000 individual holdings. Using 1971 figures from Haiti's Coffee Institute, he concludes that only 11 percent of these are more than six hectares (14.82 acres). While Girault argues convincingly that there are many large-scale coffee producers in those Haitian regions long famous for their coffee, he also follows most other students, who believe that some 65 percent of Haitian coffee is produced on holdings of less than two *carreaux* (i.e., 6.6 acres).

The vast flow of coffee from the countryside is handled by only 800—1,000 intermediaries, most of them purchasing agents for the twenty-eight officially recognized coffee export firms. Four of these exporters were handling 54 percent of all coffee exported in the early 1970s, and eight firms were handling 74 percent. Such domination of peasant production is aggravated by a heavy government tax on coffee, which comes out of peasant pockets rather than being paid by the middlemen or the exporters:

> The government of Haiti taxes coffee more heavily than any other coffee-producing country in the world. The tax is so large in proportion to the cost of production that it is considered to be a major factor in discouraging production and encouraging a shift in consumption from the export market to the domestic market. Analysis of the incidence of coffee taxes shows that the burden of tax falls squarely on the shoulders of the producers—the Haitian farmers—making them in effect the most heavily taxed group in the country. In view of their severe poverty, this situation raises serious equity problems. (DARNDR 1976:2; cited in Smucker 1982:344)

While the world coffee price was dropping (1950–71), both the tax rate and exporters' cut doubled, leaving the peasant producer with less than half of the market price to retain as his own. Not surprisingly, the incentives to produce more coffee—or, for that matter, to produce the same amount as in past years, instead of shifting to the production of other foods for the internal market for subsistence—grew even weaker. In recent years, as Haitian agricultural production has declined and as more Haitians have emigrated to escape economic exploitation and political repression, Haiti's dependence upon imported food has actually increased. No doubt it is sustained in part by the remittances that migrants send to their families; in this case, declining farm productivity, increasing importation and consumption of foreign foods, and emigration go hand in hand.

Because of the concentration here upon the role of coffee, which has bulked so importantly in the history of the Haitian peasant economy, no reference has been made so far to the massive peasant production of local foods. Until quite recently, the rural economy, poor as it was, produced the major part of all foods consumed by the national population. Complex carbohydrates such as maize, sweet potatoes, yams, millet, cassava, and rice; beans and other pulses; fruits such as mangoes, bananas, soursop, citrus, and ginep; ample fresh vegetables; fowl and eggs (but hardly any meat or dairy products) reached the towns and cities from the surrounding hinterlands by a complex, elaborate system of markets and marketing intermediaries. In spite of poor roads, nonexistent communication facilities, and inferior transport, the Haitian rural economy managed to feed not only itself but all of Haiti's nonagricultural population. It bears noting that this entire complex peasant economy was built up after the revolution, which had left the Haitian countryside in great disorder, by a peasant population that was poor, illiterate, and saddled with crushing postwar indemnities. But now a deep decline finally seems to be setting in.

There are theories concerning this now apparent unraveling of the peasant adaptation. Some scholars attribute it to growing population and land subdivision, and to the steadily eroding land upon which the system is based; or to the worsening terms of trade imposed upon the peasantry by an improvident and corrupt regime. While under some circumstances emigration can provide a double reinforcement to the peasantry, on the one hand reducing the number of mouths to feed and on the other remitting cash to help out those who stay behind, under other circumstances the growing flood of departures can eventually sap the strength of the whole peasant system, leaving a denuded or unmotivated countryside behind. It seems likely that this is now starting to happen in at least some parts of the Haitian peasant economy. Rather than making genuine efforts to restore peasant vigor, the regime is apparently content to continue to skim off a portion of the labor of the peasantry in the form of taxes, without a thought for tomorrow.

In spite of these quite ominous trends and the suffering of the Haitian rural sector, the facts are that most Haitians are cultivators to this day, and that the economy still rests largely upon the backs of the peasantry. To ignore or discount either those people or the importance—social and political, as well as economic—of their labor is to miss a central point about Caribbean economies: the historic role of small-scale agriculture in the values and beliefs of the people.

Cuba

The case of Cuba's peasantry is quite different. Prerevolutionary data on Cuban agriculture outside the sugar industry are poor; even calculations about the number of peasants in Cuba, or the amount of land held by them, are generally considered untrustworthy. The census of 1946 provided evidence that nearly 40 percent of Cuba's 160,000 farms were less than twenty-five acres, while nearly another one-third were from twenty-five to sixty-two acres. On the face of it, this statistic suggests an immense population of agricultural small holders, plus large numbers of sharecroppers and other types of tenants. That the Cuban sugar industry, for example, was manned by thousands of landless or near landless proletarians or semiproletarians is well known.

The revolution led to tremendous structural changes in the organization of Cuban agriculture, the most important being the incorporation of the sugar industry, fields and factories alike, into the state sector. Though there was early talk of a reduction in the Cuban commitment to sugar, that was eventually replaced by the insistence—certainly justified by later events—that sugar would continue to be the economic backbone of national agriculture. Since the revolution, not only have the sugar cane plantations been nationalized, but their form has been greatly changed. Far less labor intensive than during the prerevolutionary free enterprise period, today's plantations probably make Cuba "a relatively low-cost sugar producer, as it was before the 1959 revolution" (Hagelberg 1985). Heavily mechanized, from planting and cultivating through the cutting operations, with four new mills and still others being built, the Cuban sugar industry today is strikingly modern, and a world leader, in spite of its highly irregular performance in the years following the revolution.

But of course Cuban sugar had never been produced by a peasantry, whereas a noticeable proportion of its coffee and tobacco crops, and even more, its production of so-called minor crops, were traditionally peasant based. The agrarian reform of 1959 actually enabled a substantial portion of the landless rural labor force to operate the land they rented, sharecropped, or otherwise had access to, as if it were their own property. The agrarian reform of 1963 eliminated most medium-size farms but did not alter the status of the very small ones or of those who cultivated them. Research suggests that many of these were, in fact, people who had been landless before the revolution, many who had worked part-time for wages on the large estates or plantations, meanwhile also sharecropping small holdings by one or another traditional arrangement with the landowners. In 1966, 234,000 small farmers—peasants—were still independently working almost 35 percent of the arable land then in cultivation in Cuba. Between 1967 and 1971 this number was reduced to 203,000, working perhaps 32 percent of the land. Since land could no longer be inherited, a gradual decline in private holdings and in the proportion of the land worked privately was to be expected. By the end of 1975, private land was down to one-fifth of the total, while the number of private landholders stood at 162,000 (Mesa-Lago 1978:100). Nonetheless, the private sector was said to be producing 80 percent of all tobacco and coffee, 60 percent of all vegetables, 50 percent of all tubers and fruits, 33 percent of all

cattle, and even 18 percent of all sugar cane in Cuba (ibid.). In these regards, the peasant sector was apparently performing in a manner similar to that of the private farms in the Soviet Union. It seems certain that these noteworthy performances depend upon a more efficient use of land resources, more labor intensiveness, and higher motivation, under private (rather than state) ownership.

Small farmers (or peasants) are incorporated into the Cuban Asociación Nacional de Agricultores Pequeños, which supervises extension, credit, etc. and buys specified portions of agricultural yield (the *acopio*) from peasant producers at below-market prices. The fate of the unclaimed (non-*acopio*) portion of peasant production has varied a good deal since the 1960s. Though first permitted to market such surpluses without regulation, the small farmers were later cut off from free marketing. Since 1980, however, free peasant markets have been reinstituted, probably because the prohibition of marketing simply magnified the problem of controlling small-farm production. Peasant earnings from the sale of surpluses cannot be invested in land or in heavy equipment, but they can be used to buy consumer goods or deposited in savings banks. Better credit facilities, higher prices for the *acopio*, and incentives to small farmers to increase their production of key crops such as coffee and tobacco have been increasingly invoked to maintain small-farm productivity. In 1981–82, peasant farms were still producing more dry beans, coffee, tobacco, root crops, and vegetables than the state farms, and providing a higher yield per hectare, though the number of peasants continued to dwindle.

These meager facts afford us a somewhat unusual picture. The revolution actually put a substantial quantity of land into the hands of once landless rural people. It created a new peasantry, but only briefly. The readiness of the regime to sustain or nourish such a segment of the Cuban rural economy seems to have vacillated ever since. Mesa-Lago may have been overly pessimistic when he suggested that "the fate of the only private or quasi-private sector left in Cuba is clear: total absorption by the state sector" (1978:101). But the future of the Cuban peasantry is certainly not very promising, in spite of its apparently high productivity and usefulness.

THE FUTURE

These few examples only scratch the surface of the variation the peasantry exhibits in this region. Why is the nature of Caribbean peasantries not better understood, and their problems more widely recognized? The very commonness and ubiquity of peasants inclines the more privileged classes to take them for granted rather than to try seriously to understand them. Throughout the Caribbean, city folk of all classes generally show some condescension toward the rural poor. Their language or dialect, their religions, their social customs, their comportment, and their dress are ignored or viewed with ill-concealed disdain. At the same time, and perhaps paradoxically, Caribbean peasants tend to be romanticized—at least by those who think about such things at all. I know of very few Caribbean novels ostensibly concerned with the peasantry that do not glamorize the achievements (and even the sufferings) of country people.

Added to this is another, more distinctively Caribbean problem: the peculiar integration of the peasant sector with the plantation system. Though the nature and extent of this integration varies from place to place, only in Haiti may the peasant adaptation be said to have dominated the plantation adaptation for any lengthy period. Elsewhere, the reconstituted peasantries of the region have always had to struggle for their stakes against the large estates—for land, for labor, for credit, for official support and assistance. Because the plantation system was customarily regarded by the colonial power as the enterprise to be protected and sustained, peasantries rarely received any help from the metropolis. Indeed, at most times peasants were viewed as dangerous to the success of the plantations, because they inevitably competed for at least some resources (such as labor, credit sources, water, or land) with them.

In the modern world, the problems of Caribbean peasantries have been compounded. Mining, tourist developments, oil refining, real estate speculation, highways, and similar developments increasingly use up scarce Caribbean land, and inflate the costs of all local land. Synthetic substitutes for vetiver, sisal, beeswax, goats' horns, or arrowroot starch drive out the organic products, which are not likely to be as uniform, or as available at all seasons, as the synthetics. Other colonial tropical areas undertake the production of export commodities such as coffee, spices, and tobacco under the stimulus of new metropolitan interests, underselling older Caribbean producing areas in the metropolitan markets. Moreover, the worldwide trend toward larger-scale agricultural production of all commodities, including those that have been produced traditionally by peasantries, intensifies the competition Caribbean peasantries must face in selling their products. These are not problems for Caribbean peasants only, but for peasantries everywhere.

In many instances, the consequences are a gradual slackening of activity in the peasant sector, a movement by more and more of the labor force from self-employed farming to wage labor, and increased emigration to overcrowded Caribbean cities or even to developed countries in other regions in search of work. Such migration has become typical and chronic in the Caribbean region, which consistently produces more labor than its dependent and irregular economies can steadily employ. Particularly since World War II, migration on a more permanent basis has become an important "solution" to Caribbean peasant problems, and it has to some extent now redefined the nature of rural life there. In Haiti, it is estimated that nearly one-third of all locally produced food is now consumed in the capital city, which is inhabited by only about 18 percent of the national population—while food imports, totaling almost a quarter of national food consumption, are also mainly consumed in the capital. Such figures gain even more significance when it is realized that Haiti is the most thoroughgoing peasant country in the entire region.

Even in Puerto Rico, where plantations dominated the national agriculture in the years preceding World War II, there has been a complete transformation of the agricultural economy. The interest in industrialization in the 1950s there led to a complete neglect of agriculture; emigration, which was substantial, was regarded as a blessing to the local economy; and industry, which was counted upon to create new jobs, actually created only half as many as were being lost in the agricultural sector. In the end, Puerto Rico has found itself facing a denuded agrarian sector, a sugar industry in rapid decline, and an enormous (and growing) bill for imported food.

Nonetheless, critics will say, there is no way to make Caribbean peasant agriculture pay for itself, since it is not competitive with other, cheaper agricultural areas in Asia, Africa, and parts of Latin America, where both labor and land cost less. Like many other issues, this is one where other considerations besides the economic will have to be taken into account if thoughtful policy decisions are to be made. In the history of North American agriculture, the time came when the social benefits of maintaining small-scale agriculture were no longer of much interest to policy makers, and the results are to be seen not only in the large corporate agribusinesses of the modern United States, but also in the character of both our cities and our countrysides. In all likelihood, if it were ours to do over again now, we would decide to develop our agriculture in exactly the same way; but the vote would probably not be quite as unanimous today as it would have been two decades ago. It remains questionable whether, in another two decades, the vote would not be entirely reversed, as the rural environment continues to decline, the Sun Belt cities repeat the experiences of the Northeast, and the chemical content of our foods becomes yet more threatening.

The issues are of course very different in the Caribbean region; but in at least some regards, they are parallel issues. Societies such as Puerto Rico and Jamaica must decide, more or less collectively, whether they desire to subsist primarily on tourism and the remittances of emigrants—particularly after bauxite and similar reserves have been exhausted. For a society such as Haiti, not even this choice is realistic; and Haitians will surely continue to flee Haiti as long as political repression and economic corruption keep the future of the people entirely problematical.

Putting the stress upon peasant life itself can easily lead to a false romanticization of rural splendor; there is little that is easy, refined, or glamorous about Caribbean rural life. But for centuries independent cultivation offered to the Caribbean masses the most important and dignified alternative available to plantation wage labor or migration. As these alternatives now become more and more risky or difficult, the time has come for Caribbean citizens to rethink the futures of their own countrysides. A successful solution to the problems those countrysides present may well determine the political future of the entire region.

REFERENCES

CRICHLOW, MICHAELINE
n.d. [1983] "Some Notes on Land Tenure and Social Transformation in the
Caribbean. . . . the case of St. Lucia." Manuscript.

DARNDR (Département de l'Agriculture, des Ressources Naturelles et du Développe-
ment)
1976   *Agricultural Policy Studies: Coffee.* Damien, Haiti: JWK International
Corporation / Unité de Programmation de DARNDR.

GIRAULT, CHRISTIAN A.
n.d. [1980]   *Le Commerce du café en Haïti.* Paris: Editions du Centre National
de la Recherche Scientifique.

HAGELBERG, G. B.
1985   "Sugar in the Caribbean: Turning Sunshine into Money." *In* Sidney W.
Mintz and Sally Price (eds.), *Caribbean Contours.* Baltimore: Johns
Hopkins University Press.

LEFRANC, E.
1978   *Small Farming Study.* Caribbean Development Bank.

MELICZEK, H.
1975   *Land Tenure, St. Lucia Project Findings and Recommendations.* (A
report prepared for the Government of St. Lucia by the Food and
Agriculture Organization of the United Nations acting as executing
agent for the U.N. Development Programme.) Rome.

MESA-LAGO, CARMELO
1978   *Cuba in the 1970s.* Albuquerque: University of New Mexico Press.

ROCHIN, REFUGIO I., AND CAROLE FRANK NUCKTON
1980   "The Arrowroot Industry of St. Vincent: At a Crossroads." *Agribusiness
Worldwide* 1(6):20–26.

RUBENSTEIN, HYMIE
1977   "Economic History and Population Movements in an Eastern Caribbean
Valley." *Ethnohistory* 24(1):19–45.

SMUCKER, GLENN R.
1982   "Peasants and Development Politics: A Study in Haitian Class Culture."
Ph.D. thesis, New School for Social Research.

TROUILLOT, MICHEL-ROLPH
1982   "Motion in the System: Coffee, Color, and Slavery in Eighteenth-
Century Saint-Domingue." *Review* 5(3):331–88.

·5·

A Linguistic Perspective on the Caribbean

MERVYN C. ALLEYNE

A LINGUISTIC CLASSIFICATION

The languages of the Caribbean are often categorized and characterized by means of labels referring to the four European powers that dominated the region in the colonial period—*English-speaking, French-speaking, Spanish-speaking,* and *Dutch-speaking.* These terms provide only approximate references. If they are taken literally, they may be misleading, inadequate, or inaccurate in some cases, and they certainly mask a great deal of linguistic complexity.

To be exact, only the term *Spanish-speaking* has an accurate application in the Caribbean; not only do Cuba, the Dominican Republic, and Puerto Rico all use Spanish as both an official and a universally spoken language, but they also share a particular dialect (variety) of Spanish and thus constitute an important linguistic and cultural division of the Caribbean, even though they have no political ties whatever to each other. The other three terms are less accurate.

The territories often designated as English-speaking do need a term of easy reference since they constitute a significant division within the Caribbean; not only do they share English as the sole *official* language, but they also have strong political and economic links through membership in the now defunct Federation of the West Indies, in the current economic community CARICOM, and in the current supranational University of the West Indies. Five of these countries have also joined to form the Organisation of Eastern Caribbean States (OECS). They maintain important ties with Britain—individually through participation in the British Commonwealth, and collectively through the West Indies cricket team, which competes with England and some other Commonwealth countries. Linguistically, however, this group is quite diverse, as we shall see later in this essay.

The designation *French-speaking* is often used to refer to Haiti, Martinique, Guadeloupe, and French Guiana, and French is indeed the official language of these societies. However, another language—variously called Haitian Creole, Haitian, French Creole, Creole, or patois—has constitutional status in Haiti, and the majority of people in these societies do not speak French in their everyday interactions. Haiti has no political or economic links with the

others nor, having become an independent nation in 1804, any special or particularly strong links with France; the others maintained their colonial status until becoming overseas departments of France in 1946.

The Dutch-speaking territories—Suriname and the Netherlands Antilles (Curaçao, Aruba, Bonaire, Saba, St. Eustatius, and St. Maarten)—are linguistically quite complex, although Dutch is indeed the sole official language. Preparations were begun in 1983 for making Papiamentu the official national language of Curaçao, designating English and Spanish as official second languages, and preserving the role of Dutch as the language of postprimary education for at least ten years. There are no political or economic links between Suriname and the Netherlands Antilles, and the postcolonial ties between Suriname and the Netherlands are becoming increasingly tenuous not only because of the political differences caused by the Suriname revolution of 1980, but also, more fundamentally, because of increasing awareness by Surinamers of the potential isolation that the use of Dutch imposes on them in the area. There is at present very little sense in referring to the Netherlands Antilles as "Dutch-speaking," and should current trends continue, Dutch will soon cease to be in active use at any level of the national life of the Netherlands Antilles.

Beneath these simplistic classificatory designations are to be found language situations of considerable complexity. The Caribbean, which includes the South and Central American littoral washed by the Caribbean sea, is the location of almost every type of linguistic phenomenon, and of every type of language situation. For example, trade and contact jargons, creole languages and dialects, ethnic vernaculars, and regional and nonstandard dialects are all spoken. There are also ancestral languages used for religious purposes (Latin, Yoruba, Kikongo), regional standards, and international standards. And there is multilingualism, bilingualism, monolingualism, diglossia, and a postcreole continuum (see below). In "English-speaking" Trinidad, for example, several languages other than English (Spanish, French Creole, Bhojpuri) serve as media of everyday interaction in many (mostly rural) communities. And in "English-speaking" Dominica and St. Lucia, everyday interaction among most of the rural and urban population is carried on in French-based Creole, a language that is completely different from (and not mutually intelligible with) English; Dominica and St. Lucia are in fact bilingual countries. In addition, there is a rather sharp differentiation in these "English-speaking" countries between the official norm of English and the nonstandard colloquial variety of English, which is strongly influenced by the French Creole language. The language situation in Jamaica is extremely difficult to classify; even linguists are uncertain about how many discrete languages/dialects are spoken there,

In this essay *creole* refers to a type of language and *Creole* to a particular language (e.g., Jamaican Creole).

Handwritten annotation top right: Diglossia - 2 codes exist

and generally deal with this complex issue by referring to Jamaica as a "postcreole linguistic continuum."

It would be useful here to define some of these designations. It must be remembered, however, that in trying to classify countries this way, we are in many cases trying to fit quite dynamic situations into static classifications. *Trade and contact jargons* are specialized codes that may emerge in limited contact situations, such as bartering between peoples whose native languages are not mutually intelligible. They are simple (or simplified) codes matching the simplicity of the communicative context (e.g., bartering) in which they are used. They are prone to disappearance as the contact between the peoples ceases to exist. Throughout the New World, trade jargons have emerged out of the contact between Europeans and the indigenous peoples of the Americas. In other parts of the world, some of these jargons have become well known, and one in particular—*lingua franca* or *sabir*, which was used in the Mediterranean in the Middle Ages—became quite important as a vehicle for commercial exchanges in the area. It has become customary to use the term *pidgin* to refer to trade and contact jargons that are well established. Scholars claim that several pidgins were used on the coast of Africa and in the Far East during the period of European expansion. When populations in contact begin to engage in regular social interaction (leading, for example, to the establishment of households of "mixed" couples), the pidgin may become the language of the home and be learned by children of the household as their first (native or mother) language. This implies an expansion of the functions of the language and of its expressive resources as it acquires a richer vocabulary. At this point, the pidgin becomes known as a *creole*. Creole forms of speech exist throughout the Caribbean.

The Caribbean also illustrates two types of language situation that do not fit well within the linguists' traditional scheme of multilingualism/bilingualism/monolingualism. *Diglossia* refers to a language situation in which two codes exist, sharing one level of structure (vocabulary), but differing at other levels (pronunciation and grammar). The two codes (e.g., French and French Creole in Haiti) are said to be in complementary distribution; that is, they are used in mutually exclusive contexts. French is used, for example, in Parliament, in the law courts, and in secondary and tertiary education, while Creole monopolizes private informal interactional contexts and the oral tradition. The second type, called by linguists the *postcreole continuum*, is a graded continuum of variation that has developed between a creole and a standard language of the same vocabulary. Jamaica is a typical example.

THE HISTORICAL PERSPECTIVE

This diversity of linguistic phenomena and language patterns is the direct result of the modern post-Columbian history of the region, which witnessed migrations of peoples and population replacements of a scale and complexity

MERVYN C. ALLEYNE

perhaps unsurpassed in any other period of equivalent duration in human history. In most cases the new migrations completely replaced the indigenous population, which left few significant traces. The most vibrant traces are the communities of so-called Black Caribs on the Belizean coast who speak a contemporary form of the language of the indigenous pre-Columbian inhabitants of the Lesser Antilles. These Black Caribs are racial mixtures of African and Island Carib. Their ancestors were exiled from St. Vincent by the British and relocated in British Honduras (Belize) in the eighteenth century, in an attempt to facilitate the colonization of the island of St. Vincent. Some descendants of these Island Caribs still live in Dominica, where they preserve to some degree their racial and ethnic identity. But rather than a Carib language, they now speak the French-based creole of Dominica.

It was contact among immigrant groups of diverse origins (who are often simplistically condensed by outsiders as "European" on the one hand and "African" on the other) that became the most significant factor for the emergence of West Indian societies, because nowhere else in the hemisphere was the destruction of the indigenous peoples and their civilization more complete. This contact between different cultures represented by the immigrant groups has produced societies that some anthropologists and sociologists consider heterogeneous and pluralistic but others see as showing integrative tendencies. Between these two points of view the truth seems to be that these societies are contradictory, conflict-prone and insecure, ambivalent in outlook and attitudes, ambiguous in their formation and in their functioning. With very few exceptions, these societies came into being as colonies ruled by more than one European power in the course of their history. The majority are now politically independent; the others have worked out peculiar kinds of relationships with their (former) colonial masters that reflect the unevenness of their cultural history and the fragility of their present economic situation.

The language situations existing in the Caribbean are mirrors through which the complex cultural history of the region may be observed. Broadly speaking, contact was between Western Europeans and West Africans. But even within one European "nationality," regional differentiation was significant, especially in the formative years of the colonies. The Africans came mainly from a vast geographical area of West Africa stretching from Senegal in the north to Angola in the south. The linguistic and cultural diversity of this region is well known, and a large part of it was represented not only among the Africans brought forcibly to the Caribbean in general, but even among those brought to particular territories. Anthropologists and linguists assign different degrees of importance to this fact in accounting for the development of Caribbean societies and cultures (including language). One view stresses that the diversity—together with the facts that Africans were extracted forcibly, were unable to prepare themselves to migrate, and lost all contact with their homeland—meant that Africans were unable to continue their native

↳ *This is an important point*

forms of culture and language. Another view emphasizes that West Africa, in spite of its surface diversity, is a culture area with a common underlying structure and that the languages of the area belong to one genealogical family. Some scholars also argue that in many Caribbean territories a particular West African ethnic group dominated and set the cultural pattern, whether by dint of numerical superiority, relatively early arrival, cultural characteristics that resulted in stronger group cohesion and stronger leadership qualities, or a combination of these. In this view, the notion of cultural continuities from West Africa, with change arising out of contact with European culture and the demands of the new environment, is seen as the most fruitful framework for the historical interpretation of Caribbean societies and cultures. And indeed, African languages do persist today (although not as vehicles for everyday interaction).

However that may be, it is generally accepted that what characterizes and typifies the Caribbean from a linguistic point of view is the emergence and current existence of forms of speech now designated in the literature as creoles. The term *creole* is often also used to refer to the people, the society, and the culture, but its reference is both imprecise and different in the Spanish Caribbean from the British and French Caribbean. Only in the Spanish-speaking Greater Antilles (Cuba, the Dominican Republic, and Puerto Rico) is this type of language form absent. There, rather than a creole language or dialect, we find a nonstandard dialect of Spanish. In the second view presented above of the role of West Africa in the emergence of Caribbean societies and cultures, the question to be posed concerning these Spanish-speaking territories is not why a creole has or has not been reported, but rather what the conditions were that caused the relatively intense linguistic assimilation of Africans to a Hispanic norm. Indeed, the same question is to be posed in relation to English-speaking Barbados, where we find a nonstandard dialect of English whose relationship with its European ancestor is somewhat analogous to that between Spanish and the nonstandard dialect of Cuba, the Dominican Republic, and Puerto Rico. Reconstructions of historically antecedent forms and documents of the eighteenth and nineteenth centuries confirm a creole language for Barbados, which has now developed into a nonstandard English dialect under the strong culture-assimilatory conditions existing in that island. In fact, Barbados, like Cuba and the Dominican Republic, and to a lesser extent Puerto Rico, experienced the unbroken and relatively intense presence of only one European nationality throughout its colonial history.

European colonialism and imperialism may have been based fundamentally on the economic factors of trade and the control of raw materials. They certainly developed into cultural imperialism, however, and the notion of "savage," "uncivilized," and "primitive" came to be applied to civilizations and cultures with which Europe came into contact. The creole culture that emerged in the Caribbean (and in the southern United States of America) and showed a relatively high degree of acculturation to the European norm (when compared with African and Melanesian cultures) was not usually characterized as "savage" or "primitive" (except when slaves resisted through armed revolt) but rather as aberrant, simple, and pathological. Indeed it was often not considered "culture" at all; rather, slaves were considered to have been "stripped" of their African heritage, to have assimilated in an imperfect way a few "smatterings" of European traditions and to be displaying nothing more than pathological manifestations of European culture. This has come to be known in the literature as the "deficit theory" of Afro-American culture.

The languages of Africans and their descendants that developed in the New World are good examples of this. Considered bizarre, aberrant, and corrupt derivatives of one or another European language, they were not viewed as natural languages with their own rules of grammar. Rather, they were all referred to in terms of "deficiencies," "corruptions," and "mutilations." They were often likened to "baby talk" and were thought to betoken, by the poor state of their development, the inherent biological inferiority of Africans and their descendants.

An important part of the colonial syndrome is the acceptance by the colonized of the colonizer's interpretation of them. Caribbean people have largely accepted Europeans' views of their language behavior as part of a more general self-deprecation and negative evaluation of their cultural behavior. The general feeling is that creole languages and dialects are defective—that they may be suitable for the expression of "folklore" (folktales, folkmusic, proverbs, swearing, etc.), but that they are quite inadequate for the expression of complex and abstract thought.

This has created throughout the Caribbean a prejudice against local languages. Language not only is correlated with social class differences and generally used as the most widely recognized index of social class but also has become associated with backwardness and lack of "culture," whereas the use of the standard form of European languages is associated with intelligence, enlightenment, and "culture." The use of a creole language or dialect is seen not only as socially restrictive, prohibiting the social mobility of the user, but also as intellectually restrictive, leading to bad or inadequate habits of thought. This makes it possible to attribute to creole language patterns deficiencies that in fact stem from other, more serious educational problems.

CREOLE LANGUAGES IN THE CONTEMPORARY PERIOD

This negative view of creole languages was much more common a decade or so ago than it is today. The contemporary period has witnessed two factors that have led to a considerable modification of the interpretation of these languages and dialects and of subjective and national attitudes toward them. These are (1) the work of linguists in providing new insights into the history

This is interesting... and very true. Reminds me of what Guy said

Chom / Confiant / Glissant all fit here

and nature of creole languages; and (2) political and cultural developments that have led to some aggressiveness in the Caribbean in asserting political as well as cultural independence. This is not the place to deal in any detail with political and cultural movements. Suffice it to say that, politically, the territories of the Caribbean are either assuming a radical anti-imperialist posture, being careful to state their adherence to the Nonaligned movement, or, in cases where complete political independence has not been achieved (Puerto Rico, the French West Indies, and the Netherlands Antilles), developing vocal (if not always politically important) segments clamoring for independence. In the area of culture, there is everywhere a new confidence in the local norm, whether it be in religion, music, food, craft, or language; this is true even in the French and Dutch West Indies, where there are political arrangements other than complete independence. There is a new consciousness everywhere of a national identity, one manifestation of which is the attitude toward the language of the people. Thus, there is some mitigation of the traditional hostility toward creole languages and some new awareness of their communicative and integrative potential. That is not to say that current attitudes are clearly positive and unambivalent, or that there is anything resembling a national consensus on the expanded role that the creole language could or should play in the life and development of each nation. There are still large and powerful sectors in each Caribbean society that persist in viewing these creole languages as unworthy, as something less than real "languages," and as hangovers from a distant, backward past that are inhibiting national development and progress.

New consciousness of nat'l identity

The scientific work on Caribbean languages and dialects has contributed both to the development of a new linguistic sensitivity among Caribbean peoples and to the development of linguistic science itself through a new awareness of the nature of language and its role in the organization of society. Linguists now have a better understanding of the nature and scope of language change and particularly of the effect of social and cultural factors on language change. Studies in language variation have received considerable impetus from work on Caribbean language phenomena. Most sensational of all is the new insight into language universals being provided by studies of Caribbean languages. Indeed, one currently developing view is that Caribbean language forms are crucial both to our understanding of the innate capacity for language with which human beings are exclusively and uniquely endowed and to the unraveling of the mystery of the origin of language itself.

There is still much controversy among linguists about the genesis of creole languages of the Caribbean. The different current views may be summarized in terms of two main theories: the universalist theory and the substratum theory. Both of these reject the traditional view of creole languages as simplified offshoots of European languages, as indeterminate mishmashes of several languages, or as products of the slavery, discrimination, economic oppression, and lack of education to which their speakers were subjected. The most recent version of the universalist theory suggests that children growing up in a multilingual community where a pidgin is used find it inadequate as a native tongue and have recourse to their innate capacity for language in generating new language forms to meet their cognitive needs. The substratum theory considers that there are a whole series of ways in which a culture and language contact situation might develop, and that one has to look at the specific conditions of any one contact situation to understand the linguistic developments there. Many of today's internationally important languages (e.g., French, Spanish, and English) have diverged from their earlier form mainly because of contact with other languages. Some general features are common to all contact situations; there may also be specific features that make particular contact situations different from others. Some linguists are now asking whether the significant features of the contact situation that gave rise to the creole languages of the Caribbean have not also recurred in other contact situations and produced languages analogous to the creole languages. (The language of particular interest in this regard is English itself).

It would be useful here to look at the nature of creole languages and their role in the societies where they are spoken. The traditional claim is that a pidgin is the necessary precursor of a creole language. Also, pidgins are quite prone to early extinction while, in contrast, there is nothing transient or secondary about creole languages. The latter are native languages, used by their speakers in the full range of their expressive and cognitive activity and as the normal vehicle for everyday interaction in communities that know no other language. Since the lexicon of each creole language is derived predominantly from a European language, there may be a temptation to view it as some type of offshoot from that European language. However, creole languages are languages in their own right. Some of them (e.g., Haitian and Papiamentu) have now acquired written forms and a developing literary tradition. They are coming to be used in scientific discourse and as the medium of instruction at different levels of the educational structure. In short, they are following precisely the same course of development as the standard languages of the Old World and the new standard languages of the Third World (Indonesian, Filipino, Cambodian, etc.).

Creole languages were traditionally viewed as derived from European languages (through pidgins based on these languages). Linguists now tend to agree that only the vocabularies derive from such sources, and they attribute the phonology, syntax, and lexico-semantic structure to other origins. Certainly in the case of those lexically derived from English, English is more the point to which they are moving than their point of departure. This group is highly differentiated, though clearly historically related. At one extreme of differentiation are the creole languages of Suriname: Sranan (the popular vernacular of the coastal region), and the languages of the maroons of the interior (Saramaccan and Ndjuka). In the case of the mass vernaculars of

Jamaica, Guyana, Antigua, St. Kitts, Montserrat, and St. Vincent, continuing contact with English has resulted in language forms showing less differentiation. Finally, the people of Barbados and, to a lesser extent, Trinidad use forms of speech that have lost all but a few of the surface forms associated with creole language structure.

The languages based lexically on French are more uniform, and there is a high degree of mutual intelligibility among them. Certainly the popular speech of the Lesser Antilles (Guadeloupe, Martinique, Dominica, and St. Lucia) is a single language; this language is also spoken by minority pockets in Grenada and Trinidad. The creole languages of French Guiana and Haiti show slight differences from the Lesser Antillean variety but are mutually intelligible with it and with each other. It is now quite generally accepted that this language is neither a "version" nor a "dialect" of French; it is an independent language using the same lexical roots as French but not mutually intelligible with it.

Similarly, Papiamentu shares lexical roots and some syntactical forms with Spanish and Portuguese but is an independent autonomous language not mutually intelligible with either. Its closest relative may be Palenquero, the ethnic lanuage of El Palenque de San Basilio (Bolivar Province, Colombia), which is spoken by the descendants of maroons (slaves who escaped and formed independent communities).

The remarkable fact about all these Caribbean languages is that in contrast with their lexical diversity they show a high degree of structural similarity. I cite here a few examples of structural similarities giving French-based creole examples first, Jamaican Creole examples second:

1. Both verbs and adjectives are predicates, and they are used syntactically in the same way.

mwē malad *mi sick*	"I'm ill"
mwē kuri *mi run*	"I run"
mwē va malad *mi wi sick*	"I'll be ill"
mwē va kuri *mi wi run*	"I'll run"
m'ap malad *mi a sick*	"I am getting ill"
m'ap kuri *mi a run*	"I'm running"

2. Plurals are formed by placing the third personal plural pronoun after the noun.

$$\left.\begin{array}{l} \textit{nom yo} \\ \textit{di man dem} \end{array}\right\}$$ "the men"

3. Verbs and adjectives can be emphasized by being placed at the beginning of a sentence and then repeated.

$$\left.\begin{array}{l} \textit{se kuri li ap kuri} \\ \textit{a run im a run} \end{array}\right\}$$ "He is really running"

4. Verbs can be strung together without any connecting word.

$$\left.\begin{array}{l} \textit{mwẽ pote yo ale} \\ \textit{mi carry dem go} \end{array}\right\}$$ "I took them away (literally, "I took them go")

$$\left.\begin{array}{l} \textit{kuri ale lese li} \\ \textit{run go lef im} \end{array}\right\}$$ "Run away and leave him"

5. Particles are placed before the predicate to express tense and aspect.

$$\left.\begin{array}{l} \textit{m'ap kuri} \\ \textit{mi a run} \end{array}\right\}$$ "I am running"

$$\left.\begin{array}{l} \textit{mwẽ te kuri} \\ \textit{mi en run} \end{array}\right\}$$ "I ran"

$$\left.\begin{array}{l} \textit{mwẽ t'ap kuri} \\ \textit{mi en a run} \end{array}\right\}$$ "I was running"

CONCLUSIONS

A number of other forces may have been at play in the development of creole languages; but it is now very clear and widely accepted that, whatever these forces may have been, the Caribbean mass vernaculars are quite normal forms of speech and cannot be simplistically described as "corrupt," "bastardized," "broken," "ungrammatical" derivatives of European languages. It is also becoming more and more widely accepted that terms such as *patois* and *creole*, insofar as they denote or connote something special, abnormal, or pejorative, are unfortunate misnomers bequeathed to the area by the formerly dominant powers, and that the most appropriate designations are those that are based on the name of the country and nationality (e.g., *Sranan, Saramaccan, English,* and *French*). This method of naming would give rise to designations such as Dominican, St. Lucian, Jamaican, and Bajan.

Nor do linguists subscribe to the notion that some languages are "superior" in terms of their form and structure. It is now generally accepted that there is nothing inherently "wrong" or "inferior" in the present structure of Caribbean mass vernaculars. Linguists also tend to agree that these forms of speech should be described on their own terms rather than in terms of the European languages from which they are simplistically assumed to have been derived. Thus it is agreed that it does not make sense to say that a sentence such as *mi sick* or *mwen malad* is a "simplified," "corrupt," or "ungrammatical" version of *I am sick* or *Je suis malade*. These Caribbean sentences belong to, and are part of, a language system whose grammar has its own rules, i.e., its own way of structuring sentences. These rules are as legitimate and "correct" as the rules of grammar of English or French or Swahili. They allow speakers to learn the language and communicate meaning to other members of the community with as little ambiguity and misunderstanding as any other language system in the world.

Westerners have been subjected to a Greco-Roman cultural and intellectual tradition with its own peculiar value system. Inflections, concord, cases, and subordinate clauses, for example, are considered, in this value system, to be the natural indispensable property of any logical language system, and languages that do not show these features are often suspected of being "primitive," "simple," or "inadequate." The fact is, however, that all languages adequately express the thoughts of their speakers. Therefore all languages have actual and existential adequacy. Each can potentially be made to deal with any intellectual demands that human societies may make of them. This is indeed virtually the whole point of language planning.

The mass vernaculars that developed in the Caribbean encountered different conditions in each territory. In Suriname, the English, whose language was serving as the "target" of African linguistic acculturation and supplied the lexicon to the developing creole language during the settlement's first decade and a half, surrendered the colony to the Dutch at a very early date, allowing the development of languages, such as Saramaccan and Sranan, that were widely different from English. On the other hand, conditions in Barbados were favorable for a close approximation to the European "target" language; thus Bajan has become relatively close to English even though in previous centuries it was quite deviant from English and closer to Sranan. Furthermore, those groups of enslaved Africans undergoing these linguistic processes were never homogeneous and undifferentiated in terms of their experience of the conditions of contact. Some Africans (and their descendants) were exposed to quite favorable conditions for the learning of the dominant language and were highly motivated to do so. Others were exposed to less favorable conditions; in addition, their motivation to learn was relatively weak, in some cases involving actual resistance to a complete assimilation of the "target." This produced in Jamaica, Guyana, Antigua, Montserrat, and St. Kitts (societies where English, the dominant language, had already taken on a creole-type structure and seemed to facilitate linguistic fusion with the creole) a language situation described by linguists as a "(postcreole) continuum," in which different graded levels of speech show different degrees of approximation to (and conversely, deviancy from) a standard norm of English. These levels now correspond more or less to the social stratification; that is, there is a tendency for upper-class people to speak more standard English, and for lower-class people to speak a more creolized form.

In still other territories the dominant language changed in the late eighteenth and clearly nineteenth centuries from French to English and created a strict bilingual situation involving English and French-based creole. In Trinidad and Grenada, a form of English strongly influenced by the French-based creole gradually became the majority (mass) vernacular, while in St. Lucia and Dominica, the French-based creole has maintained its position as a mass vernacular although it is being threatened by a form of English similarly influenced by the French-based creole.

These different conditions of language contact have given rise to the following types of language situations:

1. *Multilingual:* Trinidad has standard and nonstandard forms of English, a French-based creole, nonstandard Spanish, Bhojpuri, Urdu, and Yoruba. Suriname has Dutch, Sranan, Saramaccan, Ndjuka, Javanese, and Hindi.
2. *Bilingual:* St. Lucia, Dominica, and Grenada have standard and nonstandard forms of English and a French-based creole. The Netherlands Antilles has Dutch and Papiamentu (with English and Spanish widely used).
3. *Diglossia:* In Haiti and the French West Indies, French and a French-based creole exist but are kept relatively separate.
4. *Continuum:* Guyana, Antigua, Jamaica, Montserrat, and St. Kitts have different graded levels of language beginning with a polar variety commonly called "creole" or "patois" and moving through intermediate levels to a standard norm of English at the other pole.
5. *Monolingual:* Barbados, Cuba, the Dominican Republic, and Puerto Rico have a standard and a nonstandard form of European languages (English in the first case, Spanish in the others).

THE SOCIOECONOMIC STATUS OF CREOLE LANGUAGES

It may be said that an association exists between creole languages and low socioeconomic status. During the formative years of Caribbean societies when the creole language type developed, there was a quite simplified division between slaves, who (with the early extinction of the indigenous Amerindian population) were African, and free people, who were European. There are reports in the historical literature that, especially in the French-speaking

Creole = symbol of national identity

islands, some members of the white creole population (i.e., persons of European descent born in the islands) adopted the creole language, and one view (old, outdated, and almost universally rejected) held that Europeans created pidgin and creole languages. However, it is clear that creole languages, from the very inception of plantation societies, became associated with African slaves and their descendants. Creole languages served to identify this population ethnically and culturally, even though it was quite a negative identity, both from the perspective of the elite of the society as they evaluated the culture of slaves, and from the perspective of the slaves as they evaluated their own culture. It is true that slaves constituted a socioeconomically homogeneous group by virtue of being slaves, but there was an occupational differentiation among them, necessary for the effective operation of a plantation. The main occupational subgroups were field workers, artisans, and domestics. There is reason to believe that this division was the forerunner of contemporary social stratification as well as of the linguistic continuum in places such as Jamaica, Guyana, and Antigua. Different levels of language, corresponding in the past to the occupational subgroupings, now correspond to the rural/urban dichotomy and, within the urban sector, to levels of socioeconomic stratification. Thus the "deepest," most pure, most extreme, most "African" form of creole is to be found among nonliterate rural people living in locations remote from urban centers. Other levels of creole representing gradual approximations to a standard norm of English roughly correspond to levels of socioeconomic stratification. Insofar as social values are attached to levels of speech, we move from extreme negative to extreme positive social values as we move from one polar level of speech to the other. To refer to these levels linguists have adopted the terms *basilect, mesolect,* and *acrolect,* which express this correlation with the social order by combining -*lect* (from *dialect*) with derivational prefixes expressing the hierarchical structure of society. Thus, basilects are spoken more by the lower socioeconomic groups and acrolects by the higher socioeconomic groups.

The basic feature of Caribbean societies is that the mass vernaculars in the vast majority of nations are creole languages having low socioeconomic status. Creole languages are coming to be viewed as symbols of national identity, but there is still some insecurity about their use and uncertainty about their worthiness. *Yes*

In spite of this low status and negative value, the interactional and transactional utility of creole languages is highly recognized, and everywhere in the Caribbean (as on the coast of Africa) they are widely learned as second languages by immigrant ethnic groups. Thus among East Indians, Chinese, Javanese, and Middle Easterners in the Caribbean, the creole language is the one first learned after their arrival in the New World. In no case, however, has it become ethnically identified with these groups. It remains the recognized cultural property of the black, African-derived population, even where, as in the case of Guyana, East Indians may speak a variety of creole containing

forms belonging to an earlier period that have disappeared from the creole of other ethnic groups.

The socioeconomic status of a creole language in the Caribbean is particularly low when it is juxtaposed in the same society with a European language that shares its lexicon. In societies where the creole language coexists with an unrelated language (e.g., Suriname, where Sranan is lexically based on English and coexists with Dutch) it may be observed that the socioeconomic status of the creole language is not as low, and, in addition, it becomes the object of relatively intense language engineering programs. There is thus a marked correlation between the structural distinctiveness of the creole language vis-à-vis the official language on the one hand and the socioeconomic status of the creole language and the intensity of language engineering programs on the other.

CONTINUUM SITUATIONS

In this regard, societies in which the creole language has the greatest structural similarity to the official language tend to be those in which there is a language continuum, such as in Jamaica, Guyana, Antigua, Montserrat, St. Kitts, and St. Vincent. There the basilectal and mesolectal forms of language are linked to Standard English (the acrolect) in a graded continuum, and it is difficult, for both linguists and native speakers, to isolate discrete homogeneous linguistic systems and therefore difficult for the population to focus on "Creole" as a separate and distinct indigenous language. All speakers understand some messages in English and all speakers to greater or lesser degree introduce into their speech forms belonging to a more or less wide zone on the continuum. As a general rule the selection of forms from a particular level within a speaker's range of competence can be correlated with (or, in some views, is determined by) the social context. Factors in the social context may be subsumed under rather broad categories such as formal/informal, or public/private, and a speaker generally uses the form that corresponds to the context in terms of conformity to the social etiquette of linguistic usage. Thus a schoolteacher conducts his class in Standard English (the acrolect), uses a mesolectal variety in the staff room when speaking informally to his colleagues, switches to the acrolect if the conversation moves to a serious subject, and, on returning home in the evening, calls upon his basilectal variety when talking to his male gardener about the work that he had earlier assigned to him for the day. He interacts with his wife in the mesolect but is careful to use a variety close to the acrolect when speaking to the maid because any usage approximating the basilect would suggest familiarity. On the other hand, a speaker may attempt to define the context and his relationship with the interlocutor(s) by the choice of linguistic form. If indeed our schoolteacher wished to indicate to the maid his desire to be on terms other than a strict employer/employee relationship, he would use a basilectal variety and the message would be clear. The master of ceremonies and a toaster at a wedding reception are obliged, by the social etiquette of linguistic usage, to begin their address in an acrolectal variety. If, however, they wish to express the conviviality of the occasion or to stimulate some measure of it, they will very soon move to a level closer to the basilect. This variable use of language through the selection of forms belonging to different linguistic levels and having different socioeconomic statuses is referred to in the literature as "code switching." It is practiced by the entire population. Successful political rhetoric has to master it and employ it, and at every other level of interactional and transactional activity it occurs with varying degrees of conscious control.

There has, however, arisen a considerable amount of variation in speech that is inherent in the language system, i.e., that does not seem to be rule-governed in terms of being in any way determined by or correlatable with factors in the social context. It is also becoming increasingly difficult to find speakers who consistently use a pure homogeneous invariable basilect. For example, the speech of two painters redecorating a room of a house was recorded without their knowledge. Since the context was well defined and there were no interruptions from outside, one might have expected that these two men (good friends of the same age, occupation, and social class, chatting informally to each other) would consistently use whatever variety corresponded to that context (presumably basilectal). This did not happen. They both used a mixture of forms from the full range of the linguistic continuum. They sometimes used *mi* for the first person pronoun, and sometimes "I" with its full range of pronunciations. They also moved freely between at least four forms of the past continuous tense:

> *mi en a go*
> *mi was a go* ⎫
> *mi did goin* ⎬ "I was going"
> I was goin(g) ⎭

This mixing leads to an even greater difficulty in separating standard usage from nonstandard and creole usage (or acrolect from mesolect from basilect) and complicates the English language teaching problem. There is also greater difficulty in focusing on a creole level (the basilect) as a separate autonomous entity and attaching to it sentiments of language loyalty or elevating it to the status of national symbol or national treasure. It must be said again, however, that other factors such as political ideology and political culture can alter the picture of the social status of linguistic levels in a Caribbean language continuum.

In Jamaica, the rise of Rastafarianism and nationalist/Socialist political movements has changed the status of basilectal forms. There is an increasing willingness to admit that the "dialect" or the "creole" or the "patois" (as the basilect is variously called in Jamaica) is indeed the native language of Jamaica and that it is one of the main forces contributing to a distinct Jamaican cultural and national identity. The use of basilectal forms is one of the chief ways by which middle- and upper-class members of the society and members of ethnic groups whose loyalty and commitment to Jamaica may be suspect (whites, mulattoes, Chinese, Middle Easterners) may seek to demonstrate their loyalty to the Jamaican nation as it develops a new and aggressive form of national culture and national posture.

As its communicative function and its role as a symbol of national identity become more fully and generally recognized, basilectal speech is entering a number of new domains from which it was previously excluded. Television, radio, and newspaper advertising and public service programs and announcements are making considerable use of it. But here it is interesting to note that the unequal socioeconomic relationship between Jamaican Creole and Standard English is still reflected in the type of advertisements that are couched in each language and the type of media context in which the basilect is used. Public service announcements that are inspirational and accompanied by serious martial or hymn-type music are done in Standard English, while the more down-to-earth practical, development-oriented types are more often done in Creole. Commercial advertisements distribute English and Creole in accordance with the socioeconomic status or connotations of the product being advertised. For example, jewelery is advertised exclusively in English, while beer or automobile parts are advertised in Creole. In advertisements that simulate real-life situations, the dialogue may be done in Creole, but the general comment by the announcer must be in English. There is thus recognition of the communicative effectiveness of Creole in reaching a certain type of audience and recognition that the natural speech of Jamaicans is Creole; but a well-rooted sense of what is "proper" and prestigious still blocks Creole from entering certain domains. One radio station—Radio Central, part of the state broadcasting system—carries some of its broadcasts in Creole. These are a fundamental part of its role and function as a regional radio station catering to regional sectoral interests and aiding in the general cultural and educational uplift of the central region of Jamaica. Its audience is, in the vast majority, peasant farmers. The radio station administration overcame some opposition from the main urban center in the region and continues to broadcast news in Creole, thereby recognizing the fact that news should be cast in the language that the target audience understands. What is also interesting, however, is that the news is not read in the customary narrative way by an announcer. Rather, there is a dialogue between two persons involving questions and answers, further explanations, and comments. Thus not only the language, but also the interactional format that is *felt* to be typical of the socioeconomic group of peasant farmers (little or no education, predominantly oral culture) are adopted by the station. *Struggle*, the newspaper organ of the Workers Party of Jamaica (a left-wing political organization), copiously interlards its columns with basilectal and mesolectal forms in order to express and assist the identification of the party with the mass of the population. However, most of the newspaper is in English, thereby reflecting the recognition that certain topics and certain formats (such as print) are still properly the domain of English. Tensions and conflicts in Jamaican society may thus be observed through conflicts existing in attitudes to, and use of, different forms of language.

DIGLOSSIA

At the next level of structural distinctiveness between the mass vernacular and the official standard language is the situation of the "French-speaking" Caribbean. In Haiti, Martinique, Guadeloupe, and French Guiana, the creole is lexically based on French, which is the official language; but there is absolutely no doubt in the minds of the people that this creole (or "patois," as it is also called) is a distinct autonomous language quite separate from French. These cases gave rise to the identification of a new classificatory type in the sociolinguistic taxonomy—diglossia. *Diglossia* is the term used to refer to the coexistence of two codes (dubbed the "high" and the "low" varieties) that share one level of linguistic structure (the lexical level), allowing the filtering down of lexical items from the high to the low, but are in complementary distribution in the total communicative network, i.e., they do not overlap in any set of domains. For example, the high variety is used in formal public domains (law courts, Parliament, etc.) while the low variety is reserved for informal private settings. Haiti constitutes a special case within this group. Although the creole language spoken in these "French-speaking" territories is relatively homogeneous and although there is mutual intelligibility between varieties of French Creole, Haitian Creole differs somewhat from the others in form because of what seems to have been its ruralization in the aftermath of Haiti's early independence. The emphasis on the development of national symbols and the failure to provide opportunities for socioeconomic advancement for the mass of the population in Haiti resulted in the more widespread use of Creole in Haiti than in the other territories. Indeed, it is clear that the majority of Haitians are monolingual in Creole, since there is virtually no opportunity for Haitians to learn French outside the school system and the schools remain quite inadequate for this purpose. French is the language of the capital, and even there, only in official communication, education, and high business and technology.

Haiti has gone further than the other French-speaking territories in raising the social and juridical status of Creole. Article 35 of the Haitian Constitution of 1957 declares French the official language but recognizes the right of Creole to be used "in order to safeguard the material and moral interests of citizens who do not command the French language." This was reinforced by the Legislative House, which in 1979 passed a law stating, "The use of

Creole, the regular language spoken by 90 percent of the Haitian population, is permitted in schools as instrument and object of teaching."

In 1983, the French Ministry of Education published a policy statement granting approval for Creole to be introduced where necessary and feasible into the elementary education systems in the overseas departments of Martinique, Guadeloupe, and French Guiana. This seems to have been the logical extension of the French law that recognizes the rights of French citizens of the Basque areas and Corsica to elementary education in their mother tongue.

Apart from these official recognitions, the status of Creole continues to rise in Haiti as a result of the long Haitian national cultural tradition and the de facto existence of many Creole monolingual communities, and in the French overseas departments as a result of new radical movements for the assertion of an identity separate from France. Missionary groups and, from time to time, government agencies have been most instrumental. In Haiti, in addition to an already long tradition of Creole usage in adult education and evangelical work carried out by missionary groups, in commercial advertisements, in the mass media, and in poetry, there is an increasing use of Creole in formal contexts for scientific discourse. At many conferences today, both local and international, Haitian intellectuals are using Creole in their speeches and comments.

BILINGUAL SITUATIONS

It is in the Netherlands Antilles and Suriname that the dominant creole language (Papiamentu in the former, Sranan in the latter) is least stigmatized and enjoys the most prestige. In the ethnically plural society of Suriname, Sranan (not Dutch) is the language first learned by the new immigrant ethnic groups (East Indians, Chinese, Javanese) as well as by maroons and Amerindians who interact with the coastal inhabitants. Although certain separatist tendencies within the component units of the Netherlands Antilles are affecting the language planning efforts there, Curaçao and to a lesser extent Aruba and the other territories are moving ahead with quite ambitious, yet totally realistic and pragmatic planning for the organization of languages within their societies. Papiamentu is regularly used, without any conscious posturing, in a whole range of contexts from which other creole languages are excluded in the other Caribbean territories. There is, for example, a daily newspaper in Papiamentu and, more remarkably, a normative grammar written in that language itself. In spite of this, there persists among some influential members of the society a negative evaluation of the intrinsic and instrumental value of Papiamentu, and this is hampering somewhat the final adoption of the language for education at both primary and secondary levels. But work toward this goal is continuing apace on both the legislative and administrative/pedagogical fronts.

LANGUAGE AND DEVELOPMENT

Much is being said today of the role of human resources in national economic and social development. This claim places great importance on mass education and mass involvement in the decision-making process through effective communication among the people and between the population and its leaders. The primary instrument in this view of development is a language shared by all the citizens of the nation. This language may then also become the symbol of the achievement of nationhood and undergoes a process called standardization. This equips it to be the effective instrument of communication and education, permits the full participation of all the people in the political, social, cultural, and economic activity of the nation, and makes the language a fitting symbol of national identity, a veritable national treasure.

The communication dilemma is that development also requires international communication, whether in higher education, trade, transfer of technology, or international agreements. There is therefore a language and communication conflict, which may in some cases reflect a wider ideological conflict expressed in terms of self-reliance on the one hand and development by inflows of capital and technology in a free market system on the other. Effective communication with the people in the language of the people and the development of national self-confidence through the removal of cultural and linguistic insecurities are the cornerstones of the self-reliance model.

However, even the strongest adherents of self-reliance have to recognize the usefulness, if not the indispensability of international contacts and communication whether in the form of trade, political alliances, or importation of technology. The formulation of a comprehensive language policy that addresses the problem of local language(s) and foreign language(s) emerges as a prime necessity chiefly, but not exclusively, in newly emerging nations, the vast majority of which espouse the notion of self-reliance, even though it may remain an abstract ideal.

Different solutions have been proposed. At one extreme, Indonesia rejected the former imperial language, Dutch, and installed Indonesian as the sole official language of the nation; at the other, Ghana has retained English as its sole official language. In between there is a variety of experiments, including those of Canada and Kenya with two official languages; those of India and Nigeria with one federal official language and a number of state official languages; and that of Norway involving the standardization and official adoption of two varieties of the same language, one based on middle-class speech and the other based on popular speech.

In the Caribbean, no less than in other parts of the world, the problem exists and a solution is required. This is not the place to enter into a discussion of development philosophies and methodologies. The notion of self-reliance and political and economic independence have the fullest support among Carib-

bean nations, and even those that are not independent nations support the notion of national identity, political democracy involving participation of all the people, and cultural revaluation. All agree that the development of human resources should be the mainstay of political and economic development. But one of the most severe constraints on the realization of all the goals associated with national development is the underexploitation of human resources brought about by the language and communication problem that exists in all but the monolingual countries.

To take the case of education, large numbers of young people have little opportunity to overcome the language barriers to adequate education. From earliest childhood, their education is conducted in a language that is not native to them, that in different cases has different degrees of relatedness to their native language, and that may in some cases be virtually unintelligible to them. Education for these people does not have the component of exploration and discovery of the environment so as to produce creative adjustments to it. What is learned becomes unquestioned and unquestionable, and it is often remarked that Caribbean children who may be quite critical, argumentative, and insightful outside the classroom are uncritical and inarticulate during school. This runs all the way through to tertiary levels of education. The reason is probably that inhibitions in free expression arise from the school's rejection of the native language of the children. There are as yet no studies of the psychological difficulties that this kind of language inhibition may cause. One can only speculate on the possibility. It is also quite probably a factor in the general dependency syndrome that some commentators have mentioned as being characteristic of the Caribbean. One of these commentators has remarked that:

> quite apart from the reduction of the rate at which the countries of the Caribbean region can generate the professional and managerial level personnel needed for their development, the psychological damage in inhibiting the growth of articulate public expressiveness reduces the capacity of the societies to generate new ideas appropriate to their needs. Instead there is persistent borrowing of "solutions" to problems, with the language/culture in which these "solutions" have been conceived. The region hence remains an importer not only of materials but of ideas.

In the specific areas of language arts, it was not until quite recently that educators, educational policy makers, curriculum development experts, or writers of educational materials have given some recognition, however small, to the language situations in Caribbean territories. There still persists some belief that the existence of these creole languages as native languages is responsible for the low performance of students in the language arts (which still requires the acquisition of skills in the official language). And this would tend to increase the general hostility toward these native languages. There is, however, an increasing awareness that it is the inappropriateness of the methods used for teaching language arts (as well as other factors of a more general nature) rather than the existence of creole languages as native languages that causes the vast majority of children to leave primary and secondary schools without achieving adequate proficiency. There is also a growing awareness that language arts education should include much more than the teaching and learning of the official language and that the goal should rather be the acquisition of what is being called "communicative competence." Needless to say, this awareness takes some time to spread, and even more time to be translated into programs that reach the majority of the school population. An example of the stage of development of this awareness is to be found in the preamble to the English language syllabus for grades 7–9 issued by the Ministry of Education of Jamaica.

> English is the official language of Jamaica. Nearly all our children learn to speak Jamaican Creole, which has taken nearly all its vocabulary from English but much of its syntax from other sources; but in order to play a productive role in modern Jamaican society, they must be able to communicate effectively and accurately in English. We must strive to make Jamaican children highly competent in the language most widely spoken in the world, while teaching them to appreciate the Local Creole.

In other areas of national life, there are similar problems of a practical and concrete nature. Agricultural extension officers, family planning workers, rural development agents, and public health workers all have to grapple with the problem of effective communication. The communicative gap existing between the elite and the masses poses serious problems of social and political organization. While the masses were quiescent and accepted their low socioeconomic status and the low status of their culture and language, the communicative gap facilitated socioeconomic exploitation and political manipulation. Today there is an increasing awareness of the value of the popular culture and of the popular language, and political and economic leaders have to come to terms with it. Yet the fact remains that Caribbean national life is characterized by a linguistic (and cultural) cleavage between the economic and political leadership and the populations at large.

The use of creole languages, the mass vernaculars of the Caribbean, is now a vital factor in the democratization of national life and institutions and in the accessibility of these institutions to the mass of the population. Only in this way will the region be able to exploit the full potential of its human resources, break down traditional elitist structures, and remove the alienation that exists in the region.

MERVYN C. ALLEYNE

REFERENCES

ALLEYNE, MERVYN C.
1980 *Comparative Afro-American*. Ann Arbor, Mich.: Karoma.

BICKERTON, DEREK
1981 *The Roots of Language*. Ann Arbor, Mich.: Karoma.

HYMES, DELL (ed.)
1971 *Pidginization and Creolization of Languages*. Proceedings of a conference held at the University of the West Indies, Mona, Jamaica, April 1968. Cambridge: Cambridge University Press.

STEWART, WILLIAM
1962 "Creole Languages in the Caribbean." *In* F. Rice (ed.), *Study of the Role of Second Languages in Africa, Asia and Latin America*, pp. 34–53. Washington, D.C.: Center for Applied Linguistics.

TAYLOR, DOUGLAS
1977 *Languages of the West Indies*. Baltimore: Johns Hopkins University Press.

APPENDIX

The following chart provides a language profile and linguistic classification of each Caribbean territory as well as a brief note on the language planning activity in each. An important caveat must be mentioned here; the classification in terms of "language situation" should be qualified in the following respects:

1. Some linguists, as well as laypersons, contend that the language situation of Jamaica, Antigua, etc. is not a "continuum," but is rather either bilingual or bidialectal.
2. The classification of Haiti as a diglossic country is widely disputed. Some claim that the overall situation is one of bilingualism, but in addition that the majority of speech communities in Haiti are monolingual (in Haitian).

TABLE A.1.
Language Profile of Caribbean Territories

Country	Language Situation	Official Language	Mass Vernacular	Minority Languages, Ethnic Vernaculars	Major Second Language	Language Planning Activity
Cuba	Monolingual	Spanish	Spanish	—	—	—
Dominican Republic	Monolingual	Spanish	Spanish	—	—	—
Puerto Rico	Monolingual	Spanish	Spanish	—	English	—
Barbados	Monolingual	English	English	—	—	—
Jamaica	Continuum	English	English Creole	—	—	Growing awareness of the creole as mother tongue and symbol of national identity
Guyana	Continuum	English	English Creole	Hindi (Bhojpuri), Amerindian	—	Same as Jamaica
Antigua	Continuum	English	English Creole	—	—	—
St. Kitts	Continuum	English	English Creole	—	—	—
Montserrat	Continuum	English	English Creole	—	—	—
St. Vincent	Continuum	English	English Creole	—	—	—
Belize	Multilingual	English	English Creole	Spanish, Mayan, Garifuna	—	Creation of bilingual population in English and Spanish
Trinidad	Multilingual	English	(Postcreole) English	French Creole, Spanish, Bhojpuri	—	—
Grenada	Dying bilingual	English	English (influenced by French Creole)	French Creole rapidly receding	—	—

Location	Type	Official	Creole	Other languages		Comment
St. Lucia	Bilingual	English	French Creole	—	—	Incipient standardization of French Creole
Dominica	Bilingual	English	French Creole	—	—	Same as St. Lucia
Haiti	Diglossic	French, Haitian	Haitian (French Creole)	—	—	Advanced standardization of Haitian
French West Indies	Diglossic	French	French Creole	—	—	Incipient standardization of French Creole
Suriname	Multilingual	Dutch	Sranan	Javanese, Hindi, Ndjuka, Saramaccan, Amerindian	—	Incipient standardization of Sranan
Netherlands Antilles	Bilingual	Papiamentu, Dutch	Papiamentu	—	English/Spanish	Advanced standardization of Papiamentu. English replacing Dutch as international language
U.S. Virgin Islands	Bidialectal	English	(postcreole) English	Small pocket of French in St. Thomas	—	—
British Virgin Islands	Bidialectal	English	(postcreole) English	—	—	—
Dutch Virgin Islands	Bilingual	Dutch	(postcreole) English	—	—	—

·6·

The Caribbean as a Musical Region

KENNETH M. BILBY

For centuries the Caribbean region has provided Europe and other parts of the world with much-desired commodities, such as sugar, coffee, and rum. The wealth of more than one European empire was built in considerable part on a system of exploitation consecrated to the production of such goods. The Caribbean, more than most areas of the world, bore the brunt of this enterprise and was shaped by its demands.

The millions of human beings who were pressed into the service of this system were drawn from nearly every continent. Whether indentured Europeans, enslaved Native Americans or Africans, or postemancipation African and Asian contract laborers, their primary reason for being there was—like that of the Europeans in control—to contribute to the machinery of production. Indeed, the plantation-based Caribbean societies of the slavery era have been characterized by some authors as little more than artificially created industrial complexes, held together only by the threat or use of force. Given such a history, dominated so singularly by bare economic considerations and populated by such a diversity of individuals thrown so suddenly together, one might be led to assume that little in the way of a cultural life could have developed in the Caribbean. In fact, such a view has been common in the past, and many people continue today to see the Caribbean as a "cultureless" region, or a region where the only culture that exists consists of fragmentary or corrupted versions of transplanted European traditions. Even in the Caribbean itself, Europocentric ideologies have penetrated at every level, and in spite of growing nationalism, this attitude is still held by many.

The great irony is that during this century, even as this ideology has continued to hold sway, the Caribbean region has become a major exporter of culture. The material products exported in previous centuries have more recently been joined by a succession of musical forms, born and bred in the Caribbean. Not only Europe, but much of the rest of the world as well, has developed a steadily growing appetite for the indigenous musical creations of Caribbean peoples. This process has unfolded gradually, one wave of musical exportation following on another, and practically every major linguistic sub-region of the Caribbean (hispanophone, francophone, and anglophone) has been represented. Afro-Cuban and Dominican music, Haitian méringue, and Trinidadian calypso have all had international success. More recently, Jamaican reggae has had the widest, and perhaps the most significant, impact of any Caribbean form to date.

The recent worldwide explosion of enthusiasm for reggae music has created a resurgence of popular interest in things Caribbean. Alongside the large Caribbean audience that has always existed, and a handful of non-Caribbean aficionados, ethnomusicologists, and other scholars, there now exists a larger public eager to learn more about the background of modern Caribbean musical forms: their origins in folk traditions, their social significance, and the contexts in which they arose or with which they are now associated. Since most of the information available on Caribbean music has been published piecemeal in scattered journals and magazines and in the liner notes of record albums, there is a need for a broad overview of the subject. The present essay is intended as a synthesis of much of what has already been published on Caribbean music, which will provide the reader with some idea of the variety of musical forms to be found in the region, their essential characteristics, their social significance, and the wider impact that some of them have achieved.

Perhaps the most remarkable thing about Caribbean music is its great diversity. As with other cultural domains in the Caribbean, there is a bewildering range of forms, showing pronounced differences from region to region. This diversity challenges the very notion of presenting an all-embracing overview of Caribbean music, but I am convinced that most of these differing traditions *can* be accommodated within a general pan-Caribbean perspective, one that takes account of what they all share as well as what sets each one apart.

The brevity of this essay allows nothing more than an introductory excursion into the world of Caribbean music. A great deal more space would be required in order to do real justice to a musical tradition that is surely one of the richest and most varied in the world and that has probably had a greater influence on world music than that of any other geographic or political region of comparable size.

THE HISTORICAL DEVELOPMENT OF CARIBBEAN MUSIC

Most Caribbean musical forms, like Caribbean language forms and other aspects of culture, are characterized by a simultaneous newness and oldness, the heritage of a historical process that has come to be known as creolization. That is, most Caribbean musical forms are the relatively recent products of a meeting and blending of two or more older traditions on new soil, and a subsequent elaboration of form. This creative process appears to have been set in motion during the earliest years of the European settlement of the area. Although the contributing peoples and their traditions varied from one part of the Caribbean to the next, the results were similar in many ways. One reason for this is that almost everywhere in the region the creolization process brought into contact a variety of European and African musical traditions.

There were, of course, exceptions to this rule. In places where large-scale plantation systems did not take root, and where the population included few persons of African descent, the process of creolization took a rather different shape. In the rural interior of Puerto Rico, for example, where smaller farms predominated and settlement was more limited to Europeans and their descendants (the native population having been decimated and/or assimilated early on), musical forms tend to be almost exclusively Hispanic-derived. In addition, there remain a few Caribbean areas (such as the coastal strip of South America that includes Guyana, Suriname, and French Guiana) where Amerindian populations have until recently remained relatively isolated and have maintained purely native musical traditions. But exceptional cases such as these notwithstanding, the initial process of creolization in the Caribbean, far more often than not, centered on the encounter between representatives of *two* major musical traditions: *European* (Spanish, French, British, and to a far lesser extent, Dutch, Danish, and Portuguese) and *African* (West, Central, and to a lesser extent, East African). It was only in later years, after the emancipation of slaves in most areas, that the picture was further complicated by the arrival of large numbers of indentured immigrants from India, China, Java, and elsewhere.

Our knowledge of music in the Caribbean during the period of slavery is limited to what can be gleaned from contemporary reports, travelogues, and local histories, almost all of which were written by Europeans. The descriptions of music contained in these sources invariably suffer from European bias and misinterpretation. Furthermore, almost all of them are concerned with aspects of musical life on the large plantations, to the neglect of other areas. Nevertheless, the available information permits us to make a number of generalizations.

The process of blending began very early on. There exist numerous reports of slaves dancing, sometimes encouraged or forced by Europeans, on board ship while en route to the Caribbean. These impromptu musical events were sometimes backed by European instruments, such as concertina or fiddle, sometimes by African percussion, and sometimes by a combination of the two. On the plantations, the initial process of creolization took several directions. Blending occurred not only between European and African traditions, but also between the varied traditions of a multitude of African ethnic groups, whose cultures and languages often differed from each other at least as much as did those of the various European colonizers. This blending of distinct African traditions, which occurred throughout the Caribbean, has sometimes been referred to as "inter-African syncretism." The new musical creations that resulted sometimes owed a particularly heavy debt to one or more specific

African ethnic groups; but even when this was not the case, they often remained predominantly African, in that they displayed very little European musical influence. During the early years of colonization, a given musical event among slaves in any part of the Caribbean, as described by contemporary observers, might have included, back to back, songs in "Koromanti" (most likely Akan), "Nago" (Yoruba), and a number of other African languages, as well as songs in the local creole language, accompanied by a wide variety of African-derived drumming and dance styles.

At the same time, there existed everywhere in the Caribbean purely European musical forms, stemming from both folk and art traditions, performed at first by Europeans on European musical instruments. As slave musicians were exposed to these forms and were increasingly integrated into the social contexts in which they occurred, a host of new and strikingly different musical forms began to emerge. In many cases these new creations were neither predominantly European nor predominantly African in form and style but rather represented a thorough fusion of the two.

In most parts of the Caribbean, then, there developed out of this creolization process a broad spectrum of musical forms, ranging from purely European-derived examples at one extreme to what have sometimes been called neo-African styles at the other. Each colony evolved its own version of such a spectrum, a fact that now makes it possible, in spite of tremendous local variation, to treat the Caribbean as a single musical region. In some respects, this notion of an African-European musical spectrum is analogous to the concept of a "linguistic continuum" that has been used by linguists to describe creole languages in the Caribbean and other parts of the world. In those parts of the Caribbean where a linguistic continuum exists, it is possible for most speakers to slide "up" or "down" a continuous scale of different linguistic forms, one end of which is closer to a European language and the other of which is comprised of a "deeper" creole form characterized by African-derived features. Where such continua are found, the different levels of speech are seen as being appropriate to different speakers and contexts and are associated with different socioeconomic strata; but most individuals are capable of making adjustments and moving across at least a portion of the continuum. Much the same forces were involved in the development of Caribbean languages and musical forms, and the linguistic analogy is helpful in allowing us to appreciate the dynamics of Caribbean music.

Music constituted only one aspect of the creole slave cultures that flourished throughout the Caribbean region, but it was an important one. The historical literature leaves no doubt that music loomed very large in the lives of the slaves. Nearly everywhere in the Caribbean, for instance, slaves regularly held their own dances—both on the plantations and in towns—accompanied by drumming and singing. These dramatic musical events (referred to as "fêtes," "plays," and so on) often took place on holidays or "off-days" when slaves were not required to work, and they sometimes continued without interruption for several days and nights. It is clear from the existing descriptions of these ceremonies that they sometimes had religious significance; they were commonly tied to slave funerals, and they often involved spirit possession. (There is also evidence that they were sometimes tied to well-organized cults.) The slaves' owners felt obliged to allow these periodic "entertainments," even though they feared that they provided opportunities for the planning of revolts, for they viewed them as "pressure valves" that helped to discharge the pent-up resentment of the slaves before it could reach the point of explosion.

The daily work regimen also had an important musical component. Field gangs often carried out their tasks to the accompaniment of work songs, performed in call-and-response style by a leader and chorus. These songs, most of them sung in the local creole language, often served—as did many of the songs sung at slave dances—as satirical vehicles, commenting on, and often ridiculing, the behavior of local personages. No one was immune to this form of social criticism, including Europeans, who frequently found themselves the butts of slave humor.

In most parts of the Caribbean, a grand theater of cultural and musical blending was to be found in local carnival traditions. These islandwide celebrations often began as traditional observances of European religious holidays but over time became increasingly dominated by slaves and free blacks, who incorporated many of their own innovations. A typical Caribbean carnival during the slavery period included participation by both blacks and whites and involved colorful troops of costumed and masked dancers (sometimes organized in competing "teams" or "sets") who paraded through the streets and lanes to the accompaniment of singing and music, which was played on a variety of African and European instruments. In many areas, such festivities coincided with brief periods of general licence, during which slaves were temporarily allowed to violate certain rules of the plantation regime with impunity.

There were also the social dances of the Europeans, which were accompanied by the various pan-European ballroom dance styles of the era. Varying versions of dances such as the waltz, mazurka, polka, reel, or schottische were found throughout the region. Slave musicians who had been exposed to the repertoire of European styles often provided the music for these dances. Although the musicians who adopted these were capable in many instances of playing them in a manner faithful to the European tradition, they tended to allow their own aesthetic preferences to transform the music into something completely new. Eventually the slaves made these European-derived dances their own, and they became part of slave performances, alongside the neo-African drum- and percussion-based styles.

These few brief examples give some idea of the breadth of the cultural foundation—shared by most parts of the Caribbean—on which the musical creolization process is based. After emancipation, new additions were made to this general foundation, further enriching the musical landscape. Intensive Christian missionizing in some areas, for instance, led to important new musical developments that drew on various European liturgies. (In some places, where religious instruction of slaves had been allowed, this had already begun to occur much earlier.) The appearance of indentured laborers from Asia, with their own cultural and musical traditions, added further to the available pool of musical resources. But the basic creole musical continuum, with its African and European stylistic poles and its large middle ground, remained central to the ongoing Caribbean musical experience.

The historical literature, sketchy as it is, rarely permits us to glimpse the creolization process in action at the individual level, where conscious creative decisions (as well as unconscious adjustments) were made. But the concrete results are nonetheless visible everywhere, both in the documented music and dance of the past and in the many continuities of context, style, and form displayed by their present-day musical descendants. The following discussion of specific modern-day folk music traditions provides abundant evidence of such continuity. And the discussion of Caribbean popular music presented thereafter will show that the sorts of creative processes that shaped earlier forms—through adaptations, adjustments, and reinterpretations made by individual musicians—remain very much alive and in force today.

A BRIEF SURVEY OF CARIBBEAN FOLK MUSIC

It is difficult to find a major island or other territory in the Caribbean where African-derived traditions showing only very slight European musical influence do not continue to exist. Whether religious or secular, these traditions are distinguished by their fundamentally African instrumentation, consisting of a variety of drums (usually of African design, and most often played in ensembles of two or more) and other percussion instruments, such as rattles, scrapers, sticks, and bells (or bell-like metallic objects). Almost always, drumming is based on a principle of interlocking leading and supporting parts. In most cases, these traditions, in their general outlines, hark back clearly to the "plays," or slave dances, held so often on the plantations in previous centuries.

Not only the centrality of drumming and percussion, but also a number of stylistic features—such as the close interaction and communication between musicians and dancers, as well as the presence of a "metronome sense," overlapping call-and-response singing, off-beat phrasing of melodic accents, and occasionally polymeter—reveal the African origins of these traditions. (For a classic discussion of these stylistic features in relation to African music, and of their absence or only rudimentary development in European music, see the article by Richard Waterman appearing in the list of suggested readings.) When there does exist clear evidence of European influence in these traditions, it is usually limited to the language and melodic shape of songs. One of the most interesting things about these neo-African traditions is that although they remain essentially African in every respect, most of them must be seen as syncretic (blended) New World creations, for with few exceptions they are not traceable in their entirety to any specific region or ethnic group in Africa. And this is the case even with traditions that bear the names of specific African places or peoples. That such syncretic styles flowered so consistently throughout the Caribbean gives eminent testimony to the fundamental affinity—and easy "meshability"—of African musical traditions south of the Sahara.

Beginning with the anglophone Caribbean, we note the presence of an African-based drumming tradition in the Bahamas, where two- or three-drum ensembles, accompanied by a saw scraped with a knife, are used to provide music for a variety of dances, such as the "jumping dance" and "jook dance."

Farther to the south, Jamaica displays a rich variety of musical traditions clustering around the African end of the stylistic continuum. The various communities of Jamaican maroons (descendants of slaves who fled the plantations in the seventeenth and eighteenth centuries to form their own societies in the forest) possess a religious tradition known as "*kromanti* dance" or "*kromanti* play," in which ceremonies revolve around the possession of participants by ancestral spirits who use their powers to help the living solve various problems. The maroons also have a large repertoire of complex drumming traditions (most often played on an ensemble of two drums) used to invoke and entertain the ancestors. Among the several musical categories employed in *kromanti* ceremonies—each of which is associated with particular dances and songs, sung both in Jamaican Creole and a number of African-derived languages—are *prapa, mandinga, ibo, dokose* (said to be the names of "nations"), and *saleone, tambu,* and *jawbone* (recreational styles).

In the western part of the island there is a religious cult known as *gumbe*. Similar in many ways to maroon ceremonies, *gumbe* dances include musically induced spirit possession, ritual healing, and complex drumming. Also in the western area are the *nago* and *etu* traditions, said to be practiced by the descendants of postemancipation indentured African immigrants, many of whom were Yoruba. The ceremonies of both groups make use of songs in Yoruba and Jamaican Creole, accompanied by distinctive styles of drumming that are found nowhere else in the island. *Tambo* (or *tambu*), found primarily in the parish of Trelawny, is a Kongo-related drumming tradition, used mainly for entertainment, that may also have been introduced by postemancipation immigrants; here, a single drummer produces subtle and complex rhythmic variations by applying the heel of his foot to the head of the drum to change

pitch. (He is often accompanied by another musician, who beats the back of the drum with two sticks.)

In the central part of Jamaica there is a tradition known as *buru* (a word used elsewhere in the island to refer to any African-derived dancing or drumming); *buru,* played on an ensemble of three drums, along with scrapers, rattles, and other percussion instruments, is associated in some areas with secular masquerade dances and is said to derive from work songs stemming from the slavery period. When this music was carried by rural migrants to the ghettos of West Kingston several decades ago, it played an important role in the development of a new kind of drum ensemble music, called *nyabingi,* created by adherents of the Rastafari religion.

Still in Jamaica, but farther to the east, we find the *kumina* cults, whose members possess a vital dance-drumming tradition that is largely Kongo-derived. Specific drum rhythms (usually played on a battery of two drums, though sometimes three or more are used) and "African country" songs are used to summon the spirits of deceased cult members so that they may possess devotees and maintain contact with the living. *Kumina,* like a number of other African-based Caribbean traditions, is thought to have evolved shortly after emancipation, primarily among recently arrived indentured African immigrants. The Afro-Christian religious tradition known as *convince* or *bongo,* limited to the eastern part of the island, also makes use of a clearly African-derived style of music. Although drums are generally not used in *convince* ceremonies, songs are backed by polyrhythmic clapping (sometimes reinforced by percussive sticks) and are performed in typically African call-and-response style. Ceremonies almost always involve possession by ancestral spirits.

The Virgin Islands, which have been under the control of various colonial powers in the past, possess an interesting dance-drumming tradition called *bamboula,* which is thought to go back at least to the eighteenth century. (Dances of the same name have also been reported, in various historical documents, from Martinique, Guadeloupe, Haiti, and Louisiana.) The *bamboula* is danced during wakes, in carnival celebrations, and on other socially important occasions. Usually played on a single drum known as the *ka* (found historically in many parts of the Caribbean), the music may incorporate a second player who beats the back of the drum with percussive sticks. The drummer, as in Jamaican *tambo* and *kumina,* and a large number of other Caribbean traditions, skillfully uses the heel of the foot in order to vary the pitch of the drum.

In the chain of islands that make up the Lesser Antilles, most of the English-speaking islands have at one time or another either been French possessions or received substantial numbers of French immigrants; the populations of some of these remain largely bilingual (in English and French-based creoles), and their musical traditions—even those closer to the African end of the continuum—continue to show varying degrees of French influence. But in some of these traditions this is seen only in the existence of songs sung in French Creole and, as in other areas of the Caribbean, there are some musical styles that display almost no French influence. This is true, for instance, of the *kutumba* and *kèlé* ceremonies of St. Lucia (the former associated primarily with wakes and the latter with memorial rites for the ancestors). These two traditions are practiced by people who claim descent from a number of African "nations," and the songs, dances, and drumming that form an essential part of all their ceremonies are, for the most part, unmistakably African-based.

African influence is also central in the "big drum dance" of Carriacou, a tiny island off the coast of Grenada, whose neo-African musical traditions are some of the best documented in the Caribbean. Big drum ceremonies are held for a wide variety of purposes, ranging from weddings to ancestral memorials, and although they do not involve spirit possession, the dead are nonetheless invoked and given offerings. Like the *kromanti* play of the Jamaican maroons, and a number of other African-based traditions in Cuba, Haiti, and other parts of the Caribbean, the big drum tradition encompasses a large repertoire of distinctive singing, drumming, and dance styles, all of which belong to the African end of the island's musical spectrum. Some of these are associated with particular African "nations" and carry religious significance; others are primarily recreational. Among them are the following stylistic categories: *kromanti, arada, chamba, congo, banda, ibo, manding,* and *temné* (all "nation dances") as well as *old bongo, juba,* and *kalinda.*

Trinidad is particularly rich in African-based traditions. One of the more notorious, because of its connection with social unrest and riots at several points in the island's history, is known as *kalinda*. (The dance carrying the same name in Carriacou is said to have been brought there from Trinidad.) Dances called *kalinda* or *calenda* have been noted as well in several other parts of the Caribbean in the past. The Trinidad tradition centers on intricately choreographed stick-fighting, accompanied by music played on two or three drums, and sometimes also by *tamboo bamboo,* a type of stamping tube that is beaten rhythmically against the ground. *Kalinda* bands and stick-fighters once competed for regional championships but, after being banned by the authorities, were forced to go underground. Long associated with the famous Trinidad carnival, the *kalinda* tradition played an important part in the development of the calypso tradition and the steel bands that are so popular today. The *bongo* is a dance found in several parts of the island, traditionally performed at wakes for the purpose of placating ancestral spirits. Like the *convince* or *bongo* tradition of Jamaica, with which it shares many musical traits, the *bongo* dance of Trinidad usually does not make use of drums. It is accompanied rather by handclapping and percussive sticks, and sometimes the *tamboo bamboo* as well. *Bongo* songs, sung in call-and-response style, often include humorous social commentary.

Trinidad also boasts a number of musical traditions that seem to have been introduced by postemancipation African immigrants. The *congo* (or *kongo)* dance, held by people who claim Kongo descent, occurs in conjunction with weddings and christening ceremonies. Songs sung by a leader and chorus are backed by a three-drum ensemble. The *rada* tradition (whose name is derived from *Allada,* a major port on the coast of what was once Dahomey) incorporates music played by a three-drum ensemble, to which are added a rattle and a piece of iron used as a percussion instrument. The drumming, as well as call-and-response singing, is used to bring on spirit possession. The *shango* cults (also known as *yarraba),* largely of Yoruba origin, make use of three or four drums, along with rattles, and a wide repertoire of songs, to invoke a number of deities (known as "powers") to come and take possession of dancers. Minor ceremonies are held throughout the year for a variety of purposes, and once a year a major four-day ceremony takes place.

Yet farther to the south and east, Guyana is the home of several predominantly African-derived traditions. *Cumfa* and *kwe-kwe* (or *queh-queh)* are two of the better known ones; sometimes the two are combined in a single ceremony. These furnish us with yet another example of the sort of syncretic tradition that has over time integrated a varied selection of "nation dances" into a single complex. *Cumfa* and *kwe-kwe,* both of which center on ancestor worship, include typically neo-African call-and-response singing, dancing, and drumming (played on two or more drums).

The Spanish-speaking Caribbean is no less rich in fundamentally African-derived musical traditions. Cuba, in particular, possesses some of the most purely African music in the entire Caribbean. Perhaps the best known of these traditions is that tied to the *lucumí* religion, which is derived primarily from religious traditions of the Yoruba people of West Africa, but which also contains influences from Catholicism. *Lucumí* worship centers on the invocation of a large number of deities (known as *orisha)* and a complicated system of divination known as *ifa.* There is a large repertoire of different songs and drumming styles associated with specific deities, such as Ogun (god of war and iron), Ochun (goddess of the rivers), and Chango (god of thunder). The hourglass-shaped drums used in *lucumí,* called *bata,* are essentially the same as those used in certain types of Yoruba music in Nigeria today. Also represented at the African end of Cuba's musical continuum is the music of several *congo* cults, such as *mayombe, kinfuite,* and *palo-monte.* All of these cults or sects are concerned with the tapping of *nganga,* a sort of magical or spiritual force that pervades the universe; but each has its own dances and songs, accompanied by several different kinds of drum ensembles. The dance known as *yuka,* for example, makes use of a group of three drums of varying sizes and pitches, played with the hands, while *makuta* employs two drums of a very different kind—played with sticks—as well as rattles and a bell. *Lucumí* (which has come to be known also as *santería)* and the Congo groups are found both in the city of Havana and in several parts of the countryside.

Another Cuban tradition, the *abakua,* must not go without mention. The *abakua,* a secret society with an all-male membership, is derived largely from the traditions of the Efik people of the Calabar region of Nigeria. The society is said to have emerged during the slavery period among free blacks, who organized themselves and pooled resources in order to help buy the freedom of slaves, who were then admitted to the society. *Abakua* music is based on a percussion ensemble, at the center of which are two or three drums, and it is distinguished by its association with a unique masked dance, performed by a character known as *ireme* or *diablito* (Spanish, "little devil").

The Dominican Republic also possesses a number of African-derived musical forms, most notably those belonging to the *congo* ensembles. Although songs are in Spanish, the drums used to back them (known as *congos* or *palos*), the call-and-response form, and the wide variety of complex drumming styles, produce a music whose resemblance to African forms is as strong as any in the Caribbean. The groups that play this sort of music are found primarily in the southern part of the island, where much of the black population is concentrated.

Puerto Rico, which has a predominantly Spanish-derived population, also has a neo-African tradition, known as the *bomba.* A recreational dance dating back to the period of slavery and documented in the historical literature, the *bomba* depends on an ensemble of two or three drums. The focal point of the dance is a sort of contest between the leading drummer and a particular dancer. The dancer challenges the drummer by improvising steps that the latter must try to match on his instrument. If the drummer is unable to follow the steps, he loses; if the dancer runs out of improvisations, he or she loses. The traditional form of the *bomba* is confined primarily, if not exclusively, to the former plantation region of the island.

In the francophone Caribbean, the most famous African-derived musical traditions are those associated with the Haitian religion known to outsiders as voodoo, vodun, or *vaudou.* (Although these names have been used by outside observers to refer to the entire ceremonial complex, the rural Haitian equivalent denotes only a kind of dance that may or may not be performed in religious contexts.) This religious system is present both in the capital of Port-au-Prince and throughout the countryside, and there is marked regional variation from one area to the next. Although the theological system of Haitian voodoo represents a syncretic blend, combining beliefs derived from a number of West and Central African religions with influences from Catholicism, the bulk of Haitian ritual music and dance styles are overwhelmingly African-derived. Throughout the country, particular categories of music are connected with different "nations" and/or *lwa* (or *loa*—possessing deities); in some areas these deities are divided into two major pantheons, known as *rada* and *petro,* each with its own type of drum and percussion ensemble and its own cycle of dance-drumming styles. Among the more widespread styles of Haitian ritual music and dance are *banda, nago, congo, yanvalou,* and *ibo.* Everywhere in Haiti these are intimately tied to the invocation and entertainment of the *lwa,* the possessing deities, but they are also sometimes employed in secular contexts.

Farther to the east, in Guadeloupe, we find a tradition called *gwoka* (or *gros-ka)—ka* being the name of the type of drum on which the music is played. Essentially a recreational music, *gwoka* is associated with celebrations of several sorts, sporting events, weekend parties, and other social events. Three or four drums, as well as rattles, percussive sticks, and sometimes tambourines, are used to back topical songs performed in call-and-response style. For a time this tradition appeared to be waning, but in the late 1960s it began to experience something of a revival, and today it enjoys renewed popularity.

French Guiana, located on the northeastern coast of South America, also has its neo-African tradition, known as *cassé-co* (said to be derived from French *casser-corps,* "to break the body"). This is the traditional dance music of the African-descended creole population, which lives primarily in the coastal region. Played on two or three drums, along with a benchlike instrument beaten with two sticks, French Guianese music includes several distinct substyles, such as *gragé, le role, belia,* and *camougué,* each of which has its own dance movements.

Finally, we come to the Dutch Caribbean. The islands of Curaçao, Aruba, and Bonaire (part of the Netherlands Antilles) possess in common a musical tradition known as *tambu,* usually making use of a single drum accompanied by a piece of iron struck with a stick or another piece of metal. The call-and-response songs, most often topical, are usually sung in the local creole language, Papiamentu, and show a certain degree of European melodic influence; but the drumming itself, often involving virtuosic displays and complex cross-rhythmic play against the patterns of the percussive iron, is quite clearly African-derived.

Suriname, the South American republic that gained its independence from the Dutch in 1975, is so well represented by musical traditions belonging to the African end of the spectrum that only the most summary mention can be made of them. The African-descended segment of the population divides roughly between the Creoles (living in the coastal region) and the maroons (descended from slaves who escaped from the coastal plantations during the seventeenth and eighteenth centuries and, at least until recently, living primarily in the interior forest). Because many of their original ancestors were slaves on the same plantations, the present-day Creoles and maroons are culturally related in many ways. (Their languages, for example, are closely related English-based creole languages that originated during the mid-seventeenth century, before the colony was taken from the British by the Dutch.)

The Suriname Creole religion known as *winti* incorporates a music and dance tradition much like many of the others I have already mentioned. Centering on the invocation of a large number of deities belonging to different categories, each with its own domain of concerns (and some connected with specific "nations"), *winti* ceremonies contain a corresponding diversity of styles. One finds, for example, such differing musical categories as *kromanti* (associated with warrior gods and healing powers), *ampuku* (connected with forest spirits), *papa* (tied with a number of other kinds of spirits), and several others. Each of these calls for different arrangements of drums and percussion, different songs, and different dance styles.

The maroons, on the other hand, can be divided into six different "tribes" or ethnic groups (Kwinti, Saramaka, Matawai, Djuka, Paramaka, and Aluku, the last being the only maroon group located primarily across the border in French Guiana), which are separated by both linguistic and cultural differences. But all of the maroon groups are historically and culturally closely related, and they share a number of ritual music and dance traditions that, in their general outlines, resemble those of the Creoles. Thus, each maroon group has its own version of *kumanti/komantí, ampuku/apúku, papa/papá,* and so on, all of them involving a variety of broadly similar styles of drumming, dance, and song, ministering to similar gods, and occurring in similar social contexts (funerals, rites honoring deities, and so forth). But there are important regional variations as well, fostered by continual stylistic innovation; and a number of music and dance forms are associated with specific groups. The dances *susa* and *agankoi,* for instance, are considered to be specifically Djuka, while *tjêke* and *bandámmba* belong to the Saramaka.

Although maroon musical traditions were clearly created in the New World, they also remain, at a general level (in their social organization, their instrumentation, their performance style, and the way in which they structure sound), some of the most fundamentally African traditions to be found in the Caribbean. The same can be said of most Creole music as well, although clearly European-derived vocal harmony is not uncommon in *winti* songs. (Although there is very little evidence of European musical influence in maroon music, there is a strong possibility of Amerindian influence, particularly in the areas of melody and vocal style—a question that has yet to be investigated carefully.) Both Creole and maroon music and dance performances also constitute probably the clearest living examples in the Caribbean of integrated traditions directly descended from the dances or plays held by slaves in past centuries. (In both the coastal language and the various maroon languages, these performances are referred to by the equivalent of the English word *play.*) In spite of the fundamental dynamism characteristic of all maroon arts, the central features of present-day maroon performances—ranging from clothing styles and specific types of dance movements to the sorts of interac-

tion occurring between dancers and drummers—have a great deal in common with the plantation "plays" recorded in eighteenth-century documents.

Before moving on to a discussion of Caribbean musical forms located toward the middle of the African-European spectrum, I wish to mention one unique tradition found in the coastal Central American country of Belize. This is the ritual music of the Black Carib (also known as Garifuna). (The Black Carib are descended from African slaves who were shipwrecked off the coast of St. Vincent in the seventeenth century and merged with the Amerindians of that island to form a new society, which was later transported by the British to British Honduras—now called Belize.) What makes the ritual music of the Black Caribs particularly interesting is that it has clearly blended African and Amerindian features and at the same time displays virtually no European influence. Drumming is rather African-sounding, but the melodic shape of many songs (some of them in the Amerindian-derived language preserved primarily by women) clearly owes much to Amerindian musical traditions; and some dance steps appear to be similarly derived.

Just as each part of the Caribbean has its neo-African music, each also has its European-African hybrids. These are forms that have their feet planted, as it were, in both musical worlds and yet belong to neither; and they occur throughout the Caribbean. The various European traditions involved in their formation were more homogeneous than the varied African traditions that contributed to Caribbean music. For this reason, pan-Caribbean comparisons and generalizations are easier to make for these hybrid forms than they are for neo-African ones. Thus, these mixed traditions may be discussed in terms of a number of overlapping larger musical genres that span the entire Caribbean region.

Perhaps the most ubiquitous musical traditions of this kind are those that grew out of the European social dance music of an earlier era. This music was pan-European, in the sense that it was shared—with local variations, of course—by all of the European countries involved in the colonization of the Caribbean. Not only did this sort of music everywhere make use of the same kinds of instrumental ensembles (including, for instance, violins, guitars, flutes, and concertinas), but it was also based on the same repertoire of pan-European popular ballroom dances. (Dances such as the polka, quadrille, waltz, or mazurka—to name only a few—were known across Western Europe.) Because this music was so widely distributed, it helped to spread shared European melodic and harmonic concepts to all parts of the Caribbean. If there is one way in which the more European-influenced instrumental music of the Caribbean shows its "Europeanness," it is in its universal use—even if in slightly modified form at times—of a system of harmony, based on a particular diatonic scale, that originally developed in Europe over the course of several centuries.

Today the direct descendants of these ballroom dance styles are still to be found in every part of the Caribbean, with names that differ slightly according to area, as part of the repertoires of local village bands. Whether in Haiti or Puerto Rico, Jamaica or Curaçao, Martinique or the Virgin Islands, one can find rural bands that continue to play their own versions of dances such as the quadrille, the contredanse, the lancer's dance, the polka, and the mazurka.

Some Caribbean village bands continue to be capable of producing less creolized renditions of these dance tunes, versions that sound very European and remain quite close to the originals. But what one hears much more often is a thoroughly Caribbean adaptation that could never be mistaken for European dance music. Many bands make use of non-European instruments, such as the banjo (an Afro-American instrument found in many parts of the New World), the "rhumba box" or *marimbula* (a large, bass version of the African instrument known as *sanza, mbira,* or thumb piano), and various kinds of drums, rattles, and other percussion. But it is the modification of style and form, even more than the instrumentation, that sets these Caribbean creations off from their European precursors. In general, one can hear in the playing of these village bands a thoroughgoing infusion of African-derived rhythmic concepts; melodies tend to be liberated from the sort of strict metrical divisions characteristic of most traditional Western European music, while European back-up instruments such as the guitar take on a new "percussive" role. The result, when played well, is a music of irrepressible vitality, combining the best of both worlds.

The Caribbean village bands that play this sort of music tend to be associated with purely secular recreational dances. However, there exist a few intriguing examples of musical traditions stemming from these same ballroom dances that have been wedded to ritual contexts. In Trinidad and Tobago, for instance, as well as some of the smaller islands of the Lesser Antilles, one finds versions of the reel and the jig performed in the context of "jumbie dances"—rites involving the invocation of the spirits of celebrated *obeah*-men (ritual specialists) of the past, who come to take possession of dancers. The music of these dances fuses clearly British-based violin playing with African-influenced rhythmic accompaniment played on an ensemble of tambourines or drums, along with a triangle. In southern Haiti, certain *lwa* (deities) are served by the performance of dances such as the *mènwat* (minuet) and *kôtrédâs* (contredanse), backed by a trio consisting of a violin, a tambourine, and a small drum. Traditions such as these show the extent to which originally European musical forms could be transformed, both in form and meaning, by the process of creolization.

In most parts of the Caribbean, the repertoires of village bands are not limited to European-derived ballroom dances. After all, it was rural ensembles much like the contemporary village bands—with their predominantly European instrumentation and their fundamentally European harmonic underpinnings—that played an important part in the development and proliferation throughout the Caribbean of other, completely original song and dance styles (ones that have no direct European antecedents). Virtually every country or island in the Caribbean has its own version of such an indigenous style, displaying its own unique blend of African-derived and European-derived features, culled from the local corpus of folk traditions. In spite of the many ways in which they differ from one another, such "national" styles as the Dominican *merengue,* the Jamaican *mento,* the Puerto Rican *plena,* the Cuban *son* and *danzón,* and the Martiniquan *biguine* all owe a great deal to the syncretic music first played by rural ensembles of the village band sort; all of them are rooted, ultimately, in creole forms developed during the slavery era. And all of them continue to grace the repertoires of present-day village bands. (Most of them have also contributed to the later development of urban popular styles—a matter that will be discussed at a later point.)

Another widespread Caribbean genre deserving mention is that of the work song. In many places, cooperative labor gangs continue to coordinate their work to the rhythm of special songs, often performed in call-and-response style by a leader and chorus. Most commonly these work songs are associated with agricultural tasks (such as the clearing and preparation of fields for planting), but their applications range from house building to rowing, and from food pounding to the cutting and hauling of lumber. A clear precedent for such musical forms is to be found in the historical descriptions of the work songs once employed by slaves on the plantations. It should come as no surprise, then, that many of the work songs heard in the Caribbean are closer to the African end of the African/European stylistic continuum (for example, in their melodic shape and in their short, repeating responsorial phrases). But because European work songs have a good deal in common with their African counterparts (such as frequent use of an antiphonal, or call-and-response, structure), it is sometimes difficult to disentangle the influences involved. In any case, many Caribbean work song traditions display a continuum of styles ranging from more African to more European. In Jamaica, for example, there are some digging songs that sound predominantly African, with their short choral litanies and highly syncopated melodies, and others whose melodic structure and use of part-singing based on European harmony attest to their European background. Unfortunately, the work song is among the more poorly documented of Caribbean musical genres. Aside from Jamaican digging songs, some of the better-known examples are the work songs associated with the Haitian *coumbite* (a system of communal agricultural labor) and those connected with the cooperative labor traditions of the Lesser Antilles, known as "lend-hand," *gayap, coup de main,* and so forth.

Throughout the Caribbean, another important context for music making is the wake. Wake traditions such as the Puerto Rican *baquiné,* the Haitian *gage,* or the Jamaican "nine-night" (or *dinky-minny*) display many similarities. Among other things, they share an association with a number of similar musical genres. A typical Caribbean wake might include, at different points through the night, the music of a village band, the performance of game songs, and the singing of European hymns or other religious choral music. The game songs—which have a special association with wakes but often occur independently—are of particular interest. Performed usually in call-and-response style (the form often being dictated by the structure of the particular game), these songs also vary in style along an African-European continuum; examples range from those clearly related to specific songs of European origin to others that can only be considered indigenous and that show all of the more common African-derived stylistic features found in other kinds of Caribbean music. Songs of this sort have been particularly well documented in Jamaica and the Lesser Antilles (where the games they accompany are known as "ring play," "pass play," and so forth), but they are found in most other parts of the Caribbean as well.

The influence of European religious music has been felt in nearly all parts of the Caribbean. In the hispanophone areas, one still finds religious "brotherhoods," or *cofradías,* whose members perform ancient Spanish-derived religious chants. In Haiti, Catholic *cantiques* (hymns) have been integrated into voodoo ceremonies. In the anglophone Caribbean, where large-scale missionization among slaves tended to take place somewhat later than in other areas, a number of independent Afro-Protestant cults or sects sprang up during the nineteenth century. Their present-day descendants, including groups such as the Spiritual Baptists (Shouters) of Trinidad, and the Revival Zionists and *pocomania (pukkumina)* practitioners of Jamaica, possess particularly interesting musical traditions. Blending Protestant devotional songs (many of them taken from nineteenth-century British and American hymnals) with polyrhythmic clapping and, in the case of the Revival Zionists, forceful drumming, these groups have invented an entirely new musical form—once again, neither European nor African—which displays a certain kinship with North American black gospel music. While the liturgical music exerting the greatest influence in francophone and hispanophone areas has in the past been Catholic, the recent spread of American-based fundamentalist Protestant sects (and in particular, Pentecostalism) to all parts of the Caribbean promises to complicate the picture further.

Finally, we come to the great street celebrations or carnivals of the Caribbean, where animated music and dance have always been central elements. Today, as in the past, virtually every island or territory observes its own annual calendar of outdoor festivities. During designated periods—usually coinciding with major holidays such as Christmas, the New Year, Mardi Gras, Easter, and a number of Saints' days—celebrants don festive apparel and take to the streets, adding their voices and movements to a folk drama in which performers and audience are one and the same. These communal manifestations have long served as meeting grounds where different musical forms normally occurring in other settings mingle and give birth to new styles. Thus, many of the musical traditions already discussed in relation to other contexts are also sometimes brought into the service of carnival celebrations. But most Caribbean festival traditions can claim certain musical forms as their own—such as the marching or parade music that is at the heart of all carnival processions.

Just a few examples from different parts of the Caribbean will suffice to show the variety and richness of these carnival traditions. The Cuban *comparsas,* or street processions, tied to the celebration of traditional religious holidays, have been a point of convergence for some of the most vital Afro-Cuban musical forms. Among the musical traditions having a special relationship with these festivities is the *rumba.* The traditional carnival music known by this name (to be distinguished from the popular style known as rumba in North America, which was actually based on another Cuban form, the *son*) in fact encompasses a variety of different dance-drumming styles, such as the *guaguancó, yambu,* and *columbia.* All of these must be placed close to the African end of Cuba's musical continuum. Although instrumentation varies from place to place, drum and percussion ensembles (including *claves,* and sometimes *congas* and boxes, or *cajones,* used as drums) are always involved; sometimes horns or other instruments are added. These carnival ensembles, or *conjuntos,* once limited to outdoor celebrations, eventually made their way indoors to the dance halls, where they contributed to a new kind of *conjunto* music using other instruments such as the piano and bass.

In Haiti, the beginning of carnival (shortly before Easter) signals the arrival of the *rara* bands. Winding through the roads and lanes from village to village, the musicians pick up crowds of dancers, singers, and spectators as they go. The *rara* bands produce some of Haiti's most compelling music. Rural bands use a wide variety of instruments. Particularly noteworthy are the *vaccines* (long, hollow trumpetlike tubes that are blown to produce single pitches); when played in ensembles of two or more, the *vaccines* produce complex interlocking melodic patterns, each instrument interjecting its own note at specific time intervals. This technique, known as "hocketing," is shared by traditional horn ensembles throughout West and Central Africa. Various kinds of drums are also employed, as well as rattles and other percussion. Urban *rara* bands sometimes add other instruments such as guitars and brass. (There is a similar carnival tradition across the border in the Dominican Republic, known as *gaga.*)

The most famous of Caribbean carnivals is that of Trinidad, which draws thousands of tourists every year. The close relationship between calypso music and the Trinidad carnival—with its calypso "tents" (makeshift theaters where contenders compete for the calypso crown), steel bands, and annual "road march" (procession)—is generally well known. But most of the smaller islands in the Lesser Antilles also have vigorous (if less famous) carnival traditions that have borrowed elements from Trinidad, such as the steel band, while retaining their own distinctive features. Almost all of the islands have mumming traditions, derived in part from European folk plays, that have been integrated into the festivities. Masked dancers parade through the streets, pausing occasionally to recite passages from Shakespeare or medieval mumming plays or, in the French-influenced islands, to sing carnival songs in French patois.

A similar carnival tradition is found, in somewhat attenuated form, in the "John Canoe" (or *jonkonnu*) dance of Jamaica, and the tradition known as *mummies* in St. Kitts and Nevis. (A transplanted version of the latter is also found in San Pedro de Macorís in the Dominican Republic, brought there by immigrants from St. Kitts and Nevis.) These last examples deserve special mention because of the unique form of music they use: a type of fife and drum music that was born out of a blending of European military drumming traditions with the music of West African flute and drum ensembles. This exciting music is paralleled by similar traditions in Haiti and other parts of the Caribbean, as well as by Afro-American fife and drum traditions found in certain parts of the southern United States, and it is thought to bear a close relationship to the sort of drumming that was used in the very earliest forms of jazz.

Traveling along the Caribbean musical continuum yet farther, we arrive at the European extreme—musical forms showing little or no African influence. As should be evident by now, many of the African-European hybrid traditions already discussed contain occasional examples of specific songs or instrumental pieces that are primarily of European derivation. Some Caribbean village bands play versions of ballroom dances that sound purely European; and it is not difficult to find particular work songs or ring play tunes whose melodies can be traced to specific European folksongs. But the extreme European end of the continuum remains largely undocumented, primarily because most researchers of Caribbean folk music have been more interested in hunting down neo-African forms—and in teasing out the African-derived strands in the more syncretic forms—than in finding less "exotic" European carryovers.

Be this as it may, there are several examples that can be cited from the literature on Caribbean music. In the hispanophone Caribbean, there are the *jíbaro* and *guajiro* traditions belonging to the rural farming populations of Puerto Rico and Cuba, respectively. Both traditions make use of small string ensembles and are characterized by a type of song based on a Spanish-derived ten-line verse form known as the *décima*. The Dominican Republic also has its fundamentally Spanish-derived music: the ancient vocal choruses known as *salves* and *tonadas,* which are found primarily in the northern part of the country. French-influenced areas, for their part, have kept alive Christmas caroling traditions (in some places, known as *quesh* [French *crèche*]), in which choral groups pass from house to house and regale the residents with

harmonized French folksongs and *cantiques de Noël.* And in most parts of the anglophone Caribbean, it is still possible to find British sea shanties that agree nearly note for note with versions recorded on the other side of the Atlantic by British collectors during the nineteenth century, as well as Irish and Scottish ballads that are still known and sung in Appalachia and parts of the British Isles.

Having finished our journey from the African end of Caribbean music to the European, it is necessary to mention that there are certain parts of the Caribbean where a strong Asian presence has also left its mark on local musical life. In countries such as Trinidad and Tobago, Guyana, and Suriname—where people of Indian descent are either in the majority or constitute a very substantial minority—there exist thriving musical subcultures based on both Hindu and Muslim traditions. And even some of the islands with much smaller Indian populations, such as Guadeloupe or Jamaica, have preserved certain Indian-derived musical traditions. Moreover, in Suriname, the only Caribbean country with a substantial Javanese minority, traditional Indonesian shadow-puppet plays (*wayang*) continue to be performed, accompanied by the music of locally made *gamelan* orchestras. Asian music, however, has been slow to enter the creole musical continuum, and there exist few well-documented cases of syncretism between Asian-derived and other Caribbean folk musical forms. Nevertheless, Indian traditions such as the *hosse (hosein)* festival of Trinidad—with its *tassa* (kettle-drum) ensembles—are attended by people of all ethnic backgrounds, and drummers of African descent are not uncommon. So it seems more than likely that these Asian-derived musical forms, in spite of having arrived later than most others and remained more or less separate, will contribute more and more to the development of Caribbean music as time goes by.

This brief survey of Caribbean folk musical traditions would not be complete without a few general remarks about some of the cultural characteristics shared by the many different varieties of music spread across the region. It is evident that the shared creolization process and the development of an African-European stylistic continuum are partly responsible for the present-day unity—broadly speaking—of Caribbean music. But this unity goes beyond the level of musical structure. It is not simply a matter of "African rhythm" married to "European melody" (a common depiction of Caribbean music, which, though oversimplified, contains a large grain of truth). For the distinctive cast of this music owes as much to its social dimensions as it does to the pool of sound resources bequeathed to it from the past. And certain cultural trends—certain tendencies that emerge when one views Caribbean music-making episodes as social as well as musical events—have been noted by many different observers, writing about different parts of the Caribbean, and at different points in time.

Most writers on Caribbean music have noticed the extent to which musical traditions are closely integrated with social and religious activities. Music as an autonomous art form, pursued for its own sake, and divorced from everyday social life—as in the Western classical tradition (or at least a large part of it)—is a concept foreign to all but the Europocentric elite sectors of Caribbean societies. As should be evident from the preceding description of specific musical traditions, Caribbean folk music is almost always embedded in some larger social context, whether this be a religious ceremony, an afternoon of communal labor, or a weekend dance where young men and women seek out prospective lovers. Music is more than mere accompaniment to such activities; in many cases, it is central to them, and their successful completion depends upon it.

The use of song for social commentary has been so widely reported in the Caribbean that one must consider this a pan-Caribbean phenomenon. The topical song, relying for its effect on such devices as double entendre, irony, and veiled allusions, is a Caribbean specialty that cuts across many musical genres. Virtually anyone or anything can be made a target of such songs, and thus several writers have surmised that this sort of sung criticism functions as a means of social control. Attempts have been made, as well, to link these songs to the widespread West African tradition of "songs of derision." But not all Caribbean topical songs fit this mold; while some are used to ridicule human foibles, others are more neutral and serve simply to channel information on local current events through the community.

One of the most salient features of Caribbean musical life is the collective nature of most music and dance performances. In most traditional settings, there is no division of participants into passive audience and active performers. To be sure, there are specialized roles; specially gifted instrumentalists, singers, or dancers are given recognition for their abilities. And individual performances, or segments of performances, may be dominated temporarily by one or more central performers. But all participants have the opportunity to contribute in some capacity. Indeed, a performance that does not inspire enthusiastic collective participation—and thus does not become "hot"—is a failed performance. What determines the success of a musical performance, then, is not only the technical skill with which it is executed, but also the degree to which it engages others in active participation; the process is circular, for the higher the level of participation, the more the leading players and dancers will be spurred on. The quality of communication and *interaction* generated—interaction between the instrumentalists and dancers, between the lead singer and chorus, between the listeners and watchers clapping and offering encouragements and the players and dancers receiving them—is what makes or breaks a musical performance. This general criterion of collective participation is something that Caribbean musical traditions share with African and Afro-American music in general, and it constitutes one of the most powerful reminders of the depth of the African contribution to Caribbean musical life. It is an aesthetic canon, a sensibility, that permeates nearly all Caribbean music. Even many of those traditions that, at the level of form, are closer to the European end of the spectrum are not exempt from this principle, as anyone who has witnessed a "hot" Caribbean quadrille dance can affirm.

At the same time, within this collective framework, there is a strong emphasis on individuality. Many writers on Caribbean music have noted the importance of individual "style" in musical performances. Performers who wish to occupy the limelight must cultivate a personalized touch—an individual "flash" or *élan*—that distinguishes their performances from those of others. Originality and flamboyant individualism are encouraged. This emphasis on individualized expression goes hand in hand with the positive valuation placed on improvisation and experimentation in most Caribbean musical traditions. In all but the most conservative traditions (most of which are tied to religious contexts), improvisation—within limits, of course—is a normal and expected part of performance behavior. Variation and novelty are consciously sought—rather than standardization and accurate reduplication, as is generally the case in the Western classical performance tradition. Needless to say, it is among individual performers—who decide when or when not to embellish a note, accentuate a drumbeat, or alter a dance movement—that this creative process is acted out. This stress on individualized expression applies not only to musical performances, but also to much of the social interaction characterizing daily life in the Caribbean. (The role of individual performance of various kinds in establishing one's social "reputation" has been noted by several authors.) It can perhaps be said that this is part of what lends Caribbean social life in general its particularly "dramatic" quality. But it must be emphasized once again that, in musical spheres, an individual's flare for performance cannot stand on its own. For the power of any individual performance flows in very large part from the collectivity within which it unfolds.

Finally, it is necessary to assess the significance of the tremendous musical diversity marking most Caribbean societies for the musicality of the individual. The Caribbean individual's musical environment is rich, a musical world whose sheer diversity is paralleled in few other parts of the globe. A tiny island such as Carriacou (seven and a half miles long by three and a half miles wide, with a population of roughly six thousand) can lay claim to as many as ten or fifteen distinct "types" of folk music, ranging from predominantly African-derived traditions such as the big drum dance on the one hand to British balladry on the other. In many of the larger islands, internal regional variation creates an even more complex situation. So the individual Caribbean musician is confronted with an unusually wide variety of musical choices.

This has led to the development in many areas of a phenomenon that may be referred to as polymusicality. In a musical environment in which it is possible for one to encounter virtually back to back the buoyant strains of string bands and the complex drumming of possession cults, the call-and-response of field gangs and the layered harmony of a Bach chorale, it is not surprising that many individuals acquire competence in more than one tradition. In the Caribbean, the individual musician who specializes in a single form or style to the exclusion of all others is a rarity; just as the instrumentalist who limits himself to a single instrument is an exception. This polymusicality of the individual Caribbean musician can be illustrated with an example drawn from my own field experience in Jamaica. One Jamaican musician whom I once trailed for a period of several days moved through the following succession of very different kinds of musical performances, never showing the least difficulty in switching from one style to another. Starting one morning by playing guitar in a coastal *mento* band for tourists, he returned later that day to his rural village to join in a fife and drum performance, playing the leading drum, and then in the evening added his voice to a Revival church chorus. The next day he treated a group of friends to an impromptu performance of British ballads, accompanying himself on guitar, and late that night played guitar and led a number of religious songs at a "nine night" (wake). On the afternoon of the third day, I found him jamming on electric bass with a local reggae band, and by the early evening he was contributing some excellent banjo playing to a village quadrille dance. The next morning found him on the coast entertaining the tourists again, this time on harmonica, and when I left him that evening he was on his way to a *kumina* ceremony, where he intended to sit in on the supporting drum. While his musical schedule during these few days may have been more fully packed than usual, the easy movement between styles was not unusual for this man; nor was the wide scope of his musicianship extraordinary for a rural Jamaican musician.

There is a temptation to see Caribbean musical life, because of its great diversity, as being made up of a rich but incoherent patchwork of different traditions. However, Caribbean musical cultures—like Caribbean languages and Caribbean cultures more generally—are perhaps better represented as integrated wholes than as jumbled assortments of separate and competing cultural traditions. The African-European musical spectrum displayed by each Caribbean country or island belongs to its entire population, with the exception perhaps of small European-oriented elites. The polymusical individual— and almost all individuals are polymusical to at least some degree—moves across the stylistic continuum with no sense of discomfort or disjointedness. (As with linguistic continua, the individual makes shifts from one part of the continuum to another according to context.) Internal regional variation in any particular country may color the local African-European spectrum slightly differently from one spot to another. But the local musical continuum remains more or less an integrated totality, a cultural pool held in common by the larger society, to which each individual has at least partial access.

The polymusicality of individual Caribbean folk musicians—who sample freely from the musical spectrum, without regard for the historical provenance of specific styles—provides the strongest evidence of the integration of Caribbean musical cultures. I offer another example from my own experience. When making a study of the music of the Jamaican maroons, who have a reputation for being the most culturally African of all Jamaicans, I discovered that one of the most knowledgeable and respected *kromanti* drummers was also the best harmonica player in the area. His lively performances of jigs, reels, and the various figures of the quadrille were without equal and would have stood up to the best that the British Isles themselves have to offer. To suggest to this man that this music, in which he took such pleasure, was any less "his" than were the *kromanti* drumming styles that he had also mastered would have been a patent absurdity. There was nothing in the least "schizoid" or incongruous about the way this individual had lent his talents to the whole range of Jamaican music. The two traditions, though tied to very different social contexts, belonged in equal measure to the integrated creole culture that had been handed down to him. Although he might divide his musical world into parts, he would have no doubt that his musicianship was equal to the demands of all of them.

With its wealth of coexisting musical styles, its history of blending and adaptation, and its polymusical citizenry, the Caribbean region has produced a series of particularly "open" musical cultures. Polymusical individuals in the Caribbean most often have no scruples about using what they have learned from one musical tradition to add something new to another. Moreover, the "typical" Caribbean citizen—regardless of class or level of formal education—shows a degree of musical sophistication and an appreciation for musical variety and innovation that are rare among North American and European audiences (whose tastes, in general, are so easily compartmentalized, harnessed, and molded by marketing strategists). Caribbean musical cultures—with their emphases on individual expressiveness, collective interaction, improvisation, and experimentation—are distinguished by their receptivity to new combinations of ideas and influences. Borrowing and blending between traditions, after all, has been occurring for several centuries; it is a part of the Caribbean heritage. Whatever else may be said about Caribbean music, it remains always ripe for change.

POPULAR MUSIC AND ITS LINKS WITH TRADITION

When speaking of Caribbean popular music, one thinks of contemporary, "modern" styles such as Jamaican reggae, Trinidadian *soka* (or *soca*), or the modern *cadence* (or *kadans*) of Haiti and the French Creole–speaking islands of the Lesser Antilles. These are the sounds of the "new Caribbean," the

Caribbean of oversized urban sprawls and rampant migration, of transistor radios and electrified sound systems. They are the sounds of music businesses, with recording studios and professional musicians. But one must be careful not to make too sharp a distinction between popular and folk music. In the Caribbean, the connections between the two have never really been severed. In spite of commercialization, Caribbean popular music styles can be considered urban folk traditions. Still largely orally transmitted, they continue to display many of the essential features of the rural traditions that have long fed into them.

It was inevitable that such popular styles should have sprung up throughout the Caribbean under the stimulus of urbanization, large-scale migration, and the spread of new technologies. The Caribbean penchant for musical experimentation and the receptivity to new ideas ensured that individual musicians would take full advantage of the new musical opportunities and influences to which these forces increasingly exposed them. The age-old process of blending and adaptation continued to give birth to new forms, which have since been further modified to create still other varieties. Yet, through all these changes, popular styles have remained firmly rooted in folk traditions, often passing through phases in which contributions from older, rural forms have surfaced (or resurfaced) with particular vigor. The basic outlines of this process can be traced for several of the better-known popular music forms, although the evolutionary paths of most styles have yet to be documented in detail.

Take, for instance, Trinidad. The island's first urban popular music form, the famous calypso (or *kaiso*), grew up primarily in and around the capital of Port-of-Spain, where the variegated folk traditions of the countryside had long been converging. It is impossible to pinpoint exactly when the musical style today recognized as calypso emerged. But one thing that is clear is that it went through a steady succession of transformations before taking on its present-day form. It appears that the origins of calypso are to be found in a number of folk traditions, such as the *bamboula* and *belair* (or *bélé*), which go back to the nineteenth century or before—making it one of the oldest Caribbean popular music styles. Apparently, the earliest songs were primarily in French Creole, but English was in use by the beginning of this century. Early on, a relationship was forged with the annual carnival, and so calypso acquired an association with the drum rhythms of the *kalinda* stick-fighting tradition. But it was not long before stringed instruments (such as guitar and *cuatro*) were adopted, and along with these, a number of stylistic influences from the dance music of nearby Venezuela. By the 1920s and 1930s, when calypso began to be commercialized and to achieve its first international exposure, the music of the calypso tents (where calypsonians performed and competed during carnival) was being played on guitars, bass, trumpets, saxophones, clarinets, and a number of other instruments. At the same time, there was also the calypso dancing of the streets, the parades or "road marches," that was backed by the rhythms of *kalinda* and *tamboo-bamboo*. When the *tamboo-bamboo* (stamping tubes made of lengths of bamboo) were prohibited as dangerous weapons during the 1930s, urban musicians responded by coming up with an entirely new instrument to replace them: the tuned steel pan, fashioned from discarded oil drums. This new instrument, in turn, sired a profusion of new techniques and substyles, which continued to feed into the larger calypso tradition.

The innovations that have figured so greatly in the development of Trinidadian popular music have not always been the result of new inventions or new introductions from outside. Trinidad's own folk musical continuum still furnishes studio musicians—many of whom are conversant with the older musical forms—with a well-stocked reservoir of local styles into which they continue to dip from time to time. The currently reigning offshoot of the calypso tradition, a style known as *soka,* provides a good example of this. According to several of the musicians involved in its popularization, the *soka* "beat" was first developed during the 1960s by studio musicians who, while experimenting, used the trap drums to fuse a number of rhythmic patterns derived from the *shango* cults and the *hosse* drumming tradition with the current *kaiso*/calypso style (by then played on amplified instruments, such as electric piano, guitar, bass, organ, and so forth). Elements of North American funk were added as well. The result was at first called the "*rotto* beat" or "*rooto* beat," and for some time it received little attention. During the 1970s, however, it resurfaced as the "*soka* beat" and contributed to the production of some of Trinidad's most vital music to date. Today, it continues to flourish.

Jamaican popular music, though much younger, has an equally convoluted history. As early as the 1940s and 1950s, a tiny recording industry had already begun to operate in Kingston. Local *mento* compositions, often influenced by the then popular Trinidadian calypso, were pressed and distributed on a small scale. This urbanized form of the *mento* achieved some popularity for a number of years, but it was not until the late 1950s and early 1960s that a completely original new style known as *ska* burst upon the scene. *Ska* was born when urban Jamaican musicians began to play North American rhythm and blues, a style that had penetrated the island via imported records and radio broadcasts from Miami and other parts of the southern United States. Whether consciously or not, these musicians began to graft certain rhythmic patterns derived from the music of the Revival cults onto the basic rhythm and blues framework, and a completely new form of music gradually emerged. Within a few years, the *ska* had slowed down its tempo and absorbed a number of further influences from North American "soul" music and other sources; in its new incarnation it was known as "rocksteady." Shortly after this, yet another new style known as reggae cropped up. Reggae retained the basic rhythmic structure of the previous popular styles but showed the influence of both *mento* and the Rastafarian drumming tradition known as *nyabingi*. (The liaison between popular musicians and the Rastafari movement had actually begun back during the *ska* era.)

Since the late 1960s, reggae has remained the dominant popular style in Jamaica, but it has passed through countless trends and absorbed numerous new influences. Reggae covers of the latest North American popular hits coexist alongside traditional Rastafarian religious chants set to a reggae beat. Romantic ballads alternate with message songs, some earnest and some humorous, dealing with the latest local and international political events. A profusion of substyles—"rockers," "lover's rock," "militant," and so forth—continue to pop up and to lead to further innovations. And the Caribbean penchant for variation and experimentation has been canonized in the Jamaican concept of "version": the practice of including on the flip side of a record a modified mix (often with vocal tracks removed) of the same song featured on the A side. This practice developed during the 1960s, when local disk jockeys began to "toast"—to improvise extended "raps"—over the sounds of the latest hits (thus the need for "versions"of these tunes minus the vocal tracks). Many North American and European record buyers interpreted this custom negatively, assuming that it was motivated solely by a desire among producers to take in as much money as possible by delivering a final product that cost less to produce. However, this practice helped spawn not only a vital and still thriving deejaying tradition, but also a very important new substyle known as "dub," in which local recording engineers and studio musicians used "version" sides to experiment with new sound recording technologies. By dropping different tracks in and out, and using various other studio tricks so as to change "spatial" relationships in the music, they succeeded in creating entirely new aural textures. Some of the most creative music to come out of Jamaica during the last few years has been in the "dub" vein. And today the concept of "version"—the idea that any piece of music may be used as the starting point for an endless series of variations, all of them performed "ina different stylee," and thus bearing an individualized stamp—remains central to Jamaican popular music.

Some of the most important Caribbean music has grown up outside the Caribbean, among immigrant communities in Europe and North America. Large-scale emigration has long been a feature of Caribbean life. For several centuries, movements of people from one part of the region to another have been resulting in interisland musical cross-fertilization. But the last few decades have seen emigration—particularly to urban centers to the north—on an unprecedented scale. There now exist sizeable Caribbean minority populations in cities such as London, Paris, Amsterdam, Toronto, New York, and Miami, to name just a few. Caribbean music remains as important as ever in the lives of these immigrant communities. And so the creolization process continues both at home and abroad. In London, young Jamaicans, Guyanese,

Trinidadians, Grenadians—as well as British-born children of immigrants from these and other parts of the Caribbean—have joined forces to create a new, and still evolving, style of "Brit reggae," reflecting their experiences in the metropole. In Paris, French Antilleans and their children have begun to cross reggae with their own styles of dance music. In London, New York, Toronto, and other cities, there are huge annual Caribbean carnivals rivaling those occurring in the Caribbean itself. The constant flow of people back and forth between the islands and the metropolitan immigrant communities ensures that the latest musical developments on either side of the ocean are rapidly circulated to all parts of the diaspora and added to the larger pool of musical resources.

New York's very large Latin community has made that city one of the great world centers of Caribbean music. So-called *salsa*—the name that began to be applied to "hot" New York Afro-Latin dance music in the late 1960s/early 1970s—is but one of the more recent developments in a long line of musical innovations stretching back several decades. Several volumes could be dedicated to this branch of Caribbean popular music by itself. In typically Caribbean fashion, New York Latin musicians have made use of the full range of musical resources available to them. Although much of New York Latin music is strongly based on Cuban folk and popular traditions (from all points on the spectrum), influences from Puerto Rican, Dominican, Panamanian, Colombian, and other varieties of music have surfaced time and again in the many stylistic permutations that the New York scene has produced.

And so Caribbean music can no longer be defined by geographical boundaries. Yet, wherever it is produced, it continues to be resolutely Caribbean, not only in its approach to structuring sound but also in its social dimensions. Collective participation remains a cornerstone of popular music performances. Although the line between performers and audience has become much more sharply drawn than in traditional contexts, a contemporary concert or dance is still not considered really satisfying unless it manages to elicit lively interaction between musicians, dancers, and listeners. Even Jamaican reggae—which until recently has been primarily a studio music, with performances by live bands being the exception rather than the rule—has always had its deejay tradition, in which the recorded output of the studios is reclaimed by live performers and made the basis of huge collective manifestations ("sound system" dances). Caribbean popular music, when performed live, has everywhere retained its antiphonal, interactive quality. This is equally evident in a Trinidadian calypso tent where the audience joins the performer in singing choruses; in a New York *salsa* party where musicians and dancers urge one another on to higher heights; or in a Kingston deejay "session" during which listening bystanders punctuate the verbal outpourings of the "man at the controls" with enthusiastic comments of their own.

The genre of the topical song—so important in Caribbean folk music—has never been healthier. The bustle and stepped-up pace of urban life and the experience of emigration have added new grist to the songwriter's mill. The frustrations, fears, hopes, and joys of life in the contemporary Caribbean—as well as in the diaspora—are given voice more clearly than anywhere else in popular song. Much of the recent popular music issuing from Haiti is dominated by images of New York City, Miami, and *lajâ* (*l'argent*). Jamaican reggae songs continue to protest as strongly as ever against injustice and to document the grinding poverty, overcrowding, and political violence that plague the lives of urban ghetto dwellers. Trinidadian *soka* numbers persist in subjecting the latest political and social developments to the incisive critiques and savage wit of the "kaisonians." And the revolution in Grenada was chronicled by local calypsos. Indeed, the contemporary topical song provides much of the Caribbean with its most effective news medium. (This takes on special significance when it is recalled that levels of literacy vary a great deal from one part of the Caribbean to the next.) Few of those current events that matter most to the man in the street escape the scrutiny of popular songwriters. In many Caribbean societies, then, the pulse of contemporary life can best be captured in local popular music. No one understands this better than Caribbean politicians, who have often felt compelled to monitor closely the latest sounds, and who have not always been above dabbling in the local genre and attempting to manipulate it for their own ends.

Caribbean popular musicians continue to be distinguished by their polymusicality. Many of the top *salsa* musicians are devotees of *santería* and double as drummers, percussionists, and singers in religious ceremonies. The names of top Jamaican reggae musicians can often be found in small print on the jackets of local Revivalist-tinged gospel recordings (this in spite of the fact that many of them are Rastafarians and are vocal in their rejection of Christianity). Some of the leading Trinidadian *soka* musicians are familiar with the drumming styles of the *shango* and *rada* cults. And many French Antillean *cadence* musicians are regular participants in *gwoka* drumming performances.

It is not surprising then that Caribbean popular music remains so firmly rooted in tradition. Yet, one of the most interesting things about the popular styles is the way they balance the old and the new. Traditional influences are absorbed so as to engender further development and growth, rather than to encourage a retreat into traditionalist purism or to cater to a nostalgiac longing for the past. And although developments in popular Caribbean music have sometimes been tied to an ideological commitment to a "return to the roots," the search for roots has most often been backed by a conscious progressivism, a determination to take older musical forms forward—to update them. In this way, Caribbean popular music manages to stay in constant motion—passing through stylistic fads, incorporating innovations, and absorbing influences from outside—while at the same time remaining genuinely tied to folk roots. Even as one stylistic trend succeeds in carrying a popular style further away from its traditional base, this is likely to be followed by a counterdevelopment in which musicians inject or reinject elements from older traditions, thus bringing about further changes. This swinging back and forth between, on the one hand, an impulse for novelty and change and, on the other, a periodic revalidation of all that is felt to be profoundly rooted in tradition (*típico, typique,* "roots," and so forth), has much to do with the dynamism of Caribbean popular music.

One does not have to search very hard to find examples of the resurfacing of traditional influences in popular music. New York Latin music, for example, has gone through several periods dominated by new introductions from traditional sources. The mambo, which grew up in the 1940s and became a fad in the 1950s, stemmed in part from Afro-Cuban religious traditions. Around the same time, traditional *charanga* music—an older, less African-sounding form of Cuban music played by ensembles characteristically consisting of flute, fiddles, bass, and piano—experienced renewed popularity, with the introduction of the cha-cha-chá. The *pachanga* rage that followed a few years later came about as the result of the fusing of rhythmic elements taken from an Afro-Cuban dance known as the *bembe* with current popular dance styles. More recently, a number of *salsa* musicians have begun to introduce the sacred *bata* drums of the Afro-Cuban *lucumí* religion, along with their distinctive rhythms, into popular music recordings. I have already mentioned the role of *shango* and *hosse* drum rhythms in the development of Trinidadian *soka.* And Jamaican popular music has been constantly nourished by contributions from the traditional Rastafarian musical form known as *nyabingi* (itself an outgrowth of several older traditional styles, such as *buru* and *kumina*).

But borrowing from traditional sources is not limited to such spectacular examples as these; it occurs continually, on a more modest scale, as a result of the input of polymusical popular artists who, whether intentionally or not, bring their familiarity with folk traditions to bear in the recording studio. And so subtle references to traditional music forms—stylistic quotations—are a regular feature of contemporary popular forms. In the latest Jamaican reggae and "dub" pieces, the attuned ear can occasionally separate out *mento*-style guitar strumming, "John Canoe"–influenced drum rolls, and Revival-like voicings. Indeed, there are particular artists who specialize in Revivalist-tinged reggae songs, others who have acquired a reputation for *mento*-based reggae tunes, and still others who build primarily on an *akete* (Rastafarian drum) foundation. Reggae singers and deejays constantly revamp and/or quote traditional *mentos,* ring play tunes, and digging songs. Moreover, rhythmic patterns belonging to one instrument in a folk music style—such as a particular drum—may be transferred to another instrument, such as organ or guitar, in a reggae piece; or such traditional rhythmic patterns can even be reproduced electronically in the studio, as happens so often in "dub" music.

This ongoing linkage between folk and popular styles is as true of Haiti as of Jamaica, of Martinique as of the Dominican Republic. The popular music of Suriname provides another good example, worth citing because it has received so little attention elsewhere. The national popular style of Suriname is known as *kaseko* (the name, as well as elements of the original style, appear to be derived from the *cassé-co* tradition of neighboring French Guiana). At first a rather calypsolike style played by an ensemble of acoustic stringed instruments and sometimes horns, *kaseko* absorbed influences from a drum-based recreational Creole style known as *kawina* and by the 1960s was being played on amplified instruments. In recent years, *kaseko* has opened up to a number of other traditional influences, and it is now beginning to reflect the diversity of Suriname folk music. Influences from traditional *winti* cult music are beginning to appear in popular music with greater frequency, and some *kaseko* bands whose members include maroons from several of the different ethnic groups have begun to record songs in the maroon languages Ndjuka and Saramaccan, and to incorporate maroon instruments and elements of certain traditional drumming styles. In view of the richness of both maroon and Creole musical traditions, Suriname promises to produce some very exciting developments in the area of popular music in the years to come.

Then there is the other side of Caribbean popular music: that which is outward-looking, which thrives on novelty, experimentation, freshness, and innovation; the side that remains always open to new influences from outside. One might even go so far as to say that many popular musicians subscribe to a "mingling ethic"—a conviction that to absorb new, external influences and create new blends is in itself normal and good, part of a natural process of musical growth. The record abounds with examples of new musical forms that have come into being when this attitude has been put into action. North American readers may recall, for instance, the "Latin *bugalú*," a blend of the New York Cuban mambo with black rhythm and blues, which managed to find a place on the AM radio playlists during a brief period in the 1960s. Or there is the *spouge* of Barbados, a new style that arose during the late 1960s and early 1970s, when local musicians began to remake Jamaican *ska* by merging it with their own traditions. Jamaican reggae is itself a product of such fusion, resulting from the blending of North American rhythm and blues with indigenous influences. The process continues in all parts of the Caribbean. At this moment, Trinidad "kaisonians" and popular musicians in the Lesser Antilles are in the process of breathing life into new musical varieties blending *soka, cadence,* and reggae. Some French Antillean musicians have been heavily influenced by *salsa,* and one can sometimes detect Afro-Cuban-style *guajeos* (repeating melodic riffs providing a base for instrumental soloing) in popular *cadence* recordings. These few examples represent only the tip of an enormous iceberg. In fact, all of the older popular styles that are still in use—such as the Trinidadian calypso, the Cuban *son,* the Suriname *kaseko,* the Haitian *méringue*, and the Dominican *merengue*—are in their modern incarnations very different from what they used to be only a few decades ago, largely because they have been open to outside influences (changes in instrumentation, amplification, new stylistic introductions, and so forth). And one need only make a brief inventory of a record store specializing in Caribbean music to get some idea of the extent to which the impulse to create new fusions prevails in contemporary popular music. Glancing over the jackets of recent releases (where the songs listed on the back are often followed, in parentheses, by the names of the musical genre to which they belong), one inevitably encounters a multitude of new experimental blends, carrying names such as "cadence-lypso," "soul reggae," "biguine funk," "rapso," "soca-highlife," "samba reggae," and so forth. Some of these are likely to remain one-shot affairs, sinking into obscurity almost as soon as they reach vinyl, while others are picked up and made the basis of further innovations.

Musical blending and cross-fertilization are of course not unique to the Caribbean. But there are few other regions where such a multiplicity of diverse musical currents have been packed into such close quarters; few other areas have been swept by such a whirlwind of musical interaction, or have given rise to so many fresh and original local musical expressions. Long before "fusion" became a self-conscious jazz fad in the 1970s, all that this term implies had already been successfully achieved a thousand times over in the Caribbean. And yet, in spite of its openness to currents originating elsewhere, Caribbean popular music remains anchored to local life; it continues to express the essential concerns of those by whom and for whom it is made. No matter how often they are temporarily co-opted by commercial or other interests, the various branches of the Caribbean musical family always manage, in the end, to stay in close touch with their constituencies. This is one of the great strengths of Caribbean popular music and part of what ensures its continuing vitality: it remains everywhere, in the truest sense, a people's music.

CARIBBEAN MUSIC AND THE REST OF THE WORLD

As much as Caribbean popular musical forms remain tied to the societies that gave birth to them, many of them have nevertheless proven—thanks to the spread of modern communications media—capable of transcending local context and of winning over foreign audiences solely on the basis of their musical appeal. Numerous Caribbean styles have managed to break through ethnic and geographical barriers. Some have succeeded in attracting substantial international followings indeed and have inspired important new musical developments by non-Caribbean musicians. In the history of Caribbean popular music, the phenomenon that has come to be called "crossover" (in the jargon of the popular music industry) goes back farther than one might think.

As early as the 1920s, there already existed a market for Trinidadian calypso in the United States. (It was during this period that North American record companies first began to release calypso recordings.) Not long after this, calypsonians were making appearances in New York nightclubs. But it was not until several years later that calypso reached its peak of international popularity, during the "calypso craze" of 1956–57 (at which time calypsos or calypso-influenced recordings represented a reported one-fourth of United States record sales).

Then there was the Cuban *rumba,* which swept North America and Europe during the 1920s and 1930s; or the Cuban-derived dance known as the conga, which followed upon its heels. The 1940s saw a great deal of interaction between Latin and black American musicians in New York, culminating in the emergence and flowering of the "Cubop" movement—which was responsible for some of the earliest successful fusions between Afro-Cuban music and North American jazz. Shortly after this, North American rhythm and blues, from New Orleans to New York, began to show subtle but important Latin influences, and by the mid-1960s, the new black-Latin fusion known as the *bugalú* was being played by both Latin and North American musicians. In their heyday, during the 1940s and 1950s, Latin dance styles such as the *méringue,* the mambo, the cha-cha-chá, and the *pachanga* spread beyond the Latin community and enjoyed immense popularity in North America. The mambo and cha-cha-chá, moreover, traveled far beyond the borders of the United States, conquering audiences in Japan, Europe, and several parts of South America. In the 1970s, a new fusion, "Latin rock," had an international impact, and by the end of the decade, a substantial market for *salsa* had grown up in Europe, Japan, and several other parts of the world.

The most recent success story is of course that of Jamaican reggae. As early as the 1960s, reggae began to make major inroads in Great Britain, thanks to the presence there of a large West Indian immigrant community; in the United States, the impact was much less marked, but significant nonetheless. By the mid-1970s it was becoming a truly international music. Through a combination of economics, politics, favorable promotion and distribution, and sheer musical attraction, reggae music has, as of this moment, succeeded in penetrating virtually every part of the planet. The ongoing association between the Rastafari movement and reggae—which led to its being thrust in the spotlight as a major vehicle of Third World protest—has been partly responsible for the music's dispersion. Active Rastafarian reggae bands can now be found in almost all parts of the Caribbean—as well as among Caribbean immigrant communities in Canada, the United States, Britain, the Netherlands, and France—and in South Africa and many West African and Central African countries. But the internationalization of reggae has not been totally dependent on this sort of cultural and political base. Today, reggae is being produced by local musicians in such unlikely places as Sweden, Germany, Japan, and Java. There is even an Australian Aboriginal reggae band. In England, moreover, reggae strongly influenced a good deal of the punk rock and new wave music of the late 1970s; and a short-lived but influential craze in British popular music at the end of the decade—the so-called Two Tone movement— was based almost entirely on a blend of rock-and-roll and Jamaican popular music styles. Through channels such as these, reggae influences have finally entered the European mainstream in a big way. The point has been reached where reggae-tinged hits are now sold in massive quantities to European and American record buyers who—in many cases—have no idea of their debt to Jamaican popular music.

The place where Caribbean popular music has had its most significant international impact is Africa. In anglophone West Africa, the West Indian calypso contributed to the development of the hardy local style known as "highlife," which—after several decades of growth and change—is still going strong, from Nigeria to Sierra Leone. Beginning in the 1930s, popular Cuban recordings began to make their way into several parts of Central Africa, and ever since, Afro-Cuban music has remained tremendously popular in this part of the continent. More recently, *salsa* has experienced a growing wave of popularity in West Africa. Finally, since the late 1970s, reggae has enjoyed increasing popularity in almost every African country south of the Sahara (once again, thanks to the wide distribution of Jamaican recordings).

These new introductions, whose African-derived components are immediately grasped by an African ear, have often played a central role in the development of major new musical fusions. African popular music, like that of the Caribbean, has been marked by an openness to new ideas from outside, a positive stress on innovation, an attitude supporting blending between different traditions, and a continual fluctuation between new introductions and traditional influences. The Afro-Cuban music that was so popular in Central Africa during the 1930s and 1940s paved the way for one of the greatest bursts of creative activity in African popular music to date. African musicians began experimenting with Cuban musical forms almost as soon as these reached their shores. By the late 1950s, popular musicians—particularly Congolese artists—had begun to develop a new style in which musical phrasings inspired by Cuban-style horn arrangements were being played on guitar. Before long, the new guitar style was picking up other influences from traditional sources and was being adapted to local techniques used in playing traditional stringed instruments. Over time, the Cuban-based music of the Congolese guitar bands was radically transformed—one stylistic innovation following on another— and by the 1970s, there existed a vital new Congolese musical genre. It was a wholly original musical form, with its lovely, fluid guitar work (three or four guitars being played simultaneously to create a rhythmically complex interlocking weave), and although Cuban influences continued to be incorporated, there was no way of confusing this new style with its Afro-Cuban ancestors.

African musicians in other countries were quick to pick up on this new music, and soon it was being played, with local variations, across the continent. During the past decade or so, Zairian music has had the widest popularity in Africa of any modern style. It is listened to and danced to from Senegal to Angola, from Mozambique to Kenya.

The "Congolese sound" is but one—albeit the most famous—of an untold number of Caribbean-inspired musical fusions in Africa. The *biguine, méringue,* calypso, and other older Caribbean popular styles have also attracted the attention of popular musicians in several parts of the continent. More recently, *soka* and *salsa* have been finding increasing numbers of admirers in Africa, and local *salsa* recordings from countries such as the Ivory Coast and Guinea are beginning to show more and more indigenous influences. The explosion of interest in reggae has also led to a good deal of experimentation in the studios. Indigenized reggae recordings, sung in local languages—and sometimes transformed so thoroughly that they are hardly recognizable any longer as reggae—have been produced in such countries as Senegal, Liberia, Ghana, Zaire, and South Africa. The themes of black consciousness and pan-Africanism that continue to dominate so many Jamaican reggae songs ring with a special resonance in modern Africa, and so it seems likely that the popularity of reggae will do nothing but grow in this part of the world during the coming years. It would not be surprising, then, if experiments in blending reggae with indigenous influences were to lead in the future to a durable new fusion that, like the "Congolese sound," could take the entire continent by storm. For reggae, like much Afro-Cuban music, rests on a generalized African musical base that appeals to listeners in virtually all parts of sub-Saharan Africa.

Meanwhile, back in the Caribbean, local musicians, largely oblivious to recent musical developments in Africa, continue to push forward with new innovations of their own. Caribbean popular music remains in as close touch as ever with its local audiences. There has been some initial contact and cooperation between farsighted Caribbean and African popular musicians, and the growing musical dialogue between continents promises to lead to some of the most exciting music of the future. Whatever may happen to Caribbean music in the coming years, two things seem certain: it will remain a people's music; and it will not stay still for long.

The story of Caribbean music is a remarkable one. For this relatively small geographical region, ravaged by centuries of European colonial domination and long looked upon as a region of "colonial backwaters," "deracinated" peoples, and societies that had supposedly produced nothing indigenous of any value, has over and over brought forth unique and vibrant musical creations to which the entire world can dance. That the story is far from finished means that the lives of music lovers in both the Caribbean and other parts of the world will be that much the richer in the years ahead.

REFERENCES

ABRAHAMS, ROGER D.

1983 *The Man-of-Words in the West Indies: Performance and the Emergence of Creole Culture.* Baltimore: Johns Hopkins University Press.

BAXTER, IVY

1970 *The Arts of an Island: The Development of the Culture and of the Folk and Creative Arts in Jamaica, 1494–1962.* Metuchen, N.J.: Scarecrow Press.

BILBY, KENNETH

1981 "Music of the Maroons of Jamaica" (notes to Folkways phonograph record FE 4027). New York: Folkways Records.

1983 "Black Star Liner: Reggae from Africa" (notes to Heartbeat phonograph record HB 16). Cambridge, Mass.: Heartbeat Records.

BILBY, KEN, AND ELLIOTT LEIB

1983 "From Kongo to Zion: Three Black Musical Traditions from Jamaica" (notes to Heartbeat phonograph record HB 17). Cambridge, Mass.: Heartbeat Records.

BRATHWAITE, EDWARD

1970 *Folk Culture of the Slaves in Jamaica.* Boston: New Beacon Books.

CARPENTIER, ALEJO

1972 *La música en Cuba.* Mexico City: Fondo de Cultura.

COURLANDER, HAROLD

1939 *The Drum and the Hoe.* Berkeley and Los Angeles: University of California Press.

1960 "Caribbean Folk Music" (notes to Folkways phonograph record FE 4533). New York: Folkways Records.

CROWLEY, DANIEL J.

1957 "Song and Dance in St. Lucia." *Ethnomusicology* 1(9):4–14.

1959 "Toward a Definition of Calypso." *Ethnomusicology* 3:57–66; 117–24.

DAVIS, STEPHEN, AND PETER SIMON (EDS.)

1983 *Reggae International.* New York: Knopf.

ELDER, J.D.

1969 *From Congo Drum to Steel-Band: A Socio-historical Account of the Emergence and Evolution of the Trinidad Steel Orchestra.* St. Augustine, Trinidad: University of the West Indies.

HANDLER, JEROME S., AND CHARLOTTE J. FRISBIE

1972 "Aspects of Slave Life in Barbados: Music and Its Cultural Context." *Caribbean Studies* 11(4):5–46.

HERSKOVITS, MELVILLE J., AND FRANCES S. HERSKOVITS

1936 *Suriname Folk-Lore.* New York: Columbia University Press.

HILL, DONALD R.
1980 "The Big Drum and Other Ritual and Social Music of Carriacou" (notes to Folkways phonograph record FE 34002). New York: Folkways Records.

HILL, ERROL
1972 *The Trinidad Carnival: Mandate for a National Theatre.* Austin: University of Texas Press.

LAFONTAINE, MARIE-CÉLINE
1982 "Musique et société aux Antilles." *Présence Africaine* 121/122:72–108.
1983 "Le Carnaval de L''Autre.'" *Les Temps Modernes* 441/442:2126–73.

LEAF, EARL
1948 *Isles of Rhythm.* New York: A. S. Barnes.

LEWIN, OLIVE
1968 "Jamaican Folk Music." *Caribbean Quarterly* 14(1–2):49–56.

LOWENTHAL, IRA P.
1978 "Ritual Performance and Religious Experience: A Service for the Gods in Southern Haiti." *Journal of Anthropological Research.* 34:392–414.

MALM, KRISTER
n.d. "Music from the West Indies: The Lesser Antilles" (notes to Caprice phonograph record CAP 2004). Stockholm: Caprice Records.

MIDGETT, DOUGLAS K.
1977 "Performance Roles and Musical Change in a Caribbean Society." *Ethnomusicology* 21(1):55–73.

MINTZ, SIDNEY W.
1974 "The Caribbean Region." *In* Sidney W. Mintz (ed.), *Slavery, Colonialism, and Racism,* pp. 45–71. New York: W. W. Norton.

MINTZ, SIDNEY W., AND RICHARD PRICE
1976 *An Anthropological Approach to the Afro-American Past: A Caribbean Perspective.* Philadelphia: ISHI.

ORTIZ, FERNANDO
n.d. *La africanía de la música folklórica de Cuba.* Havana: Cardenas.

PEARSE, ANDREW
1955 "Aspects of Change in Caribbean Folk Music." *Journal of the International Folk Music Council* 8:29–36.

PRICE, RICHARD, AND SALLY PRICE
1977 "Music from Saramaka: A Dynamic Afro-American Tradition" (notes to Folkways phonograph record FE 4225). New York: Folkways Records.

PRICE, SALLY, AND RICHARD PRICE
1980 *Afro-American Arts of the Suriname Rain Forest.* Berkeley and Los Angeles: University of California Press.

ROBERTS, HELEN H.
1925 "A Study of Folk Song Variants Based on Field Work in Jamaica." *Journal of American Folklore* 38:149–216.

ROBERTS, JOHN STORM
1972 *Black Music of Two Worlds.* New York: Praeger Publishers.
1979 *The Latin Tinge: The Impact of Latin American Music in the United States.* New York: Oxford University Press.

WARNER, KEITH Q.
1982 *Kaiso! The Trinidad Calypso.* Washington, D.C.: Three Continents Press.

WATERMAN, RICHARD ALAN
1952 "African Influence on the Music of the Americas." *In* Sol Tax (ed.), *Acculturation in the Americas,* pp. 207–17. Chicago: International Congress of Americanists.

SUGGESTIONS FOR LISTENING

Many of the folk musical traditions discussed in this paper can be heard on widely available commercial recordings. It is recommended that the reader check the Caribbean section in any of the larger local record outlets, as well as local libraries. Particularly noteworthy for their large and interesting catalogs of Caribbean folk music (including rare field recordings) are Folkways Records (New York), Cook Records (Norwalk, Connecticut), and Sonodisc Disques (Paris); these companies will send copies of their catalogs on request.

In the section on popular music, I have purposely refrained from mentioning the names of particular artists in order to encourage readers to visit the nearest outlet stocking Caribbean music and to sample the tremendous richness of contemporary popular music for themselves. For every acknowledged "giant" of Caribbean popular music—such as Bob Marley, Francisco Slinger (Sparrow), Frank Grillo (Machito), Mario Bauza, La Perfecta, and so many others—there are literally dozens of very talented, but lesser-known, individual artists and ensembles working in the same genres who are equally deserving of attention. The amount of material issued every year is astounding, and levels of quality vary a good deal, so it is necessary to be selective. But this is a matter that must be left to individual taste.

· 7 ·

The Contemporary Caribbean: A General Overview

GORDON K. LEWIS

THE PHYSICAL BACKGROUND

All societies, of course, have been shaped by geography and history. The Caribbean of today is no exception. And, as in all societies, the impact of geography and history on the Caribbean has been unique. An understanding of the society as it stands today must be founded in a full appreciation of that cardinal truth.

From Cuba and the Greater Antilles in the north to the Guianas in the south, the Caribbean consists of islands or, in the case of the Guianas, coastal South American regions that are islands in every sense except the strictly geographical. With the exception of Barbados, which is a coral reef formation, the islands of this region are part of a one-thousand-mile stretch of volcanic formations set in a subtropical setting of sun-drenched luminosity; they are subject to the vagaries of both volcanic eruption and hurricane assault. The 1902 eruption of Mt. Pelée in Martinique destroyed the (then capital) city of St. Pierre, killing 30,000 people; in 1979, the killer hurricanes David and Frederick destroyed the entire agricultural economy of the small island of Dominica within a few days. Just as California is earthquake country, so the Caribbean is volcano and hurricane country. And like Californians, the peoples of the Caribbean seem to accept their geographical environment with a sense of fatalistic equanimity. All of the archipelago's territories enjoy a rich, fertile soil, which allows the cultivation of a wide variety of raw tropical products; but just as the economic culture of the American Midwest has centered on corn and that of the Middle East on oil, the economic culture of the Caribbean has traditionally been one of sugar. For the best part of their history since Columbus's arrival in 1492, these have, with few exceptions, been the "sugar islands."

Moreover, and perhaps more importantly, these societies have been, and for the most part still are, small island societies marked by a psychological insularity, an inward-turned communal life in which everybody seems to know everybody else. That is obvious, of course, in small island capital towns such as Bridgetown, Barbados, or Castries, St. Lucia; but, surprisingly, it is also a marked feature even of larger cities such as Havana, or San Juan, Puerto Rico. Whereas North American life is continental, Caribbean life is island-oriented. This is not to say that Caribbean people are backward island folk, for in fact, the processes of internal and external migration have made them widely traveled individuals; it is, rather, that however much they may live outside the Caribbean (Martiniquans in France, Surinamers in the Netherlands, West Indians in Britain and Canada), they retain a passionate attachment to the island home. Many Puerto Ricans living in North America see themselves not just as another minority group in American life but as a separate Puerto Rican nation for whom home is still the island *patria*. Island life seems to do something to the communal psychology. And many families who participated in the Cuban exodus of the 1960s would willingly return to Cuba if there were a change of regime; however Americanized they may have become in their Miami enclave, the gravitational pull of the island home is still almost irresistible. Nor is all this at all surprising to anyone who has meandered through the region. To wander through the *el Yunque* tropical rain forest in Puerto Rico, to climb Mt. Soufrière in St. Vincent, to fly by small plane over the Kaieteur Falls in Guyana, or to hike through the Blue Mountains or "cockpit country" in Jamaica is to realize to the full the riches of the *magie antillaise*. It is a pity that so many tourists miss all this because advertising persuades them that the thing to do is to get a suntan on the tropical beaches.

The islands of the Caribbean have the delicate and fragile ecology of island environments. Much of it has already been destroyed through uncontrolled "development" by both private investors and local governments, who are rarely conservation-minded. The Freeport development in the Bahamas is an appalling example of what reckless greed can do to nature. The Institute of Puerto Rican Culture is unusual in promoting efforts to retain the old architectural heritage of Spain; what more typically happens can be seen in the mindless destruction of the old town houses of Port of Spain. Even so, perhaps, the very size of islands puts limits to despoliation. Urbanization and the spread of cars create congested housing conditions and traffic jams in Caribbean cities, but there is nothing comparable to the appalling environmental nightmare of Mexico City, where some sixteen million people (comparable more or less to the total population of the Caribbean basin) struggle to survive in a high-mountain valley plateau of soft subsoil, earthquake prone and dangerously isolated from supplies of water, food, and energy. (See the *New York Times*, 15 May 1983, pp. 1, 12). The small-island balance between the people and their environment is much more manageable and human. Georgetown, Guyana, for example, is a bicycle town, and Bermuda rigorously controls the importation and size of automobiles. However citified they have become, most middle-class Caribbean people—as conversation with them readily shows—are intensely proud of their small-town birthplaces and keep in touch with them. And however much the peasant as an economic type may be disappearing, the individual peasant's dream of owning a small piece of land on which to build a house still remains with Caribbean people of all class levels.

In a sense, geography has been kind to the Caribbean, for all of these island territories are close to each other in terms of nautical miles, being divided by narrow passages (such as the Mona Passage, which separates Puerto Rico from Santo Domingo). This is not Polynesia or Melanesia, where thousands of ocean miles separate the various groups of islands from each other. Once Columbus had made his first landfall at Watling's Island, it was easy for him to discover the other islands (unlike Captain Cook, who discovered the isolated islands of Tahiti only by accident). This geographical closeness has led to a regular movement of people among the islands, by schooner, steamboat, and, today, small interisland aircraft. Intraregional migration has been the order of the day, especially in the Eastern Caribbean where, for example, laborers go south to work in the oil refineries of Aruba and Trinidad and others go north to seek jobs in the tourist industry of the U.S. Virgin Islands. Whole settlements of contract workers, both bonded and illegal, become part of their adopted homes: Grenadians in Trinidad, Antiguans in the Virgin Islands, Jamaicans in Panama, and Dominicans in Puerto Rico. Add to this the more recent influx of political immigrants, e.g., Cubans in Puerto Rico, and a general portrait emerges of a regional society marked by the vast cyclical movements of peoples who have been uprooted—sometimes voluntarily, sometimes involuntarily. This, of course, has not yet expressed itself in any form of stable political union; the West Indies Federation collapsed after four brief years in 1962. But, short of that, the peoples of different Caribbean societies know each other as much as Europeans from different countries do. It is in this sense that geography is the mother of regionalism.

THE HISTORICAL BACKGROUND

After geography there is the shaping force of history. Like the United States and the Latin American republics, the Caribbean, in linear historical terms, is a young society. From a European perspective, 1992 will mark its 500th anniversary. Unlike other regions of the modern Third World, it does not possess a cultural foundation that goes back thousands of years, like Hinduism in India or Islam in the Middle East or Confucianism in China. As independent nations, the states of the Caribbean are even younger. Haiti became the first black republic of the Americas in 1804; Santo Domingo celebrated its break from the hated Haitian yoke in 1844; Cuba dates its independence from 1902; and it was as late as the 1960s and 1970s that the former British West Indian colonies (as someone once noted, the first to enter the British Empire and the last to leave) were granted independence by a war-weary Britain. This means that the majority of the fifty to sixty territorial societies in the region are still engaged in the difficult art of nation building, and much of their day-to-day politics centers on that problem. Resembling more the new nations of Africa than the older nations of Europe or North America, these polities are taking on their characteristic form at different rates and, to some extent, by different processes. Ceasing to be colonies only yesterday, as it were, they must now learn to become viable nation states. A U.S. observer can perhaps best understand this period of Caribbean history by comparing it to the age of independence in the post-1787 United States.

For convenience, the region's history may be divided into three periods: (1) the postdiscovery period, covering the sixteenth, seventeenth, and eighteenth centuries; (2) the postemancipation period, that is to say, the period following the abolition of slavery (1833 in the British colonies, 1848 in the French colonies, 1863 in the Dutch colonies, 1873 in Puerto Rico, and 1886 in Cuba); and (3) the postindependence period. The three major episodes of the society are thus identified as discovery, emancipation, and independence.

Each of these distinctive periods established forms and structures appropriate to its particular institutional principles in the three main areas of life: economic, social, and political. Many of those forms, of course, have disappeared, such as bonded slavery and metropolitan colonialism. But many of them still remain, albeit necessarily changed.

In social terms, discovery established the early foundations of Caribbean social structure. The colonial powers put into place the traditional black-brown-white triangle of human types. European immigration brought the white planter and the white indentured servant, while African immigration, through the infamous slave trade, brought the African slave. It established the system of "racially" determined social status, with the whites on top, the blacks at the bottom, and the brown mulatto groups (the so-called people of color or free coloreds) in between. There were, of course, poor whites and rich blacks then just as there are today; but these were the exceptions to the rule and always marginal to the central system of "racially" determined power. The postemancipation period added to this cornerstone a new set of social-ethnic relationships. Some ex-slaves became estate wage laborers, still tied to economic exploitation (for although slavery had gone, capitalism still remained); others joined a new quasi-independent peasantry, forming a new life in the "free villages" of Jamaica and the Guianas, thus contributing to the genesis of the present-day marginal peasantries; the middle-class "people of color" established themselves more firmly in trade, commerce, and the professions, thus becoming the ancestors of the modern-day Caribbean "black bourgeoisie"; the white groups—with the old plantocracy in decline—rearranged their ranks to become a new property-owning class in trade, commerce, and real estate, their white presence reinforced by the continuing European white control of government, as in the British Crown Colony system. Finally, the postindependence period ushered in a quiet social revolution, with the advent of industrialization, modernization, and Westernization. It shattered the old rigid structures in which everybody "knew his place," at once determined by class origin and ethnic identification. The modernization of postwar Puerto Rico—as Henry Wells has shown in his definitive book

(1969)—is only the best-known example of this success story. Status has been replaced by contract; what you are is more important than who you are, reflecting a quite massive process of social democratization. The key factor has been the enormous expansion of popular and higher education; today in Puerto Rico, for example, there are at least a dozen centers of higher collegiate education. Over the years these institutions have enabled a whole new class of middle-class professional persons to rise up from the social echelons of the poor. As they say in Puerto Rico, these people are only one generation away from the cane fields. There is nothing like mass education to foment silent social revolutions. Readers from the United States may recall how a similar process was unleashed by the land-grant college legislation of the Civil War period.

In economic terms, the early postdiscovery period established the typical sugar plantation economy based on imported slave labor. (Philip Curtin's book [1969] on the demographic distribution of slaves estimates that in the period of the slave trade, 1451–1870, some ten million Africans were imported into the Americas, with the vast majority in the cane-producing areas.) Sugar became a classic monocrop culture, producing the tropical raw product for refinement and sale in the metropolitan markets. It was tied structurally to European capitalist mercantilism, with profits flowing to the metropolitan absentee planters and merchant houses; the well-known "colonial pact" compelled the colony to import all from the relevant metropolis and export all to the same source. The postemancipation period, in turn, ended the tyranny of the master over the slave, but it did not end the continuing economic control of the old planter oligarchy. That oligarchy continued to hold its monopoly of the choice lands of the old plantation economy; and indeed the economic history of this period is in large part the history of a sort of social civil war between planters and peasants for control of the land. In that long struggle the peasants lost out. They were forced to become small proprietors or small peasants working the less productive areas. Furthermore, as North American sugar companies entered the scene, buying up the estates—in the later part of the nineteenth century in Cuba and in the early twentieth century in Puerto Rico—land shortage, as well as the decline of the old traditional economies such as coffee, drove the highland peasants down to the coastal regions to find work in the new sugar *latifundia*. They became proletarianized workers, forced into the new world of impersonal capitalist relationships; Sidney Mintz (1960) has shown what that meant in terms of the lowered quality of life in his biographical study of a typical Puerto Rican worker in the period between the 1920s and the 1940s. Finally, the postindependence period after the 1940s completed this general proletarianizing process. The agricultural districts became denuded as peasants and farm laborers moved to the big urban areas to become hired factory hands; today the vast majority of Trinidadians live in the southern San Fernando area and the northern east-west corridors of Port of Spain, while the vast majority of Puerto Ricans live in the six urbanized areas of San Juan, Carolina, Bayamón, Caguas, Mayagüez, and Ponce. Of course, one can still find local native craftsmen and small farmers: the nutmeg growers of Grenada, the banana growers of Dominica, the fishermen of Guyana riverine interiors, and the boat builders of Carriacou. But they are an endangered species. Increasingly, as governments embrace industrialization as their main developmental tool, the factory displaces the farm. Ironically, the peasant type becomes degraded into a romanticized figure in the seductive advertising of the new tourist industry.

Finally, the three Caribbean time periods were equally distinctive in political terms. The first period set the habit of colonial autocratic government. Each colonizing power—Spain, France, Britain, and the Netherlands—established an overseas politico-administrative machinery with policies set unilaterally by the respective metropolitan colonial offices. Local legislative councils and assemblies had their own limited rights but very little real power to shape policy. The appointed governor or captain-general was top man in both local colonial government and local upper-class life. The grand ball at Government House became the great event of the local season, all for the whites, of course; as late as the 1940s the Duke of Windsor, as governor of the Bahamas, forbade any black person to cast a shadow in Government House. The postemancipation period continued all this, although local black and brown dignitaries gradually entered public life in the local assemblies and executive councils—especially in the more liberal British Crown Colony system. But it was not until the postindependence period that this kind of colonialism became enfeebled. The British and (in Suriname) the Dutch evacuated. The old white colonial administrative class gave way to the educated brown-black middle class, so that today the majority of the regional governments are run by the native politicians, government ministers, civil servants, and administrative technicians. That, of course, had always been the case in post-1804 Haiti—where in the words of a nineteenth-century observer, "black rules white." Black now rules white in government and politics all over. If you attended a Commonwealth Caribbean summit meeting such as that held in Ocho Rios, Jamaica, in early 1983, you would find that most of the attending prime ministers had black-brown faces. It is, of course, a little different in Cuba, Santo Domingo, and Puerto Rico, where, in physiognomic terms, white and near white are the predominant skin color for people in positions of leadership. But, in general terms, much of the Caribbean is Afro-American. The difference from U.S. society is again marked. For whereas in the United States blacks, like Hispanics, are minorities, the Afro-American in the Caribbean is, in most societies, in the numerical majority. And in many cases this has been true for centuries; Jamaica, for example, was overwhelmingly black by 1700. In political terms, Afro-Americans are self-confidently master in their own houses—governor-general, prime minister, leader of the opposition.

This is markedly different from the racial scene in the United States, where no black or Hispanic has become president and where the highest elected political post achieved by blacks has been that of big-city mayor (e.g., in Cleveland, Philadelphia, Atlanta, Chicago, and Los Angeles).

THE POLITICAL CONTEXT

All this, then, is the geographical-historical background to the Caribbean basin. What does it all mean in contemporary terms? Geography is a permanent variable; the U.S. Metereological Service in Miami cannot change the direction of Caribbean hurricanes. Of course, people can destroy the creations of nature; the most infamous case in the Caribbean is that of the denuded, skeletonlike ranges of Haitian mountains, destroyed by generations of relentless soil exploitation in the slave period and of indiscriminate bush-burning methods by the peasantry in the post-1804 period. Nature, here, becomes the innocent victim.

But history is different. It is manmade. It changes things. In the Caribbean, as elsewhere, its results have been a mixed bag. At its worst, it gave rise to the evil system of chattel slavery, at its best to the history of successive slave rebellions, culminating in the Homeric epic of the uprising of the Saint-Domingue slave masses between 1793 and 1804. The present-day Caribbean is the end result of all of its processes.

In the first place, the Caribbean of the 1980s remains a region of political fragmentation. It is, in truth, a crazy patchwork quilt of different political and constitutional forms. There are older independent republics such as Haiti, Santo Domingo, and Cuba, arising out of the republican enthusiasms of the great age of democratic revolution in Europe and America between 1770 and 1830. There are later, post-1945 independent states such as the former British West Indian territories, as well as the former Dutch colony, Suriname. There are Puerto Rico and the U.S. Virgin Islands, both of them unincorporated territories, where the seat of authority in innumerable areas of public policy still remains with the president, congressional committees, and federal agencies. There are the French Antilles (Martinique, Guadeloupe, and French Guiana), which, following the French National Assembly legislation of 1946, are overseas *départements,* enjoying all of the rights of the departments in France itself somewhat like the individual states in the U.S. federal scheme. The Dutch colonial possessions, including the so-called ABC islands (Aruba, Bonaire, and Curaçao), still remain governed by the Hague, under the terms of the Dutch Kingdom Statute of 1954. The student of constitutional curiosities will recognize in Bermuda and the British Virgin Islands archaic remnants of the old British system, where London-appointed governors or administrators still do daily battle with local legislative assemblies; or see, in the division of old Hispaniola into Haiti and Santo Domingo and in the even more curious division of the tiny island of St. Maarten into French and Dutch sides, survivals of the old European habit of settling wars by dividing the spoils. Much of all this is the consequence of the wave of anticolonialism that swept the colonial world after 1945. But it is obvious that much remains to be done before full sovereignty is attained throughout the Caribbean. If to all this there is added the linguistic fragmentation of the region, divided between the four Caribbean working languages of English, French, Spanish, and Dutch (not to mention the various creole languages), it is equally obvious that it is misleading to think of the region as a single, monolithic whole—a delusion present in much of the scholarly literature on the area. (For further discussion of this point, see Lewis 1971.)

In the second place, the region is characterized by what has been aptly termed a syndrome of "ideological pluralism." It has been shaped by Europe, Africa, and—in the twentieth century—the United States. So, not surprisingly, ideas from all over the world proliferate richly, making the region a gold mine for the political scientist. Ideologies flourish like the green bay tree. There is, in Puerto Rico, the predominant social liberalism that the Popular Democratic party learned from the Rooseveltian New Deal in the 1940s. In the French Antilles there are French communist and socialist ideas; it is no accident that Aimé Césaire, the great Antillean poet, was for a long time a member of the French Communist party as well as being a powerful mayor of Fort-de-France. There is the Christian socialism of the Caribbean Conference of Churches, which embraces both Catholic and Protestant denominations. There is the pervasive ideology of new black Afro-American pride, ranging from the *négritude* movement in Haiti and the French Antilles as early as the 1920s to the Black Power movement of the 1970s imported from the U.S. civil rights movement, on to the *africanía* of the Jamaican reggae musical revolution. There is, finally, the tremendous intellectual influence of the Cuban Revolution of 1959, especially in the region's intellectual elites centered in the area's universities—so great that even in Puerto Rico, which is generally liberal-conservative, socialism has become an accepted and respectable term in the island's political vocabulary. And there are other tributaries to this general stream: British Fabian socialism, which has shaped the older Labour parties in the English-speaking region; the current of *noirisme* (black race consciousness), which has been espoused by a whole generation of Haitian writers; and what one writer has termed the "Marxist populism" of C.L.R. James, the aged Trotskyite who is today the guru of a whole group of younger West Indian radicals.

There are two points to make about this configuration. First, it is uniquely Caribbean. There is nothing quite comparable to this mental ferment in the older industrial societies. In the United States, for example, much of which still lives, ideologically and religiously, in the Victorian period, to be a socialist is still to be regarded as an eccentric or as a dangerous subversive (despite little pockets of fringe radicalism). Much U.S. radicalism is single-factor politics, taking the larger capitalist society for granted: black power, gay rights, the abortion and antiabortion movements, the defense of Israel, the women's liberation movement. The Caribbean intellectual ferment, in contrast, sees the society as a whole and seeks to change it in its fundamental elements. One has to go back to the United States or Britain of the 1930s to meet a comparable situation. The Caribbean is on a different intellectual wavelength.

Secondly, and all that conceded, it would be grievously erroneous to believe that the Caribbean radical movements have it all their own way. The revolution is not just around the corner. Despite Cuba, Grenada, and Suriname, the region remains remarkably stable, in political terms. This is not yet Southeast Asia, or even Central America. Leaving Grenada aside (since it is a special case), the anglophone Caribbean seems passably satisfied with its condition; the imported British parliamentary model works well enough, despite the local critics of the "Westminster model." Even where colonial vestiges remain, as in Puerto Rico and the U.S. Virgin Islands, or where there are new forms of neocolonial assimilationism, as in the French Antilles, the majority of the electorates—if voting habits are any index—accept the status quo. The Puerto Rican Independence party espouses a sort of Scandinavian socialism; the Puerto Rican Socialist party has recently dropped its Marxist/Leninist title in order to attract less doctrinal voters; and the independence groupings in the French Antilles are as yet unable to break the popularity of majority parties, such as Césaire's Progressivist party, which champion some form of internal autonomy for the departments. Even Jamaica supports this point of view. For in a deep structural crisis since the oil crisis of 1973–74, the existing structure of parliamentary democracy (supported by a radical as sincere as Michael Manley) has not in any way been challenged by a revolt of the masses. Everybody, of course, knows why: as the Jamaican scholar Carl Stone has shown (1973: 50-53, 79-84), the Jamaican ruling groups have been able to anesthetize popular discontent by a politics of clientelism, keeping the masses quiet by a politics of "jobs for the boys" at every social level. In Puerto Rico, similarly, the drive for political independence has been softened by a massive food stamp program, funded from Washington (with some 65 percent of all island families receiving these benefits), thus playing a role similar to Jamaican client-patron politics. For in Jamaica, as elsewhere, the peasants are deeply religious, conservative people. Even in Haiti, the peasant majority, which has never known democracy in the Western sense, continues to accept the oppressive Duvalier regime with stoic equanimity, as they have accepted all similar oppressive presidential regimes since 1804; after all, the first act that the new emperor, Henry Christophe undertook was to recruit the ex-slaves as forced labor in order to build, with Napoleonic grandeur, his great fortress of La Citadelle. (The town disturbances of 1984 in Haiti may, however, indicate some erosion of that passivity.) The lesson is clear: except for Cuba, Grenada, and Suriname (admittedly, not unimportant exceptions), the regional electorates have, so far, chosen the constitutionalist path for change rather than the revolutionary path. It seems unclear at this point whether that trend will continue. As noted earlier, the Caribbean intellectual climate is already full of revolutionary ideas. It remains to be seen how successful they will be in recruiting popular support.

All this may perhaps be put in a slightly different way. What is the real nature of the Caribbean? Can the Caribbean be lumped together with Central America? The question is not academic, because that mixing together of the two districts has become a cardinal article of faith in the United States Caribbean Basin Initiative, launched by the Reagan administration in 1981. Seen as a single whole, the two regions are perceived by the Washington policy makers as "unstable," "ripe for revolution," anti-U.S. "dominoes" ready for the "Communist takeover." Is this true?

A number of facts suggest that these ideas constitute a fatally erroneous view. Caribbean history has been one of colonies; Central American history, at least since the close of the eighteenth century, has been one of what became known, derisively, as "banana republics." Slavery was the foundation pillar of Caribbean society; not so in Central America. Central America was shaped by Spain, the Caribbean by Britain, Spain, France, the Netherlands, and North America. Central American social structures have been semifeudal, with the masses governed autocratically by an alliance of a reactionary landlord class, an inquisitorial Catholic Church, and an army specializing in the art of "palace revolutions." Certainly since emancipation, the Caribbean has been a far more open society than Central America. The explanation is no mystery. It relates to the historical experience of the respective metropolises. The liberal revolutions succeeded in France, Britain, the Netherlands, and the United States, and all of these colonizing powers, with all their imperfections, have brought their liberalism into the conduct of their colonial policies. Spain, by contrast, never really saw the victory of the liberal spirit, except for brief republican moments. It is an interesting consequence of this difference that whereas Spain was hated by the local intelligentsia in nineteenth-century Cuba and Puerto Rico, the other colonizing powers have never really been perceived in the same way. West Indians today continue a love affair with British culture, as do French Antilleans with French culture; and it might come as a surprise to some of the U.S. architects of what the Santo Domingo writer-politician Juan Bosch has termed *pentagonismo* that most Caribbean people, however suspicious they may be of the U.S. government, have a real liking for Americans as a people. Naturally, there are exceptions to every rule; Costa Rica in Central America is a unique Western-type democracy, just as Haiti in the Caribbean is an example of the Latin American style of personal *caudillismo* that Gabriel García Márquez has wonderfully satirized in his novel, *El otoño del patriarca*. Yet, speaking in generally conceptual terms, Central America remains a region struggling to emerge from a semi-feudal condition into the first stage of industrial capitalism, while leading, more developed Caribbean economies, such as Puerto Rico, Trinidad, and Jamaica, have already reached that stage and are moving toward the next. And even in the less developed Caribbean economies—with perhaps the signal exception of the primitive conditions of life of the Haitian cane cutters, the so-called *congos,* who trek annually across the border to work in the Santo Domingo sugar plantations—it would be difficult to find any cultural minority that is treated with the barbarous cruelty that has been the traditional lot of the submerged native Indian peoples in El Salvador, Nicaragua, and Guatemala.

If we are correct in pursuing the general agreement that the Caribbean is a civilization *sui generis* that can be understood only in Caribbean terms, then nothing illustrates the theme better than the general political style of the region. Politics everywhere is a national pastime. But in the Caribbean it has its own particular tropical flavor. Caribbean societies (even Cuba, the largest) are small societies—intimate, personal, small-town; not even San Juan, perhaps the most sophisticated of the Caribbean cities, is anything like New York or London. So, people turn for recreation to what comes naturally; almost everywhere, sex and politics are the only games in town. In Britain or the United States, the political fever breaks out only at election times; in Caribbean societies it is an unending, year-long bacchanal. Sexual scandal and scabrous political gossip: this is the name of the game. It is almost as if—if readers in the United States will pardon the analogy—the Caribbean were one enlarged, regional Washington, D.C.

The institutional basis of the political style is the organized, mass-based political party. These are of recent growth, for the process of political democratization, incorporating the people into the electoral process, goes back only to yesterday, so to speak, with the introduction of universal suffrage and national free elections: 1936 in Puerto Rico, 1944 in Jamaica, 1961 in Santo Domingo (after the assassination of the dictator Trujillo). Representative government is thus comparatively young. The characteristic feature of the new political parties is one of Caribbean *personalismo,* the intimate bond that unites charismatic leader and adulatory followers in a form of political messianism. Grand oratory flourishes, for West Indian politics are nothing but oral. Examples abound. Governor Romero Barceló leaves his San Juan palace to ride horseback in the hills, meeting the people. In Trinidad, Prime Minister George Chambers rides his motorcade to visit the outlying villages of the Northern Range or the hamlets of the south. In Martinique, Aimé Césaire, mayor of Fort-de-France, holds informal court with his constituents in the mayoral parlor; and in Santo Domingo, President Jorge Blanco breaks precedent by doing the same thing in the presidential palace, much to the alarm of the older type of politicians who have been brought up in the authoritarian tradition of Trujillo and Balaguer. In the smaller island townships, in turn, it is possible to listen to the local politicians in their regular nightly market square meetings preach and orate for hours on end, murdering their opponents with a scurrilous wit inspired with its own vivid spontaneity: these are the West Indian "men of words" responding to the unlettered West Indian crowd eager to appreciate any display of "learning" that the orator can show, all the better if accompanied with a few Latin tags or bookish allusions. This type of political chieftain walks and talks with his followers, plays dominoes, eats and drinks in the roadside restaurants. It is a human politics, quite different from the mass media politics of the developed countries, where the mass political rally is almost a thing of the past, killed by an orchestrated television politics in which the growth of character has been replaced by the auction of personality. The Caribbean political leader of this populist style is not a packaged product. With all his limitations, he is a man of the people. He made the political history of the last generation in the region: Uriah Butler in Trinidad and Alexander Bustamante in Jamaica, who led the workers in the 1937–38 labor riots; Albízu Campos, who organized the Puerto Rican Nationalist party against the Americans in the 1930s, and, after him, Luis Muñoz Marín, who became the architect of modern Puerto Rico in collaboration with the Americans; and Papa Godett, the union leader who helped organize the Curaçao riots of 1969.

But things are changing. As electorates become more educated, they demand more educated leaders. There is, then, a higher level in which the practicing politician is poet, artist, intellectual, and university graduate. Muñoz himself was known in Puerto Rico as the "poet in the fortress." His relationship with his beloved *jíbaro* countrymen was founded on a bond of mutual love and respect that nothing could stain or pollute. The late Eric Williams in Trinidad, the leading West Indian historian, and prime minister after 1956, brought his learning into politics, converting the main downtown plaza into the "University of Woodforde Square," a mass forum where in lecture after lecture he educated his audiences in the realities of Caribbean life, creating a truly remarkable alliance of intellectual and crowd. It is no small measure of the way in which both Muñoz and Williams towered over all other political figures in their respective societies that they built up political machines that held power for a whole generation or more: the Popular Democratic party in Puerto Rico from 1940 to 1968, and the People's National movement in Trinidad from 1956 until the present time—a record unmatched elsewhere in the region.

There is, finally, the charismatic figure of Fidel Castro. No one can have listened to one of his lengthy, hour-by-hour addresses to hundreds of thousands in the Plaza de la Revolución, mixing the Marxist/Leninist language with the rich idiom of the orator (for which Cuba has always been famous) without being impressed at how, even in such a carefully arranged scenario, an electric magic of feeling, thought, and affection flows between the magnetic leader and the adoring crowd. This, in fact, becomes all the easier to understand when it is remembered that Fidel is the least bureaucratic of state leaders. He is what the Latins call *muy simpático*. He is, in fact, a warm, outgoing person more at ease with people than with institutions or office work. The portrait that his friend Ernesto Cardenal draws of him in his book *En Cuba,* reveals him as a thoroughly gregarious Cuban really at ease only when he is out of the office talking endlessly with his people outside of Havana; it is as if, Cardenal (1977) remarks, he is still psychologically with his comrades in the Sierra Maestra. Cuba may indeed be the Soviet surrogate in the Caribbean; but in its political style there is a tropical *brio* worlds apart from the dour-faced gerontocracy that rules the Soviet Union.

It would seem, on the face of it, that this argument might be invalidated by the events that took place in Grenada between 13 March 1979—the date of the coup d'état against the Gairy regime—and 19 October 1983—the date of the execution of Prime Minister Maurice Bishop and some of his colleagues. But on closer investigation that does not seem to be the case. For both of those events arose, generally, out of the special character of developments in Grenada after 1951, with the growth of a repressive state regime, under Gairy, that introduced into the English-speaking subregion the habit of Latin American *caudillismo.* This is not to say that comparable events could not occur, in the future, in other island societies that face, generally, the same socioeconomic problems that Grenada faced. But it is worth noting that in the case of Jamaica, during the Manley regime of 1972–80, where a government was in charge that was as radically socialist and antiimperialist as the People's Revolutionary government in Grenada after 1979, the habit of constitutional government was retained intact and not seriously compromised. Until there is evidence to the contrary, the Grenada experience between 1979 and 1983 must be regarded as a tragic aberration, terrible enough in its events, that does not warrant pessimism about the future of traditional democratic-parliamentary forms within the region. Indeed, it might be argued that those events, as one studies the general reactions throughout the region to October 1983, might have strengthened, for good or ill, the resolve of the West Indian electorates not to play with the fire of Marxist/Leninist ideas. (For further commentary on the Grenada case, see Centre de Recherches Caraïbes 1983, EPICA 1984, Jacobs and Jacobs 1979, and Pearce 1982.)

The style of Caribbean politics is naturally related to the nature of Caribbean government. The two intermix with each other. As already noted, constitutional government and popular democracy are of recent growth, but they are now firmly established. There are few governments that can say, like the Renaissance Pope Leo X, "Now that we have the Papacy, let us enjoy it"; except Duvalier's Haiti (where three-quarters of the people still live in poverty and illiteracy), or, earlier (before it was overthrown by the coup d'état of

1979), Eric Gairy's repressive regime in Grenada, in which the Gairyite state, by means of its infamous Mongoose Gang (aping the feared Tonton Macoutes of Haiti), terrorized its opponents and Gairy cast himself arrogantly in the role of the playboy of the Western world. And, of course, there is the special and sad case of President Burnham's Guyana. For most observers agree that over the last dozen years or so the Burnhamite regime has converted that country into a police state: rigged elections; judicial and political harassment of opponents (including the murder of the young radical historian Walter Rodney); elimination of an independent free press; and the construction of a monolithic one-party state. It is a measure of the way in which the present-day Guyanese government has absolved itself of any sense of accountability to public opinion, both inside and outside, that up to now it has remained stubbornly silent on the matter of the Jonestown holocaust of November 1978. Yet, even with these dismal exceptions, the Caribbean region remains an area in which constitutional government is alive and well. Most of its leadership would agree with the observation of former President José Figueres of Costa Rica that "we are convinced that it is better to have a bad government rather than a good revolution, so long as the electoral path remains open."

So Caribbean government, in general, is positive government: that is to say, it is obligated to the task of improving the general living conditions of its electorates. That is for two reasons. First, most of them have grown up out of the post-1945 anticolonial nationalist struggle. In that struggle the leaderships promised their followers that they would end the indignity of colonial rule, which so blatantly denied the sovereign right of self-government, and that, once successful, they would organize a better life for everybody. The revolution of anticolonial struggle went hand in hand with the revolution of "rising expectations." As already noted, the struggle is not yet completed. Both the U.S. Virgin Islands and Puerto Rico are still in colonial status; as a visiting U.S. senator once remarked in a congressional hearing held in St. Thomas, we are still the chairman of the board. It is estimated that the local Commonwealth government in San Juan lacks jurisdiction in at least thirty-eight areas of public life, including civil aviation, federal labor relations, defense, maritime transportation, and foreign relations, all exacerbated by the fact that Puerto Ricans, while being U.S. citizens, cannot vote in U.S. congressional and presidential elections, so that they lack a congressional delegation in Washington to look after their interests. That is why Puerto Rican politics center almost exclusively on the so-called status issue, which is debated with a ferocity that astonishes every visitor. In Puerto Rico, the status of politics is the politics of status (see Heine 1983).

Second, most Caribbean government is positive government because it has to deal with a myriad of social problems of a truly intimidating magnitude. These, in the prenationalist period, were "slums of empire," and they inherited the problems. There is still mass structural unemployment and underemployment in the regional labor force—according to recent statistics, 22 percent in Puerto Rico, 25 percent in Suriname and the French Antilles, nearly 40 percent in the Dominican Republic, and, in the fourteen countries of the British Commonwealth Caribbean, ranging from 14 percent (in Trinidad and Tobago) to 23 percent (in Jamaica). That reservoir of unemployed helps to breed the well-known social problems. There are squatter communities bred by a serious housing shortage. There is both incest and illegitimacy; it is estimated that 60 percent of all births in the Commonwealth Caribbean are to young unmarried girls. Michael Beaubrun has opined that alcoholism is the one major disease that ravages the same Commonwealth Caribbean. Drug addiction, prostitution, and crime are rampant; the ironwork grilles that cover every house in middle-class urban areas, whether in Jamaica or Puerto Rico, were originally decorative in intent but are now protective against crime, which in a sense represents the revenge of the poor against the well-to-do. Heavy drinking is almost a way of life, with the West Indian rum-shop serving as the equivalent of the American bar and the English pub. Brana-Shute has described the typical drinking shop in the poorer sections of Paramaribo (Suriname), which becomes a male-centered congregation point for social drinking, gossip, banter, and political argumentation and a refuge from the endless pressures of daily life (see Brana-Shute 1976). Juvenile delinquency, in turn, becomes a serious problem; and Lieber's account of the organized street gangs of hustlers and "limers" in Port of Spain has shown how many young lower-class males enliven their humdrum existence by, among other things, plying the underground marijuana trade (see Lieber 1981). All in all, there are many thoughtful Caribbean social critics who would be prepared to say that theirs are morally sick societies and that it is the main task of governments to put their peoples to work in socially meaningful ways.

THE SEARCH FOR DEVELOPMENT

It would not be unfair to say that, on the whole, most governments have not succeeded brilliantly in that task. Why is this so? It is certainly not for want of trying or indeed wanting. Many of those governments, after all, have come into power as progressive trade union–based political parties, including the Jamaica Labour party of the present Seaga administration, which, despite its name, is conservative in its social ideas. They have all more or less accepted reforming programs of industrialization and modernization as a means of increasing the national wealth and income. Their general developmental model there has been that originally set out by the economist Arthur Lewis in the 1950s; this approach posits that in order to modernize the backward tropical economies it is necessary to bring in outside investment capital and to draw a work force from the labor-surplus economies. First applied to Puerto Rico (and thereafter known to some as the "Puerto Rican model"), it required the creation of a new statewide fiscal-administrative apparatus designed to attract outside capital. Only by building an infrastructure (roads, port systems, leased factory space, etc.) and by instituting vocational training of the work force and, most importantly, tax incentive schemes allowing easy export of the profits of the investing companies, could the scheme be made to work. In effect, it was this model that created the typical modern Caribbean state—a governmental structure designed to plan fiscal and economic developments without relying too much on traditional free enterprise economics. As a result, the Caribbean is characterized by its own version of the system of planned, directed state capitalism that is now so familiar to the advanced industrial economies, including the United States. The system controls the traditional essential public services in health, housing, and education, as well as in new areas (for instance, national air carriers including Avianca Dominicana and British West Indian Airways). Governments such as those of Trinidad and Puerto Rico are themselves employers, providing jobs for more than one-third of the national labor force.

What, then, has gone wrong? The answer in part has been provided over the last decade or so by the new schools of Caribbean radical-liberal economists and more specifically by Marxist economists. Briefly, their critical literature emphasizes four major weaknesses of Arthur Lewis's developmental model. (1) Rather than local capitalist classes taking charge once the so-called take-off point has been reached, the investing multinational corporations have come to stay, repatriating their profits rather than plowing them into derivative local enterprises. (2) The cheap labor incentive, initially successful with labor-intensive industries such as textiles, has dwindled in importance as wage rates rise in the established industries. (3) Most industries, as a result, are now capital-intensive and thus do not absorb labor supply as originally intended. (4) The general industrializing program, by denuding the agricultural sector, has in fact increased rather than decreased unemployment levels. But the social scientist, going beyond the economists, would be tempted to note, in addition, one signal defect of the whole process: that governments have planned rapid industrialization without taking into account in any serious way the massive social dislocations that flow from it—uncontrolled urbanization, disruption of family life, psychological alienation, persistent poverty, the general breakdown of established habit and custom, and the collapse of the old supportive institutions, both secular and religious. It is the history of industrial machine technology everywhere that it erodes traditional ways of life, whether this is done in the service of capitalism or socialism (a point not always fully appreciated by the more left-wing critics of the Caribbean condition). It must be remembered, too, that whereas the British Industrial Revolution took some seventy-five years or more to work itself out, the modern Caribbean industrial revolution has been compressed into a brief twenty-five years or so. If ever the constitutional fabric of Caribbean life weakens, it will be because of the social discontents unleashed by that process.

THE SOCIAL STRUCTURE

It is at this point that the discussion enters, logically, into an examination in a little more detail of the Caribbean social structure. For the recent economic history of the region cannot be separated from the social structure. Both of them are causes and effects, intermingling with each other. The structure has been shaped, basically, by the twin lodestars of race and class. It has been divided horizontally in race-ethnic terms and vertically in social class terms. Both are inimical to effective nation building, since class generates class conflict and race can breed the ugly habit of communalism.

Class is endemic, whether in terms of property ownership or income. In Jamaica, the so-called twenty-one families, many of them Jewish and with a lengthy history on the island, control the private sector. Some 147 individuals, many of them belonging to the old French and Portuguese Creole groups, many of them descendants of the earlier French and Portuguese immigrants, are the effective decision makers in the Trinidadian private sector. The mercantile-commercial economy of Martinique-Guadeloupe remains in the hands of the *gran béké* (perceived as an upper-class white group by the rest of the society). The private tourist industry of the U.S. Virgin Islands is run by the white American residential group known derisively as the "Continentals." Many of these are clannish upper-crust groups, typified by discriminatory employment practices and endogamous marriage habits. Speaking more generally, there are throughout the Caribbean three main class divisions, each divided into two subgroups. There are the old rich and the new rich; the old middle class and the new middle class; the old poor and the new poor. The old rich—such as the French Antillean *gran béké* class and the Trinidadian French—still remain politically conservative. The new rich—the *nouveaux riches* of business, tourism, and real estate speculation (profiting from a veritable explosion of land values something like that in the U.S. Sun Belt)— are too busy making money to be concerned with the social emancipation of anyone but themselves. The old middle class—the doctors and lawyers and small merchants of the old small towns—has practically disappeared. Its successor, the new middle class, consists of the motorized salariat of both government service and private firms, high-fee lawyers and doctors, and new technocrats, who are anxiously on their way up, materialistic, full of social fear of those beneath them, often trying to hide their own recent lowly social origins. The more affluent of them can be seen every day, wearing sharp business suits and carrying snazzy briefcases, in the air-conditioned offices of the new glass-concrete high-rise buildings in every Golden Mile section of the expanding cities. Finally, the old poor of the old rural sectors still survive in the form of the peasantry, but they are marginal at best. The new poor, partly recruited from the old, partly newly created by the modernization process, now live in crowded slums and neglected public housing projects. The new middle class is what a Puerto Rican critic has called *una clase televisada* (born and bred in the television age). But the new poor have also shared in the process of *embourgeoisement*. For too many members of both groups, life becomes the anxious pursuit of material possessions: a new house, a new car, a television set and, if possible, furniture-mart household appliances, fashionable boutique clothes, and shopping sprees to Miami. In the words of a 1983 Trinidadian calypso, it is capitalism gone mad. It is almost as if every social echelon were trying desperately to catch up with the affluent U.S. way of life, which they see all the time in their mass media: newspapers, radio, television, and movies. For the Caribbean is the backyard of the United States; and U.S. cultural imperialism is pervasive (see Maingot 1971).

Even so, this is not just a straightforward society of class stratification. There is also race stratification. Race is added to class. Historically, that goes back to the fact that from the very beginnings the twin processes of ethnic admixture and cultural assimilation resulted in the typical Caribbean multilayered pigmentocracy: white, black, brown, yellow, and red, with every gradation in between. So today, the society is a fantastic rainbow, in terms of both color and culture: whites, blacks, East Indians, Hindustanis, Javanese, Amerindians, Arabs, Chinese, Portuguese, Christians, Muslims, all live together in a general mélange. The early slave society set all this in a rigid form of categorization, where race defined occupation: whites were owners, blacks workers, mulattoes in between, Chinese relegated to the food industry slot, and East Indians to small trading. As in all such societies, this distribution generated the usual baggage of stereotypes with which each group viewed the others: blacks were spendthrift, East Indians money-loving, and Jews and Chinese clannish. And there developed epithets of *nigger, coolie,* and *white man* as group protective mechanisms.

Naturally, both the postemancipation and the postindependence periods have changed much of all this; 1984 is not 1784. The basic ethnographic pattern remains; Guyana is sometimes called a nation of six peoples. In *The Plural Society in the British West Indies* (1965), the West Indian anthropologist M. G. Smith has termed the more mixed societies of the region "pluralist societies," that is, those where different ethnic groups form separate cultural communities that mix but do not combine; Guyana, Trinidad, and Suriname are the leading examples. The old granite walls of institutionalized prejudice and discrimination have disappeared; there is nothing here of South African apartheid. Public life is a far more representative mirror of the different groups. East Indians have penetrated into education and government service, once black strongholds. The eminent Chinese Sir Solomon Hochoy was governor-general of Trinidad in the 1960s; Prime Minister Edward Seaga, of white Lebanese ancestry, is leader of the Jamaican majority political party, which is overwhelmingly black in its membership; José Francisco Peña Gomez, of reputed African Haitian descent, is secretary-general of a major political party in Santo Domingo, a society in which anti-Haitianism has for generations been a veritable article of faith; and the old cultural prejudice of St. Thomians against Crucians in the U.S. Virgin Islands has not prevented Jan Luis, a Crucian of Puerto Rican origin, from becoming elected governor. Clearly enough, Smith's pessimistic conclusion that, once the old colonial sovereignty was ended, the absence of any common governing power would send the various groups into mutual strife, has been proven wrong.

There is one cardinal feature of Caribbean life that helps to explain much of this. It is the fact that the trajectory of the development of race relations in the Caribbean has been different from that of, say, the United States. Patterns of discrimination and prejudice in the United States were rooted in a simplistic black-white dichotomy; any person was perceived as either one or the other. The classificatory system in Caribbean societies has been different—more subtle, more benign, based essentially on the concept of "shade." It is the degree of skin color, not the possession of "negro blood," that has been the criterion of social acceptance, so the prejudice that arises, although real, is at least more sophisticated, and therefore perhaps more tolerable, than the negrophobia secreted in the North American variant of race relations. Prejudice can thus be softened by education, speech habits, and social status. This is the factor of "social color." In U.S. society, money talks; in Caribbean society, money whitens. It is possible to be black in physiognomy yet white in social terms. In the United States a Jew can pass as a Gentile if he wants to; a black cannot pass as a white, unless he becomes like Ellison's "invisible man." The difference is crucial; and stories abound in many Caribbean societies of how local black persons, usually middle-class, have visited the United States and found their white self-image shattered by the U.S. classificatory system.

Yet when all this is granted, it does not mean that these societies, so apparently tolerant and easy-going in these matters, are happy racial democracies. There is another side of the coin. There may not be open intertribal and intercommunal violence as in Uganda or Angola or Nigeria or India. But there still remain mutual dislike, suspicion, and distrust. The studies of Bahadoorsingh in Trinidad (1968) and Greene in Guyana (1974) reveal that voting habits in those two mixed societies are still shaped by ethnic preferences: the Trinidad People's National movement (notwithstanding the fact that it has token Indian members such as Errol Mahabir) has never really conquered the Indian enclaves of the south; in Guyana, Cheddi Jagan, for all his sincere international Marxism, remains the chieftain of the Indian groups of all levels, while President Forbes Burnham represents the Afro-Americans. The case of Suriname is even more telling: thousands of Hindustanis evacuated from Suriname to the Netherlands after 1975 in the fear that independence would subject them to a new Creole (Afro-American) governing majority; today, two years after Desi Bouterse's violent takeover of power, the continuing plots and counterplots in the new power game are often interpreted in terms of continuing interethnic rivalry. Even in Puerto Rico, where race has played a much less important role and where most Puerto Ricans suffer from the nice conceit that they are "white," studies such as those of Zenon Cruz reveal a continuing pattern of subtle discrimination against the black minority: while the history of Roberto Clemente proves that a black lower-class Puerto Rican can make it in American baseball, it is generally agreed that Ernesto Ramos Antonini, a leading political figure, was never allowed the power in the Popular Democratic party that was rightly his (see Zenon Cruz 1974).

But the situation is even more serious than this, for racial acceptance is tied to social status. There is a certain delusory quality to all the stories of blacks and Hispanics who "make it" in U.S. society and of blacks and Indians who "make it" in Caribbean society; in neither case have individual success stories meant the social and economic emancipation of a whole race. In the United States the outcome of the civil rights movement has been the creation of a small but highly visible black middle class, celebrated in publications such as *Ebony* magazine. In the Caribbean the general loosening-up of the occupational structure has led to the creation of a "black bourgeosie" and an Indian middle class, especially in the professions, in the political system, and in the governmental bureaucracies. The general condition of the nonwhite majorities remains effectively untouched, partly because of continuing racial prejudices, but even more because the neocolonialist economic order still requires a large reservoir of cheap, unskilled labor. Within that order, illiterate lower-class blacks can hope to escape only if they can struggle into the world of big-business sports or entertainment, like Roberto Clemente in baseball, Gary Sobers in cricket, Angel Cordero in horseracing, Wilfredo Benítez in boxing, or Bob Marley in reggae music. As these people become millionaires they tend, like the Beatles, to lose touch with their lower-class origins. Whether they realize it or not, they become co-opted into a business civilization that has always known how to mollify discontent by welcoming a chosen few. The vast majority of the Caribbean common people still remain a proletariat, in either agribusiness or industrial employment, suffering at once from economic exploitation and racial obloquy.

What does all this mean? It means, simply, that class and race still operate as functional mechanisms of minority rule–majority subordination in a society that has become a sort of modified plantation economy, not very different in its fundamental structural characteristics from the old slave-based plantation economy. For the Caribbean historian, it means the surprise of recognition; as they say in the movies, this is were we came in. For the people in the Caribbean who seek to change the system—whatever ideological label they may give themselves—it means a proper conceptual understanding of the ideological dualism of race and class. To emphasize one to the exclusion of the other is to risk theoretical imprecision. There is no better illustration of that dualism than the new Caribbean big-business tourist industry—in Bermuda, the Bahamas, the Virgin Islands, Barbados, and Jamaica. Its lush pictorial advertising in the North American press does not belie its reality of black waiters, busboys, and chauffeurs catering to white patrons, reinforced by the fact that the managerial staff are white expatriates or local whites, while the work force is black. The employer-worker relationship thus continues as a white-black relationship. The St. Lucian playwright Derek Walcott's *Pantomime,* in which a white expatriate hotel owner and a black *maître-chef* trade racial insults with each other, each playing the old skin game, is not altogether inaccurate in portraying what goes on in Caribbean high-life tourist enclaves such as Montego Bay and Freeport.

The ongoing popular struggle in the region, then, must take account of this ideological dualism of race and class. The theoretical weakness of the Black Power movement (along with Haitian and French Antillean *noirisme)* is in being too preoccupied with reclaiming Afro-American cultural dignity, and too neglectful of the class issue, almost as if it only wanted to replace white capitalism with black capitalism in the manner of the old Garveyite movement of the 1920s. Similarly, much of the Marxist/Leninist literature has tended to emphasize the class struggle only, dismissing racism as simply a distracting issue invested by the white ruling class—just as the old European left of the interwar period misinterpreted antisemitism as a distracting issue invented by the fascist enemy. Both of these Caribbean groups in turn—the black power advocates and the Marxist/Leninist ideologues—have tended to ignore the "Indian question." They have tended to draw up a general picture of the "black revolutionary masses," gratuitously including the East Indians and other groups. But one only has to read the letters in the Trinidadian press to realize that East Indians are incensed at the idea that they are "black." They see themselves as culturally different, which, of course, is true. In all of the "pluralist societies," East Indians and black Creoles, despite interaction at the economic and political levels, still conduct their lives apart in terms of family life, friendships, social customs, and religion.

The Caribbean progressive forces, in sum, must recognize that apart from the class question there are also those of "culture" and "race." The culture question is particularly relevant to the more heterogeneous societies and less so to the more homogeneous societies of the Hispanic Antilles. (A notable exception to this generalization is Puerto Rico, where a very real culture question influences the struggle of the more nationalist and autonomist groups to defend the Spanish language against the linguistic colonialism of Americans who refuse to learn Spanish, just as the British in India refused to learn Hindi.) In these pluralist societies the leading problem, in one way, is the need to establish, so to say, a concordat of peaceful coexistence between the different communities. No single community can speak for all; as has been well said, these are societies made up completely of minorities. The ultimate desideratum may well be some form of ethnic federalism in which cultural identity may be expressed in the areas of family life, courtship and marriage, social customs, religious practices, and even perhaps language, while loyalty to the new nation state may be expressed by cooperation and common activity in the economic and political areas. This would avoid the danger of compelling all groups to surrender to some sort of spurious mainstream culture that could only be a bogus mixture of everything, rather than something culturally rich and special in its own right. For in culture as in everything else, variety is the spice of life.

The race question, so closely linked to the culture question, is equally of paramount importance. Since the blacks, the Indians, and the other groups are largely lower-class groups, any appropriate strategy to solve the "race problem" must be concerned with social and economic emancipation. For these people—in Jamaican popular parlance the "sufferers"—have always been the chief victims of racism. The appropriate strategy has been well put by Norman Girvan in a perceptive essay (1981).

> It would be wrong to conclude that revolutionary politics and ideology can be "de-racialized" in content to any significant degree. In the Caribbean and in the Americas generally, there remains a high correlation between income, occupational status, ownership of property and socio-economic power on the one hand, and "physical" and "social" race on the other hand. To that extent it is inevitable that class conflict should be expressed at least partly in racial terms. Furthermore, in so far as an ideology of physical and cultural racism is used to legitimize the socio-economic order, ideologies of racial pride and self-assertion are essential to the generation of the collective self-esteem amongst the population at large which is a psycho-cultural precondition to their challenging the system. We believe therefore that black nationalist ideologies remain relevant not only in the Caribbean but all over the Americas where black communities are to be found, and that it is necessary for non-blacks who claim to be revolutionaries to understand this.
>
> Hence in this context, revolutionary ideology must provide an effective counter not only to what the different racial groups have been made to believe about themselves but also to how they have been conditioned to regard other groups, especially groups which they have been taught to regard as their enemy but which are in a structurally similar position. Furthermore, we hold the view that strategists for revolutionary change cannot assume that the "race question" will be solved as a derivative from the resolution of the "class question." Rather they must explicitly recognize the special significance of "racial castes" as a mechanism in the political economy of exploitation, and develop strategies which speak directly to this condition and seek to ensure that it must not reproduce itself, albeit in more subtle form, in a revolutionary situation.

THE INTERNATIONAL POLITICAL CONTEXT

Finally, the Caribbean has to be seen within the general framework of its hemispheric and international relationships. It is, after all, not Marco Polo's

China or old Tibet. Few districts of the Third World are less isolated from the outside world than this. It has diplomatic relationships with both Latin America and North America. Its governments are members of the United Nations Organization and related agencies; and some of them are members of the Organization of American States. It is a leading tourist area. Its export industries link it to the global trade market: sugar in Santo Domingo, bauxite in Guyana and Jamaica, oil in Trinidad. It is one of the most heavily trafficked maritime routes in the world; recent reports estimate that the leading oil-producing countries of the basin (the United States, Mexico, Venezuela, and Trinidad) together ship a total of some 4,700,000 barrels daily through the region's maritime passages. Migration patterns, both internal and external, have made the people of the Caribbean incessant travelers, and vast informal networks of relationships link the island populations and the overseas migrant congregations. It is not for nothing that many observers, then, have compared the Caribbean to the Mediterranean.

But the region has paid a heavy price for this incorporation into the world system. From the sixteenth century on, joined after 1898 by the United States, the European colonizing powers carved up the region. The Caribbean thus became the cockpit of European rivalry and war. There was, as the saying went, "no peace beyond the line," and it would be a grievous mistake to think of all that as past history. For it is the sad tragedy of the contemporary Caribbean that it has become the arena of the new geopolitical rivalry of the modern superpowers, the United States and Soviet Russia. It would be an equally grievous mistake to imagine that this new rivalry is just a tedious repetition of the old. For it is both quantitatively and qualitatively different in at least three different ways. (1) The old rivalry involved at different times five major powers—London, Paris, Madrid, the Hague, and Washington, and the Caribbean political movements and forces could hedge their bets, as it were, by playing one metropolitan center against the other. Today it is simply Washington versus Moscow, making it a much more dangerous situation for the Caribbean governments because there is less room for maneuver. (2) The old rivalry was geographically limited, with each metropolitan power merely seeking to retain its particular "sphere of influence" among the different island groups of the region. The new rivalry is truly global, with both powers seeking to dominate the larger world itself. (3) Most ominous of all, this power struggle is characterized by the possession of a new thermonuclear weaponry, which means that each power has the awful capacity not merely to defeat its rival in the Caribbean, but to exterminate human civilization. The old rivalry merely concerned what was called the "enterprise of the Indies." The new rivalry threatens a planetary holocaust.

The region is thus marked by a different climate of opinion. The healthy condition of ideological pluralism is threatened by a new ideological polarization. Both Washington and Moscow have escalated their military and naval forces; as the U.S. commander of the Roosevelt Roads complex in Puerto

Rico put it recently, the Soviet triangle of Cuba, Grenada, and Nicaragua is now matched by the U.S. triangle of Puerto Rico, Guantanamo Bay, and the Panama Canal Zone. Each side builds up its favorite client state: Cuba for the Russians, Puerto Rico for the Americans. This, too, introduces a new form of neocolonialism, especially in financial terms. For whereas the old colonial powers, following mercantilist policies, invested little in their Caribbean holdings, the new global powers pour massive subsidies into the region. The figures in themselves are telling: a recent North Atlantic Treaty Organization report finds that total Soviet aid and arms deliveries to eleven client countries in 1980 totalled $6.3 billion, with half of that amount going to Cuba alone (see the *Trinidad Express,* 23 January 1983, p.8); while reports from the U.S. Council of Economic Advisers estimate that for the fiscal years 1981–84 total federal funding for Puerto Rico runs annually to the amount of $4,447 billion (see the *Puerto Rican Business Review,* January-February 1983, pp. 2-15, 35). This kind of fiscal dependency naturally encourages political fealty. So it is natural that Cuban foreign policy follows Soviet interests. It is equally natural that, as is generally agreed, the independence movement in Puerto Rico has been frustrated by the pervading fear of the Puerto Rican electorate that independence, with the loss of federal funds, would mean a disastrous decline in living standards. The economic appetite kills the political appetite.

This, furthermore, has to be set within the politics of imperial destabilization, as part of the politics of superpower realpolitik. The U.S. record, of course, is the better documented, for it goes back some eighty years to persistent U.S. intervention in the region: President Theodore Roosevelt's illegal creation of the Panama republic in 1902–3, President Wilson's occupation of Haiti and the Dominican Republic in 1915–16, President Eisenhower's intervention in Guatemala in 1954, and President Johnson's intervention in the Dominican civil war of 1965 (Langley 1982). The current effort of the Reagan administration to upset the Sandinista regime in Nicaragua thus is the continuation of a long record.

All of this, of course, ended with the United States invasion of Grenada on 25 October 1983, condemned, interestingly enough, not only by the Soviet Union and radical Third World governments, but also by the Organization of American States, the British Commonwealth of Nations, the world Nonalignment movement, the United Nations General Assembly, and local Caribbean governments such as those of Guyana and Trinidad and Tobago, as a flagrant violation of national sovereignty and of the rule of law in international relationships. This long record of U.S. imperialist intervention has been documented for years by a voluminous literature, the latest being a 1982 report by the London-based Latin American Bureau. There is—up to now at least—no comparable Soviet record; the Soviets have limited themselves to military and civilian aid. But that does not preclude more direct action; the cases of Hungary, Czechoslovakia, and Afghanistan show that the Russian leaders do not suffer from any serious moral scruples when they feel that their vital interests are endangered. Any such Caribbean action on their part would mean, inevitably, a new Cuban missiles crisis and open confrontation. It is a grim thought that the Third World War may well start in the Caribbean.

The Caribbean becomes the victim of all this—not completely innocent, but helpless nonetheless. A new temper of ideological intolerance makes itself evident. The local followings of each side view each other in conspiratorial terms. People are assigned opprobrious labels and viewed as either a CIA agent or a subversive communist. To be critical of one side, however mildly, is to be dismissed as a defendent of the other. It becomes increasingly difficult to take a middle ground. On both sides rigid ideological stances defend the indefensible; so, the right defends the Haitian Duvalier regime on the specious ground that it is only authoritarian, not totalitarian, while the left defends the wholesale murders of 1982 by the new Bouterse regime in Suriname on the ground of "revolutionary morality." The healthy temper of ideological pluralism, which allows the free play of all in the market place of ideas, thus gives way inexorably to a sort of fanatical zealotry that is reminiscent of the old religions of the early modern period and that Catholic and Protestant imported at that time into the Caribbean. The observation of Lord Acton on the seventeenth-century Jesuits (Paul 1904) could be applied equally well to the situation in the Caribbean. "It is," he wrote, "this combination of an eager sense of duty, zeal for sacrifice, and love of virtue, with the deadly taint of a conscience perverted by authority, that makes them so odious to touch and so curious to study."

Two minor tributaries contribute to this general stream of intolerant temper. The first is terrorism—the murder of a Cuban diplomat in Washington; the bombing of a Cuban aircraft off Barbados; and the clandestine activities of various Puerto Rican underground groups (most notably the FALN, *Fuerzas Armadas de Liberación Nacional*). All these point to an escalation of terrorist activity by both extremist left and right. Some Marxist elements will deplore in private, but rarely condemn in public, what their more extremist confreres are doing, despite the fact that terrorism is not Marxism, if only because it ignores Mao Tse Tung's dictum that in the revolutionary struggle the party must be in control of the gun, and not the gun in control of the party. The second phenomenon is that of adventurism, pure and simple. The region has in recent years seen the appearance of groups of soldiers of fortune ready to invade and overthrow established governments; at least twice in recent years the small island of Dominica has been the target of such groups organized in Miami and New Orleans and reputedly serving a defeated ex–prime minister. Once again, Caribbean continuities assert themselves, for these condottieri are the modern versions of the early pirates and buccaneers. Terrorism and adverturism thus help to add to the insecurity of the region.

GORDON K. LEWIS

THE FUTURE

What is the way out of all this? Can anything be done to avoid a new international anarchy in the region? Can the political genius of the region organize itself efficiently and rapidly to build up a *pax Caribbeana* that will ensure peace, security, and freedom for its citizen bodies? And if it can, how is this to be done?

The serious and concerned student of the region may perhaps—without indulging in excessive optimism—answer those questions with a series of categorical imperatives.

1. Any kind of politics of isolationism is out of the question. We live in one world, in which the only rational unit of effective planning is the world itself. No one region can insulate itself from the rest of the world, cultivating a sort of heliocentric isolationism, as modern China demonstrates. The modern revolutions of global communications and travel make it impossible. When a modern jetliner can traverse the whole Caribbean from Miami to Paramaribo in five hours, it is palpably obvious that, for good or ill, the region is part and parcel of a world system. That, indeed, was the inherent logic of the three historic voyages by Columbus to the New World, for they shattered once and for all the old medieval European vision of the world.

2. It follows from the above that the modern nation state is obsolete—especially Lilliputian states such as St. Vincent or St. Kitts–Nevis in the Caribbean. These are island entities confronted with regional problems. A major oil spill can affect half a dozen of them; but none of them can deal with its effects alone. The National Hurricane Center in Miami monitors the region's hurricanes; but there is still no regional organization capable of planning posthurricane aid and relief programs. The regional tourist industry badly needs rationalization in order to avoid, for example, a simultaneous surplus of tourist beds in San Juan and a shortage of them in St. Maarten. A regional planning system is necessary to control the flow of interisland migration, so that the idle hands of Barbados could be rationally organized to develop the idle lands of Dominica. Intraregional trade and commerce are similarly fragmented. Despite their common membership in the Caribbean Economic Community (CARICOM), the three leading members of this organization engaged in a sharp trade war in early 1983: Jamaica started by setting up a two-tiered exchange rate for its currency; Barbados retaliated by allow-

ing its dollar to float against the Jamaican currency; Jamaica responded by suspending trading in Barbados dollars; and Trinidad finally moved to protect its manufacturers trading in CARICOM by placing all CARICOM imports under license. The episode demonstrated that protectionism is still strong enough to weaken the regional economic integration movement.

3. The lesson is clear: the Caribbean must strengthen its integration processes and institutions: CARICOM, the Organisation of Eastern Caribbean States, the University of the West Indies, and so on. Any Caribbean progressive must be, of necessity, a regionalist. The historic fragmentation of the region—political, economic, and linguistic—must somehow be overcome. This, let it be noted, is not an argument for political federation or confederation. There are still too many governments and politicians jealous of their own little slice of sovereignty to surrender it to any central regional authority. In any case, the experience of the European Economic Community shows that it is more prudent to build up the economic institutions before attempting common political institutions such as a federal parliament or a federal council of ministers. In any case, there must also be common purposes in any federal exercise, which, by definition, do not exist, for example, between socialist Cuba and capitalist Jamaica. What is needed is much less ambitious—the long, hard work of planned cooperation between like-minded governments concerning concrete, detailed, and functional matters: oil pollution, higher education, the development of agriculture and fisheries, civil aviation, and tourism.

4. Politically, cooperation must mean the search for a regional collective defense and security system. That must include recognition of and adherence to the doctrine of nonintervention in the affairs of member states. There is need, too, for a proper system of interstate arbitration of disputes particularly in relation to those longstanding boundary disputes that threaten territorial integrity—the Venezuelan claim to one-third of Guyana territory and the Guatemalan claim to the whole of Belize. The tendency of governments to adopt the bilateral approach with governments outside of the region must give way to a genuinely multilateral policy; much of the damage done by the U.S. Caribbean Basin Initiative has come from the fact that the eligible Caribbean recipients have lobbied in Washington on their own, thus jeopardizing the

common regional interest. And in the long run, of course, the regional leadership must sooner or later address itself to the problem of the escalating arms build-up in the region, in order to make it a demilitarized "zone of peace."

5. As cooperation thus grows, the region will be enabled to deal on a regional basis with both of the superpower presences. It will be able to give priority to its own local interests rather than those of the superpowers, which are frequently alien and irrelevant; as has been well said, much of the Caribbean–Central American crisis arises from the fact that North-South problems are dealt with in East-West terms. As things now stand, a common regional foreign policy is vitiated by polarization: Fidel Castro makes the Moscow tour, as did Maurice Bishop, while Edward Seaga and Romero Barceló make the Washington tour. It is, indeed, one of the comic absurdities of the Cold War that American presidents and Russian leaders meet each other at top-level summits while their satellites remain aloof from each other. Caribbean intellectuals, of all different persuasions, visit Havana; Cuban athletes participate in the Pan-American Games in San Juan. It is high time that the politicians followed those healthy examples.

6. A similar ameliorative process must take place in the intellectual life of the region. Pluralism must not be swept away by polarization. That places a special responsibility upon the liberal-democratic-socialist elements to map out a middle ground between the two warring extremes. They have a Caribbean precedent in the record of the old democratic left, organized by the liberal triumvirate of Muñoz Marín of Puerto Rico, José Figueres of Costa Rica, and Romulo Betancourt of Venezuela. In the 1940s and 1950s this coalition fought against the dictatorial regimes of the region while even Rooseveltian New Deal America, for its own foreign policy reasons, maintained friendly relations with those regimes. A generation later, the problems remain. A new democratic left, in seeking a new social order, must ensure that it is a mixture of social radicalism and democracy. It must expose the fallacy of the argument that free elections, a free press, and open intellectual enquiry are "bourgeois" inventions that can be readily discarded. It must challenge a new orthodoxy that asserts that armed revolution, after the Cuban manner, is the only correct method of change, for the effective majority of the regional societies still offer the alternative method of change by constitutional process. As Aneurin Bevan once

remarked in the British debate, there is no immaculate conception of socialism. In a way, indeed, it is surprising that this point should have to be made at all, for the growth of Eurocommunism shows that the Western European Communist parties have been able to retain their ideology intact while at the same time rejecting the thesis that the Moscow Comintern is to be accepted as the infallible pope of the international revolutionary movement. What the Caribbean left needs, perhaps, is a Caribbean variant of Eurocommunism.

7. In any case, the geopolitical face of the region is changing. Ever since 1898 the United States has been able to treat the region as its own *mare nostrum,* under the protection of a Caribbeanized Monroe Doctrine; the other powers in the region accepted that claim. Today, however, an internationalization of the region is taking place. Not only is there now a new Soviet presence, but other forces have entered as new actors. Latin secondary powers such as Mexico and Venezuela officially recognize the Cuban regime and have developing trade relationships with the region; and these bring with them the traditional Pan-American apprehensions about the Colossus of the North. The United Nations Special Committee on Decolonization annually debates the Puerto Rican question, against angry U.S. objections. The Socialist International, moving away from its traditional Europocentrist preoccupations, has held at least one meeting in Santo Domingo and includes three Caribbean leaders in its membership—Michael Manley of Jamaica, Jorge Blanco of the Dominican Republic, and Ruben Berríos, leader of the Puerto Rican Independence party. All of this reinforces the regional progressive movement, for it enables it to make friends and influence people on a larger scale.

8. Finally, all this confronts U.S. leadership with a serious challenge—learning to adapt to a new Caribbean. The Cuban Revolution alone, apart from the other forces here mentioned, has made that inevitable, for just as the Haitian Revolution of 1793–1804 accelerated the slavery abolition movement in the region, so the Cuban Revolution has accelerated, for good or ill, the movement for social justice in the region. That means, at the least, the diplomatic recognition of the new regime, just as France finally recognized Haiti in 1825. It means that the winds of change in the area are the result of a complex myriad of forces and ideas; they cannot be reduced, simplistically, to a communist conspiracy. It is the

essence of statesmanship to accept the inevitable with grace. The 1979 Panama Canal Zone treaties show that that spirit is deeply embedded, still, in the best of the U.S. liberal tradition. Again, the proposed congressional amnesty legislation for undocumented aliens shows that the moving lines of Emma Lazarus on the Statue of Liberty still mean much to many Americans. It is not too late for the United States to abjure its crass conviction that the only way to combat communism is to support the reactionary forces of the Caribbean–Central American region and to become the champion of those other forces that seek to make the region safe for democracy and freedom. That is the only way consonant with the tradition of the United States.

The Caribbean, beyond contradiction, is on the move. This means that the Americans who visit the region, whether as tourists, businessmen, government officials, or professional experts, must be psychologically prepared to meet the region and its peoples on their terms. They cannot come as conquerors, or culture carriers, or experts with the "quick fix," or entrepreneurs looking for an easy profit. Granted the right attitude, they will find a ready response, for Antilleans share many of the Americans' traits: they are warm, gregarious, outgoing, curious to learn, and eager to adapt. Visitors will find much to enjoy and admire in the rich mixture of Antillean languages, cultures, and religions. But they must come, above all, prepared to give rather than to take; as the early Spanish conquistador chronicler Oviedo observed, "he who would possess the wealth of the Indies must first have the wealth of the Indies in his own heart."

REFERENCES

BAHADOORSINGH, KRISHNA
  1968 *Trinidad Electoral Politics: The Persistency of the Race Factor.* London: Institute of Race Relations.

BRANA-SHUTE, GARY
  1976 "Drinking Shops and Social Structure: Some Ideas on Lower-class West Indian Male Behavior." *Urban Anthropology* 5(1) :53–68.

CARDENAL, ERNESTO
  1977 *En Cuba.* Mexico: Ediciones ERA.

CENTRE DE RECHERCHES CARAÏBES
  1983 *Special on Grenada / Spécial Grenade.* Montréal: Université de Montréal.

CURTIN, PHILIP D.

1969 *The Atlantic Slave Trade: A Census.* Madison: University of Wisconsin Press.

EPICA

1984 *Death of a Revolution: An Analysis of the Grenada Tragedy and the U.S. Invasion.* Washington, D.C.: EPICA.

GIRVAN, NORMAN

1981 *Aspects of the Political Economy of Race in the Caribbean and in the Americas.* Kingston: Institute of Social and Economic Research, University of the West Indies.

GREENE, J. E.

1974 *Race vs. Politics in Guyana: Political Cleavages and Political Mobilisation in the 1968 General Election.* Kingston: Institute of Social and Economic Research, University of the West Indies.

HEINE, JORGE (ED.)

1983 *Time for Decision: The United States and Puerto Rico.* Lanham, Md.: North-South Publishing Co.

JACOBS, W. RICHARD, AND IAN JACOBS

1979 *Grenada: The Route to Revolution.* Havana: Cuadernos de Casa de las Americas.

LANGLEY, LESTER D.

1982 *The United States and the Caribbean in the Twentieth Century.* Athens: University of Georgia Press.

LEWIS, GORDON K.

1971 "The Politics of the Caribbean." *In* Tad Szulc (ed.), *The United States and the Caribbean,* pp. 5–35. Englewood Cliffs, N.J.: Prentice-Hall.

LIEBER, MICHAEL

1981 *Street Scenes: Afro-American Culture in Urban Trinidad.* Cambridge, Mass.: Schenkman.

MAINGOT, ANTHONY P.

1971 "Social Life of the Caribbean." In Tad Szulc (ed.), *The United States and the Caribbean,* pp. 36–68. Englewood Cliffs, N.J.: Prentice-Hall.

MINTZ, SIDNEY W.

1960 *Worker in the Cane: A Puerto Rican Life History.* New Haven, Conn.: Yale University Press.

PAUL, HERBERT (ED.)

1904 *Letters of Lord Acton to Mary Gladstone.* London: George Allen & Unwin.

PEARCE, JENNY

1982 *Under the Eagle: U.S. Intervention in Central America and the Caribbean.* London: Latin American Bureau.

SMITH, M. G.

1965 *The Plural Society in the British West Indies.* Berkeley & Los Angeles: University of California Press.

STONE, CARL

1973 *Class, Race and Political Behaviour in Urban Jamaica.* Kingston: Institute of Social and Economic Research, University of the West Indies.

WELLS, HENRY

1969 *The Modernization of Puerto Rico: A Political Study of Changing Values and Institutions.* Cambridge, Mass.: Harvard University Press.

ZENON CRUZ, ISABELO

1974 *Narciso descubre su trasero.* Humacao, P.R.: Editorial Furidi.

Notes on the Contributors

MERVYN C. ALLEYNE is chairman of the Department of Linguistics and director of the Language Laboratory at the University of the West Indies in Jamaica. His research has been concerned with both historical linguistics and sociolinguistics, with special stress on the origins, variation, and sociology of Caribbean and Afro-American languages. Among his recent publications are *Comparative Afro-American* and *Theoretical Issues in Caribbean Linguistics*. His *Aspects of a Culture History of Jamaica* is being published this year in both English and Spanish.

KENNETH BILBY is a Ph.D. candidate in the Department of Anthropology at the Johns Hopkins University. He has conducted field research in New Mexico, Sierra Leone, and Jamaica, published articles in academic journals, made a number of ethnomusicological phonograph recordings, and produced (with Jefferson Miller) a documentary film about the Jamaican Maroons, *Capital of Earth*. He is currently carrying out research among the Aluku (Boni) Maroons of French Guiana.

G. B. HAGELBERG is the author of *The Caribbean Sugar Industries: Constraints and Opportunities* and many other publications on sugar. He is adviser to the government of Barbados and to F. O. Licht, the West German sugar information service, neither of which is in any way responsible for the views expressed in his essay.

H. HOETINK is professor of Caribbean and Latin American sociology at the University of Utrecht. He is a past director (1969–75) of the Institute of Caribbean Studies at the University of Puerto Rico and has been a visiting professor at a number of universities in the Caribbean, the United States, and Europe. His books include, among others, *The Two Variants in Caribbean Race Relations, Slavery and Race Relations in the Americas,* and *The Dominican People 1850–1900* (originally published as *El Pueblo Dominicano: 1850–1900*).

GORDON K. LEWIS is professor of political science at the University of Puerto Rico, director of the Institute of Caribbean Studies, and a specialist in the Caribbean region, where he has lived and worked for thirty years. His books include *The Growth of the Modern West Indies, Gather with the Saints at the River: The Jonestown Holocaust,* and *Main Currents in Caribbean Thought*.

NOTES ON THE CONTRIBUTORS

SIDNEY W. MINTZ is William L. Straus, Jr. Professor of Anthropology at the Johns Hopkins University. He has done fieldwork in Puerto Rico, Jamaica, and Haiti, dealing particularly with the social and economic history of the Caribbean region. He is the author of *The People of Puerto Rico* (with Julian H. Steward and others), *Worker in the Cane, Caribbean Transformations,* and *Sweetness and Power.*

SALLY PRICE, assistant professor of anthropology at the Johns Hopkins University, has conducted field research in a rural pueblo in southern Spain, a Mayan Indian community in Mexico, and a fishing village in Martinique, but her most extensive research has been with Maroons in Suriname. Her books include *Afro-American Arts of the Suriname Rain Forest* (with Richard Price) and *Co-wives and Calabashes* (1982 winner of the University of Michigan's Hamilton Prize). She is currently working on a study of Western perceptions of "primitive art."

CARL STONE is professor of political sociology at the University of the West Indies in Jamaica. In addition to teaching, he serves as a newspaper columnist, labor arbitrator, and public opinion pollster. Among the many books and articles he has written about Caribbean and Third World politics, some of the more recent are *Democracy and Clientelism in Jamaica, Profiles of Power in the Caribbean Basin,* and *The Newer Caribbean* (co-edited with Paget Henry). He is currently completing a book on contemporary power and policy in Jamaica.

Books in the Series

The Guiana Maroons: A Historical and Bibliographical Introduction
Richard Price

The Formation of a Colonial Society: Belize, from Conquest to Crown Colony
O. Nigel Bolland

Languages of the West Indies
Douglas Taylor

Peasant Politics: Struggle in a Dominican Village
Kenneth Evan Sharpe

The African Religions of Brazil: Toward a Sociology of the Interpenetration of Civilizations
Roger Bastide, translated by Helen Sebba

Africa and the Caribbean: The Legacies of a Link
edited by Margaret E. Crahan and Franklin W. Knight

Behold the Promised Land: A History of Afro-American Settler Society in Nineteenth-Century Liberia
Tom W. Shick

"Alas, Alas, Kongo": A Social History of Indentured African Immigration into Jamaica, 1841–1865
Monica Schuler

"We Come to Object": The Peasants of Morelos and the National State
Arturo Warman, translated by Stephen K. Ault

A History of the Guyanese Working People, 1881–1905
Walter Rodney

The Dominican People, 1850–1900: Notes for a Historical Sociology
H. Hoetink, translated by Stephen K. Ault

Self and Society in the Poetry of Nicolás Guillén
Lorna V. Williams

Atlantic Empires: The Network of Trade and Revolution, 1713–1826
Peggy K. Liss

Settlements, Trade, and Polities in the Seventeenth-Century Gold Coast
Ray A. Kea

Main Currents in Caribbean Thought: The Historical Evolution of Caribbean Society in Its Ideological Aspects, 1492–1900
Gordon K. Lewis

BOOKS IN THE SERIES

The Man-of-Words in the West Indies: Performance and the Emergence of Creole Culture
Roger D. Abrahams

First-Time: The Historical Vision of an Afro-American People
Richard Price

Slave Populations of the British Caribbean, 1807–1834
B. W. Higman

Between Slavery and Free Labor: The Spanish-Speaking Caribbean in the Nineteenth Century
edited by Manuel Moreno Fraginals, Frank Moya Pons, and Stanley L. Engerman

Caribbean Contours
edited by Sidney W. Mintz and Sally Price

THE JOHNS HOPKINS UNIVERSITY PRESS

Caribbean Contours

This book was set in Times Roman text
and Florentine Script display type by
BG Composition, Inc., Baltimore, Maryland.
It was designed by Cynthia W. Hotvedt
and printed on S.D. Warren's 50-lb. Sebago
Cream White paper. It was printed and
bound in Holliston A-grade cloth by
R.R. Donnelley and Sons, Chicago, Illinois.